CLASH OF EAGLES

In the Hawker Tempest V the RAF had the fastest low to medium level fighter available. Powered by a 2200 hp Napier Sabre IIB 24-cylinder liquid-cooled engine, it had a maximum speed of 392 mph. (630 km/h) at sea level, 416 mph. (670 km/h) at 4600 feet (1400 m) and 430 mph. (690 km/h) at 17 000 feet (5180 m). It could climb to 10 000 feet(3050 m) in 2.7 minutes and had a service ceiling of 36 000 feet (11 000 m). In the closing stages of World War II, Tempest squadrons suffered serious losses to concentrated and accurate German flak. (IWM)

CLASH OF EAGLES

DENNIS NEWTON

Kangaroo Press

Cover pictures:
Upper: Panorama scene of the dogfight in which an RE8 of 3 Squadron AFC was attacked by 6 DVa scouts over the Western Front on 17 December 1917. (From a painting by Keith Swain, Australian War Memorial Gallery.)

Lower: EMU Slicks depositing members of No. 1 RAR for an operation in Vietnam.

Designed by Wing Ping Tong

© Dennis Newton 1996

First published in 1996 by Kangaroo Press Pty Ltd
3 Whitehall Road Kenthurst NSW 2156 Australia
P.O. Box 6125 Dural Delivery Centre NSW 2158
Printed in Hong Kong through Colorcraft Ltd

ISBN 0 86417 793 3

CONTENTS

INTRODUCTION

The purpose of this book is to highlight the achievements of a cross-section of Australian airmen in various conflicts throughout the world. This is appropriate in this year of the Royal Australian Air Force's Seventy-fifth Anniversary.

Australians have always occupied prominent places in aviation and military service. The particular conflicts covered here range from those in World War 1, during which Australian airmen served in Britain's Royal Flying Corps (RFC), Royal Naval Air Service (RNAS), Royal Air Force (RAF) as well as their own Australian Flying Corps (AFC) — the embryonic RAAF; World War II when they could be found not only in the RAAF but in huge numbers in the RAF and were even spread thinly in the Royal Navy's Fleet Air Arm (FAA) and could also be found (often unofficially) in some units of the US Army Air Force (USAAF); Korea in both the RAAF and RAN; and Vietnam where again they were not only in the RAAF but also on exchange in the USAF and, as we shall see, RAN personnel served with both the RAAF and the US Army. Wherever they served, their accomplishments matched and often excelled the deeds of those around them.

In many instances the airmen featured in this work have been overlooked by history. They did not bask in the glare of publicity which was given — not undeservedly — to others. Yet, they achieved much — as much as, and sometimes more than, their better known contemporaries — and they were therefore no less deserving our attention and gratitude.

This book is a way of giving them some long overdue credit. Their stories are just a few among so many exploits still waiting to be told.

ACKNOWLEDGMENTS

A book such as this cannot reach its fruition without the help and cooperation of many people and organisations. Over the years of researching and writing there have been many. Individuals and organisations that have given help and support include: William Evans, Joan Bowden, David Bowden, Gordon Olive, Beryl and Maria Olive, Pat Caban, Jim Heron, Doug Peterkin, Norman Macmillan, James Brown, R. J. Brownell, Reg Moore, Trevor Mear, Bruce Mear, John Wallen, Alan Bolton, Bill Air, Bay Adams, Cec Sly, George Hale, Margaret Drummond, Bryan Philpott, Bob Geale, George Hunt, Australian War Memorial, Australian Archives, National Library of Australia, RAAF Historical Section Department of Defence, RAN Aviation Museum Nowra, RAAF Museum Point Cook, *Sydney Sun*, *Newcastle Sun*, *Mufti* (Victorian RSL Official Journal), *Wings* (official organ of the RAAF Association NSW, QLD and WA), State Library of NSW, UK Ministry of Defence, UK Public Record Office, Commonwealth War Graves Commission, Imperial War Museum, Battle of Britain Museum, RAF Museum, *Kent Messenger*, Battle of Britain Fighter Association, the Caterpillar Club, the Goldfish Club, *Air Mail*, *Aviation News*, Military Aircraft Photographs (MAP), Bundesarchiv-Militararchiv and Carl Harrison-Ford of Kangaroo Press for the conversion of a raw manuscript into this publication.

Last, and by no means least, I give special recognition of the support and patience of my wife, Helen, and son, Scott, without which the book could not have been finished.

Dennis Newton
June 1996

ABBREVIATIONS AND CONVERSIONS

A/C	Aircraftsman
AFC	Australian Flying Corps (World War I)
	Air Force Cross
Air/Cdr	Air Commodore
AWM	Australian War Memorial
CAC	Commonwealth Aircraft Corporation
CGM	Conspicuous Gallantry Medal
CPO	Chief Petty Officer
Cdr	Commander
DAF	Desert Air Force
EATS	Empire Air Training Scheme
EMU	Experimental Military Unit
FAA	Fleet Air Arm
FEAF	Far East Air Force
F/Lt	Flight Lieutenant
F/O	Flying Officer
F/Sgt	Flight Sergeant
Fw	Feldwebel (Flight Sergeant)
G/Capt	Group Captain
Hpt	Hauptmann (Flight Lieutenant)
IWM	Imperial War Museum
KIA	Killed in Action
LAC	Leading Aircraftsman
L/Cdr	Lieutenant Commander
L/Cpl	Lance Corporal
LG	Landing Ground
Lt	Lieutenant (German: Leutnant)
Lt/Cdr	Lieutenant Commander
Lt/Col	Lieutenant Colonel
MAP	Military Aircraft Photographs
Oblt	Oberleutnant (Flying Officer)
ORB	Operations Record Book
OTU	Operational Training Unit

P/O	Pilot Officer
	Petty Officer (Navy)
RAAF	Royal Australian Air Force
RAF	Royal Air Force
RAN	Royal Australian Navy
RFC	Royal Flying Corps
SAAF	South African Air Force
Sgt	Sergeant
2/Lt	Second Lieutenant
SSAF	South African Air Force
S/Ldr	Squadron Leader
Sub/Lt	Sub-Lieutenant
TAF	Tactical Lair Force
USAAF	United States Army Air Force
USAF	United States Air Forc
WAG	Wireless Air Gunner
W/Cdr	Wing Commander
W/O	Warrant Officer

All events described in this book took place at a time when Australia used the Imperial system of weights and measures and these have been retained. Some conversions to metric are also supplied in the text, usually for aircraft specifications, and for measures of speed and altitude. Below is a table of conversions:

1 inch	2.54 cm
1 foot (ft)	30.5 cm
1 yard (three feet)	0.91 m
1 mile	1.61 km
1 pound (lb)	454 g
1 ton	1.01 tonnes
1 gallon	4.568 L

COMMONWEALTH CA-13 BOOMERANG

SIDE VIEW (PORT)

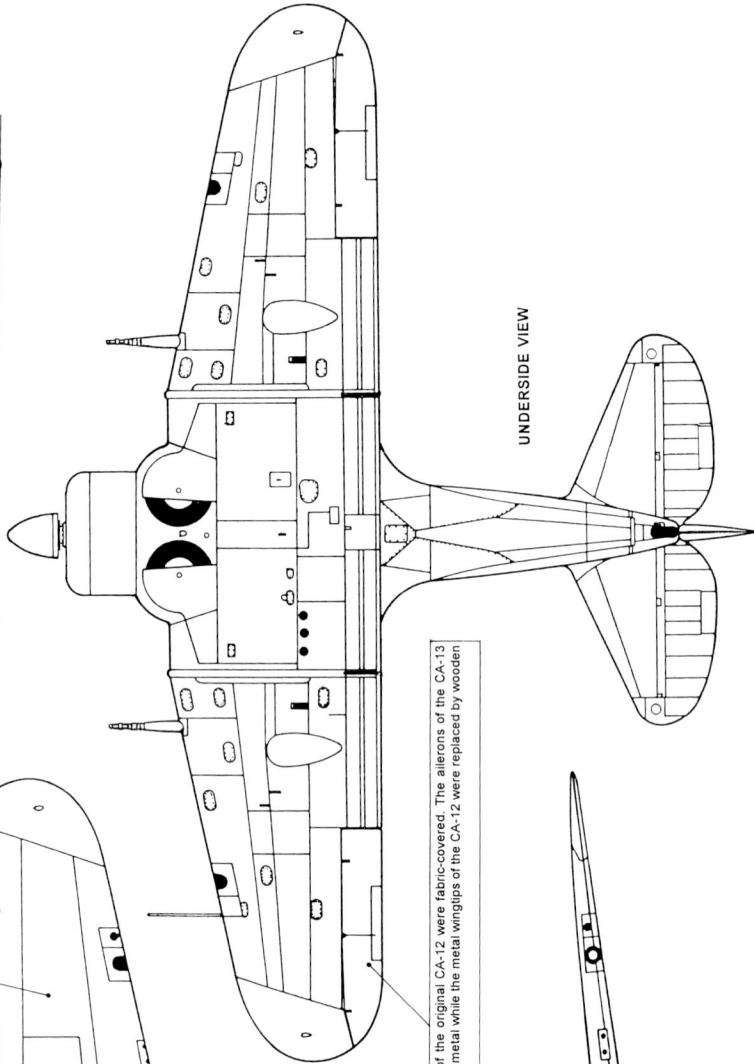

UNDERSIDE VIEW

TOP VIEW

FRONT VIEW

Wings: Single-spar structure with stressed-skin covering.

Control surfaces of the original CA-12 were fabric-covered. The ailerons of the CA-13 were skinned with metal while the metal wingtips of the CA-12 were replaced by wooden ones.

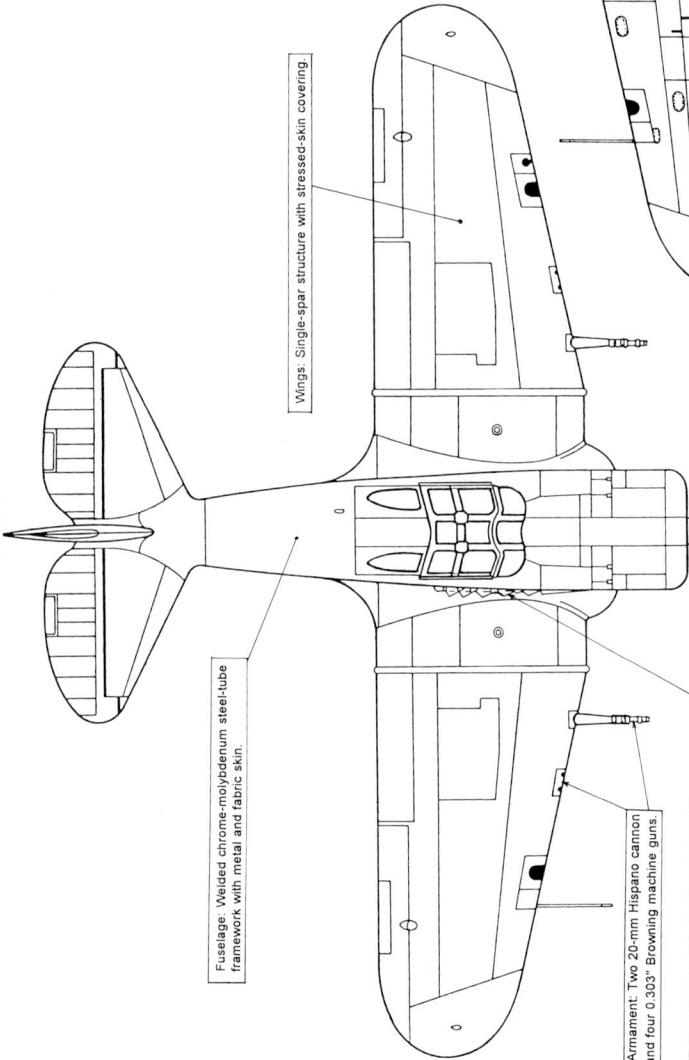

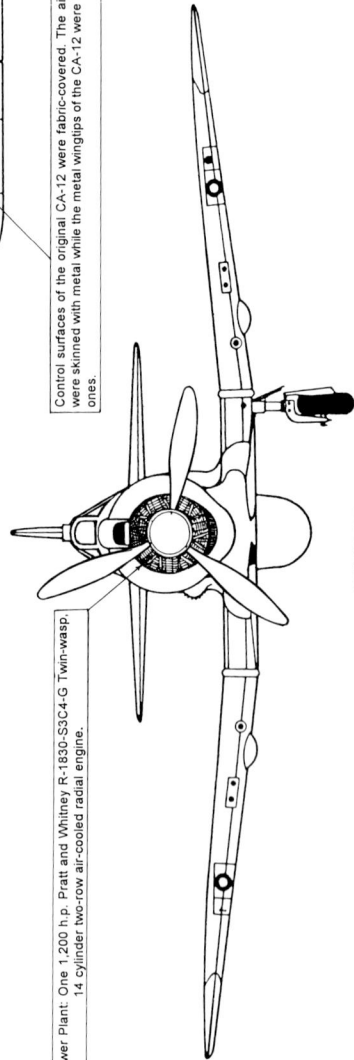

Fuselage: Welded chrome-molybdenum steel-tube framework with metal and fabric skin.

Armament: Two 20-mm Hispano cannon and four 0.303" Browning machine guns.

The CA-13 was in essence the same as the CA-12 with a flame damper exhaust from a Beaufighter fitted. Although this reduced the aircraft's performance by around 3 m.p.h. the earlier straight through exhaust had been prone to cracking and had given off considerable glare during night flying.

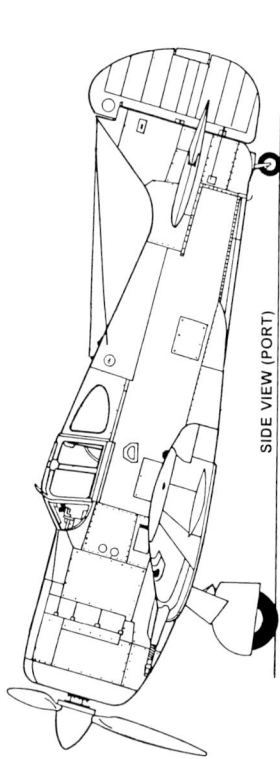

Power Plant: One 1,200 h.p. Pratt and Whitney R-1830-S3C4-G Twin-wasp, 14 cylinder two-row air-cooled radial engine.

1

THE RED BARON'S KILL

Before 1914, few people believed that the aeroplane had any military use except for reconnaissance. Experiments in firing guns from aeroplanes, and dropping bombs and torpedoes from them, were not at first taken very seriously by senior officers of the world's armies and navies. As a result, at the beginning of World War I when Britain's Royal Flying Corps (RFC) crossed the English Channel to support the British Expeditionary Force in France, its pilots flew unarmed aircraft. However, military leaders did not take long to appreciate the value of aerial reconnaissance: it reported and photographed every movement of the armies on the ground and directed artillery. The same leaders soon began to press for methods of stopping the reconnaissance activities of their enemies. Eventually, aircraft designers devised ways of firing a machine-gun from an aircraft without shooting off its own propeller in the process. Reconnaissance aircraft began to suffer heavy casualties at the hands of the new scout planes. One of the most successful types was the Fokker Eindecker, which caused so many casualties among the British and French that it became known as the 'Fokker Scourge'. Friendly scouts began to accompany the reconnaissance machines to protect them from attack. So began the clash of eagles — air-to-air combat.

Pilots often found themselves involved in great swirling dogfights as whole squadrons engaged in deadly combat. Those who were victorious and succeeded in shooting down five or more of their opponents became known as 'aces'. This is the story behind one of the victories of one of the greatest aces.

A translation of his Combat Report presented the cold bare facts of the engagement:

Requesting Acknowledgment of My 17th Victory
Date: Jan. 23, 1917.
Time: 4.10 P.M.
Place: Above trenches south-west of Lens.
Plane: No details as plane dropped on the enemy's side.

About 4.10 p.m., together with seven of my planes, I attacked an enemy squadron west of Lens. The plane I had singled out caught fire after I had discharged 150 shots into it from a distance of 50 metres.

The plane fell burning.

The occupant of the plane fell out of it at a height of 500 metres.

Immediately after it crashed on the ground, I could a see heavy black smoke cloud rising. The plane burned for some time with frequent flares of flame.

(Signed) BARON VON RICHTHOFEN

Floyd Gibbons, noted journalist and biographer of Manfred von Richthofen, wrote a dramatic account of the incident in *The Red Knight of Germany* in 1930:

Richthofen's victim that day was another young second lieutenant like himself, except that he was so new to the war in the air that the English Air Ministry

Manfred von Richthofen, the dreaded Red Baron of Germany, highest scoring ace of World War I. (Dennis Newton)

FE8. pusher scout, armed with a forward-firing Lewis machine-gun. (IWM)

had not yet made the customary record of his civilian address or the names of his next of kin.

Somewhere, presumably in the British Empire, a family is waiting for word about what happened to John Hay after his letters stopped coming, and this publication of Richthofen's report, in conjunction with the notations on the Royal Flying Corps casualty lists for that day, will supply some of the missing information.

John Hay and several planes from the Fortieth Squadron RFC left the aerodrome west of Lens shortly before three o'clock in the afternoon. He was flying an F.E. 8 armed with a forward-firing Lewis machine-gun. It was Hay's job to escort two slow flying camera planes on a patrol over the lines.

The report of the Canadian artillery observers coincides with Richthofen's account of Hay's last flight. They saw the English single-seaters, among which his was one, protecting the rear of the camera planes, when five planes of the German formation dived down from the blue.

While the camera planes flew away, the single-seaters engaged the enemy fighters. The opposing planes flew round and round, each endeavouring to bring his gun to bear on the tail of the other.

Watching through their glasses, the Canadian gunners saw a burst of smoke at the tail of one of the hard-pressed English planes.

'God! He's a goner,' said a mud-grimed Tommy, with uplifted head and open mouth.

It was John Hay. His plane nosed downward in a dive. The smoke changed to flames. It came down like a bolt of glowing fire, leaving a sooty streak against the grey winter sky.

While still more than a thousand feet above the trenches, a black bulk shot out from the ball of fire.

Falling slightly to one side, the dark satellite turned over and over in the air, revealing arms and legs.

Charred fragments of the plane fell over a wide area.

The Canadians picked up what was left of Hay about two miles south-east of the little village of Aix Moulette, and buried it. The exact spot on the military map is R.30, A.92

That night in the mess at Squadron Forty's aerodrome, the sergeant-major packed up a bundle of letters, photographs, an extra pair of boots, and some trinkets and marked the bundle:

2nd. Lt. J. Hay, Pilot 40th Sq. Killed in action, 23.1.17.

The story of Manfred von Richthofen, the fabled Red Baron, with 80 kills the highest scoring air ace of any side in World War I, is the stuff of legends. It is not proposed to retell it here. All aspects of his life, and his controversial death, have been carefully examined and studied in the minutest detail by aviation enthusiasts and military historians from all over the world. The work continues even now, and I confess to being one of those caught up and intrigued, particularly by the Australian connection.

So who was this Lt John Hay from 'somewhere, presumably in the British Empire'?

Information on 2/Lt J. Hay of 40 Squadron RFC which I obtained from official sources in England proved to be exceedingly sketchy, in common with many other records dating back to the 1914-18 War. On 1 April 1918, the RFC was officially combined with the Royal Naval Air Service (RNAS) to form a completely new and independent service, the Royal Air Force (RAF). Prior to this, RFC organisation had been the responsibility of the British Army

The first successful single-seater scout aircraft was the Fokker Eindecker which, by means of designer Anthony Fokker's synchronised interrupter gear, could fire a machine-gun forward through the arc of its spinning propeller while the blade was out of the way. It caused so many casualties among British and French aircraft that the period became known as the 'Fokker Scourge'. (MAP)

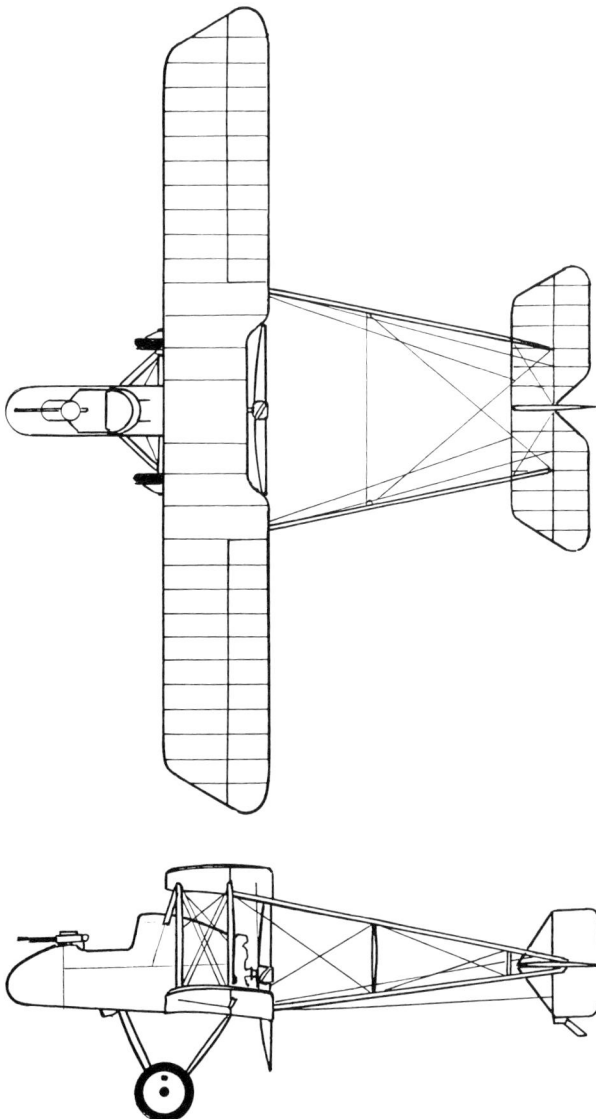

and records from this tumultuous and confused time are held by the Public Records Office, Surrey, along with all British government records dating back more than 30 years. Surviving information found there consisted of several forms, references in 40 Squadron's Flying Record Book, a number of Combat Reports and a couple of letters written by the commanding officer. There was little on John Hay to provide a comprehensive picture.

His place of birth was not stated but there was a clue, an Australian connection, mention being made that he was educated in Sydney. Probably, he was single, because his mother was given as next-of-kin with the address of a long-defunct firm of solicitors in Bishopsgate, London. He reputedly served as a quarter master-sergeant in the Seaforth Highlanders (but this is disputed) and was commissioned in the RFC on 3 January, 1916. No dates seemed to exist for his original enlistment or for his posting to 40 Squadron.

He was apparently on squadron strength when it went from England to France in August 1916. The squadron moved in two parts and both had arrived by the end of the month. According to the Record Book, their first flights there took place on 2 August but it was not until the 31st that John Hay logged his first flight, a short 10-minute hop. This suggests that he arrived with the second party.

LEFT Two-view layout drawing of an FE8. At first unable to invent an interrupter gear of their own, Allied aircraft designers had to devise various other ways of firing a machine-gun from an aircraft without it shooting off its own propeller in the process. One method used was to move the propeller out of the way to the back so that it pushed rather than pulled the aircraft along. (Dennis Newton)

Thereafter, he apparently flew on every possible occasion except for intervals which could be attributed to bad weather and a longer blank period in early December 1916 which could have been due to a period of leave. On some days he was in the air more than once, as were many others of the squadron. Treizennes airfield was the squadron's base during that bitterly cold winter of 1916-17.

References in *Military Aircraft of Australia 1909-1916* by W/Cdr. Keith Isaacs, AFC, CRAeS, RAAF (Ret'd), (Australian War Memorial, Canberra, 1971), listed John Hay as an Australian air ace with six victories to his credit. It also noted his place of birth as Double Bay, NSW, and his date of birth as 22 January 1889. An inquiry directed to the NSW Registrar of Births, Deaths and Marriages confirmed that a John Hay had indeed been born at that place, on that date.

My inquiries had reached this stage when contact was established with another of those of us 'caught up and intrigued', who was on the same path. American air historian William T. Evans of Cleveland, Ohio, has made research into the Red Baron's victims his special project and I am endebted to him for his willingness to share information.

In the 80 aircraft shot down by the Red Baron there was a total of 124 men, the planes being a mixture of single and two-seaters. Over the years, Bill Evans has endeavoured to find out the details of every one of them by establishing contact with their families and friends, or even the survivors themselves if still alive. It has been a mammoth and time-consuming task for him, following up leads to be found in many countries. Whenever 'official' channels drew a blank, he turned to advertising in newspapers. He managed to acquire a copy of John Hay's entry in the Register of Commonwealth War Graves Commission and a copy of his Royal Aero Club Certificate from London. On the latter, Hay gave his 'home address' as the Union Club of Sydney.

Evans contacted the Union Club's Membership Secretary, who revealed that 2/Lt. Hay's actual home address was Mullengudgery, NSW.

In subsequent correspondence, Bill Evans informed me that John Hay's family and friends called him Jack, and supplied some family background:

In Jack Hay's case I wrote to five newspapers before I hit 'pay-dirt'. The first contact was one that you could never imagine! A niece of the lady Jack was engaged to marry saw one of my write-ups in her paper and she wrote to me. She sent me the name and address of one of Jack's nieces today and that niece has opened up the whole family to me. ... We have become almost personal friends. I write to two of Jack's nieces — his two sisters' children, and to two of the nieces of the lady he had intended to marry. Both families had kept in touch after Jack was killed...

Jack had one brother and two sisters and they all lived a happy (and I gather prosperous) existence at their place 'Gunningbar', near Mullengudgery. It is a region that produces very fine wool and lots of early families live there. His brother, William, was in the First War in the army and survived Gallipoli. He survived the war and afterwards married twice but there were no children — so there are no descendants named 'Hay', although they all have the name somewhere in their names. 'Gunningbar', sadly, is no more. It burned down in 1936. I believe the family no longer lived there.

A line up of Albatros DII scouts, superior to all of its opponents in late 1916. By the time RFC pusher scouts capable of combating the 'Fokker Scourge of 1915 were available, the Germans had introduced the deadly Albatros series which were the first on any side to successfully carry twin synchronised forward-firing machine guns. (IWM)

Even two-seater reconnaissance aircraft such as this Aviatik BII were fast enough to outrun the British 'pushers' of late 1916 and early 1917. (MAP)

No. 40 Squadron was commanded by Major Robert Loraine who is described in Sholto Douglas' Years of Combat, Volume. 1 of his autobiography, (The Quality Book Club of London), as 'a handsome and very well known actor of middle age' and 'a first rate airman'. Douglas goes on to describe how Loraine's imposing character dominated and inspired the squadron but he makes no mention of John Hay. It was, however, Loraine who co-signed Jack Hay's combat reports.

The FE8 type flown by the unit was an anachronism. It had been designed to combat the 'Fokker Scourge' of 1915 but was delayed in entering service and introduced too late, well after Fokker had ceased to be a menace. It was not in the same class as the deadly Albatros DII which confronted it in September 1916. Powered by an unreliable 100 hp Gnome Monosoupape engine, the FE8 had a maximum speed of 90 mph (140 km/h) and carried one Lewis gun for armament; the Albatros was at least 20 mph (32 km/h) faster and carried twin Spandau machine-guns.

Richthofen's aircraft may have actually been an Albatros DIII, the latest of the line, which he had brought with him from Jasta Boelcke to Jasta 11, his new new command. It had arrived decorated in the standard colour scheme of that time — natural wood finish on the fuselage with olive green and brown, or lilac mauve, on the upper wing surfaces —but he decided to have it painted glaring red. It was an improved version of the existing scout with a sesquiplane layout to increase manoeuvrability and the range of vision from the cockpit. An increase in the compression ratio of the Mercedes engine boosted power by about 10 hp. The result was that German squadrons were presented with an aircraft which would cause brutally heavy losses to the Allies in the first half of 1917.

The FE's shortcomings were clearly demonstrated during the morning of 22 September 1916 when Jack Hay attacked an unidentified German biplane north of Arras. He came in from behind and a little below and emptied a drum of his Lewis gun in two bursts. The enemy plane's engine stopped and it began a glide to the south. Hay tried to follow to deliver the coup de grâce but could not overtake it because his own engine was misfiring and would not give full power. Finally, he had to break off pursuit.

A month later, on 22 October, while flying an escort mission east of Pont-à-Vendin, Hay spotted a BE2C, a slow British two-seater reconnaissance aircraft, fleeing westward with a German plane in close pursuit. He dived, closed in to 20 yards and fired off 20 rounds. The enemy plane, which he identified as a Roland scout, immediately turned over and fell in flames until it crashed into the ground — his first confirmed victory.

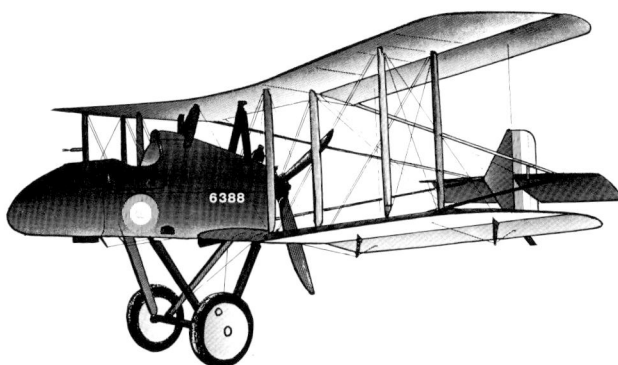

F.E.8 No.6388 of 40 Squadron RFC, the aircraft flown by Jack Hay on 23 January 1917. (Dennis Newton)

Because of this and subsequent actions, on 21 January 1917 Major Lorraine recommended Hay for the Croix de Guerre for 'his gallantry and devotion to duty'. Two days later the Australian was killed in action.

Jack Hay filled in his last combat report around 12.30 p.m. on 23 January 1917, the day he died. That morning the six FE8s of 40 Squadron's 'B' Flight prepared for an escort and line patrol mission. At exactly 9-30 a.m. five of the six took off. Jack Hay's machine proved difficult to start but a few minutes later he was airborne and trying to catch up.

At 8000 feet (2400 m) over Pont-à-Vendin he saw an Albatros two-seater flying in a northerly direction 2000 feet below. He dived and zoomed up under the enemy's tail to avoid fire from the rear gunner. At 20 yards range he opened up with his Lewis gun. The Albatros turned over and fell into a nose dive. Suddenly its wings broke away and its fuselage plummeted to earth and crashed just west of La Bassée. Shortly afterwards Hay rejoined his patrol, which he found to be two planes short. Both had aborted, one because of a badly misfiring engine and the other because of mechanical pump failure.

The four remaining FE8s then attempted to attack six German scouts which evaded them by diving away using their superior speed. Hay and the others reported that the leader of this formation had been 'painted entirely red'. The flight landed back at Treizennes around noon.

Jack Hay was up again on a similar mission at 1.12 p.m. but from this one he never returned. There were witnesses to what happened. At 2.45 p.m. he was seen by two other members of 40 Squadron shooting down an enemy aircraft which smoked, burned and crashed near Lens. Twenty minutes later, the same two pilots saw another plane fall in flames and it too crashed near Lens. It was Jack Hay's machine, FE8 No. 6388. The victorious enemy plane was coloured red.

There were no parachutes for pilots in those days. An airman had two choices: stay with the burning plane and face an agonising death by fire, or jump to swift oblivion. Jack Hay either chose to jump or was thrown clear.

Soldiers on the ground, also witnessed his grim death. According to Floyd Gibbons, the Australian's broken body was found by Canadian troops and buried about two miles south-east of the village of Aix Moulette. However, Bill Evans has warned me to treat this account with some scepticism:

Don't take as gospel Floyd Gibbons' description of the death of Jack Hay as he wrote it up in 'The Red Knight of German'. As one of the nieces says, he over-dramaticised it somewhat. Old Floyd, being a newspaper correspondent, wasn't above making a good story of it. There was a hot enough fight, all right, but when Jack was brought down his body was recovered almost immediately and buried next day. I have copies of the letters to Jack's mother from the two Canadians who recovered his body, from several of his fellow officers (he seems to have been universally loved and respected), from his mechanic who was with him the six months he was in France, from his CO, Major Lorraine, and from the minister who conducted his Funeral serrice. The minister wrote to Mrs. Hay, "Perhaps you may not know that he was in no way disfigured by his fall. You can think of him still just as he was. I conducted the funeral service, and there was a full turn-out of officers and men to show their honour of him and esteem...'

As for knowing whether or not Jack fell or jumped from his plane — as von R. states — I have no information. I see no reason for the Baron to say that if it were not so. However, as you know, his body was recovered almost immediately and buried the next day. Mrs. Hay's cousin (I believe that was the relationship) was in the lines and saw the fight and, as far as I know, didn't say that a body came out of the plane — but then, perhaps he didn't want to tell that.

Such was the man and such were the circumstances surrounding the death of 2/Lt Jack Hay of 40 Squadron RFC, the seventeenth confirmed victim of Manfred von Richthofen, the Red Baron, on that cold January day.

2/Lt Jack Hay of 40 Squadron1 RFC. (Bill Evans)

2

DEATH FLIGHT

The Australian Flying Corps (AFC), forerunner of the Royal Australian Air Force (RAAF), was established in 1912, followed in 1914 by the formation at Point Cook of the Central Flying School (CFS). By doing this, Australia became the only dominion to act on a decision taken during the 1911 London Imperial Conference that the armed forces of the British Empire should exploit the air as a means of warfare.

Following the outbreak of World War I, and after the first Australian units were sent overseas during 1914-16 — these included the famous Mesopotamian Half Flight and No. 1 Squadron which went to the Middle East — further negotiations between the Australian and British governments led to the formation of another squadron at Point Cook. This unit, established on 19 September 1916, was initially designated Squadron AFC, later in England redesignated 69 Squadron (Australian) RFC, and finally in France became 3 Squadron AFC. The squadron began with eighteen officers and 230 airmen. Squadron officers came from serving Australian Military Forces (AMF) officers who had volunteered for active service overseas following completion of a CFS instruction course, and from selected civilian volunteers with previous flying experience. Equipped with R.E.8 aircraft, in September, 3 Squadron moved to Savy in France where its role was to conduct artillery shoots as well as bombing, strafing, tactical reconnaissance and photographic missions in support of British and Canadian troops. In November 1917, 3 Squadron moved to Bailleul in Flanders where it became the corps reconnaissance squadron to the 1st ANZAC Corps at Messines and as such supported Australian troops for the remainder of the war.

At night, preparing an RE8 of 3 Squadron AFC for a sortie. (AWM)

The aeroplane drones on, scribing wide circles in the sky. Its engine tone does not change. The breeze is gentle and from the north-east. It causes the plane to drift to the south-west as it continues to circle lazily. Nothing appears to be wrong.

An observer familiar with the outlines of various aircraft would be able to identify it as a two seater biplane, one of those types used for bombing and artillery spotting. It is an RE8, a 'Harry Tate', in British markings. The peacock's-eye wing roundels can be clearly seen from the ground. It continues to circle lazily. There appears to be nothing unusual happening.

An observer in another aircraft could move closer for a more detailed inspection. The aircraft flies normally although it is obvious that it has been in a fight. It has battle damage but the controls do not seem to be affected. The aeroplane's number, A3816, now becomes visible and identifies it as a machine from.3 Squadron, Australian Flying Corps, stationed at Ballieul. In their cockpits, the pilot and observer are very still. They do not acknowledge the presence of anyone else nearby in the sky. They are on reconnaissance and appear to be concentrating on their work. Nothing seems to be wrong and an observer in another aircraft, if he was a friend, would leave them to their task.

But all is not as it seems. The RE8 flies normally in wide circles to the left. The pilot and observer are very still in their cockpits because they cannot move. They do not acknowledge the presence of anyone else nearby in the sky because they are not able to do so. No living hand is guiding the aircraft home...

December 1917 found the fliers of 3 Squadron AFC in action over the Messines Ridge, France. Their duties included photographic reconnaissance, artillery observation and offensive bombing patrols — when the weather permitted.

During November, the weather had almost invariably been either dull or raining and as December progressed it deteriorated further. Flying in these conditions was stress filled and dangerous. On 2 December, an RE8 was taking off on an artillery patrol when a sudden squall caught it and carried it into the brick wall of Bailleul cemetery. Both the pilot and the observer were killed.

Meanwhile, on the ground to the north the Third Ypres offensive had reached the final stages of exhaustion, drowning itself in a sea of mud — the swamps of Passchendaele. British and Canadian troops had occupied the site of Passchendaele village, but only after staggering losses. The weather had caused the mud to become so deep that the men could barely move, let alone fight. An order to go over the top and attack became regarded as a sentence of death and the best a soldier could hope for was that it would come swiftly and cleanly. But at last the army could go no further and the offensive had bogged down. Now the common enemy for both sides was the foul nature of the weather.

On 6 December flying was possible. One RE8 flown by Captain W. H. Anderson, with Lt J. R. Bell as observer, took off on an artillery spotting mission. Anderson also took the opportunity to drop two 20-pound bombs on a German strong point. An enemy aircraft, a DFW. two-seater, also appeared on the scene. Anderson manoeuvred the RE8 into a position which allowed Bell to fire off 90 rounds of Lewis at it. The enemy plane went down and was seen to crash just behind the German lines by an artillery officer on the Messines Ridge. It was 3 Squadron's first confirmed victory.

The weather closed in again and continued to be 'dud' for the best part of two weeks. Then, during a fine spell on the afternoon of 17 December, several aircraft went up on artillery work. Among them was A3816 flown by Lt L. Sandy of Burwood, NSW, with Sgt H. F. Hughes, formerly a civil servant of Prahran, Victoria, as his observer. Their duty was to observe and correct for an 8-inch howitzer battery. Sandy was well aware of the value of their task because, prior to joining the AFC, he had been an artillery officer.

Artillery observation entailed recording from the air the results of bombardments on enemy batteries or other targets. Attached to the squadron was an artillery liaison officer (ALO) on loan from the army. Based on the latest possible information received each evening, the ALO kept files of aerial photographs of known enemy batteries on the corps' front. He then prepared for each pilot a photograph of the prospective target marked with a 'clockface', or provided a celluloid 'clockface' disc, to help him in making corrections. The pilot was also informed of the number of guns in the shoot, the time of flight of the shells, the position of ground strips and any other available relevant information.

In the aircraft, it was the pilot's duty to record the fall of the shells. He did this by referring to his map or photograph with his 'clockface' in position and transmitting the bombardment results back to his battery. Aircraft were fitted with wireless equipment for sending but not for receiving. All signalling from the guns to the RE8 was done by the means of large strips of white cloth laid out next to the battery wireless station. If the ground was covered with snow, red or black ground strips were used. Meanwhile, the observer's job was to constantly search the sky in case of enemy attack. His Lewis gun was the aircraft's major defence. These duties of pilot and observer sometimes varied so that the latter recorded the fall of shells, but of the 515 'shoots' carried out by 3 Squadron in 1917-18, only six were conducted by observers.

CLOCK-FACE METHOD
OF
CHECKING
ARTILLERY FIRE

The pilot on an artillery observation mission was given a photograph, or map, of his target marked as shown to assist him in making corrections. Due north was regarded as being 12 o'clock. The distance of the shots from the centre of the target was noted with reference to the smallest circle within which they were contained and to the nearest clock hour. A letter code was used to speed up the transmission of results.

OK = exact centre
Y = 10 yards out
Z = 25 yards out
A = 50 yards out
B = 100 yards out
C = 200 yards out
D = 300 yards out
E = 400 yards out
F = 500 yards out

For example, transmission of "A6" would tell the battery that its shells had landed within 50 yards south of the target. Necessary corrections could then be made before firing the next round.

Clock face method of checking artillery fire. (Dennis Newton)

In 3 Squadron ,'A' Flight was known as the artillery flight and 'B' Flight as the counter-attack flight. During periods of static warfare, both these flights were used for artillery patrols and artillery observation, and 'B' Flight also continued with counter-attack patrols. 'C' Flight was the infantry flight or trench flight. All flights were available for photography, although this duty was usually given to pilots who showed a particular aptitude for the work.

Sandy and Hughes were in position between Deulement and Armentières by 2.15 p.m. and the 'shoot' commenced. For over half an hour they circled and noted the positions of the exploding shells and signalled back these results to the howitzer battery. Then, at exactly 2.52 pm, the transmissions from A3816 abruptly stopped ... Sandy and Hughes were in trouble. They had been attacked by a formation of six of the latest German Albatros DVa fighters.

By no stretch of the imagination could an RE8 be considered to have been a match for even one of these sleek German machines. This version of the Albatros had a top speed of 117 mph (188 km/h) and for armament it carried twin Spandau machine-guns synchronised to fire through the propeller. It was the successor of the deadly Albatros D.III which had so severely mauled the Royal Flying Corps

in April 1917 that the month became known as 'Bloody April'. These were also an improved version of the Albatros DV which was in service at the same time.

On the other hand, the RE8's 150 hp RAF 4a engine gave it a maximum speed of 102 mph (164 km/h) and for armament it had one synchronised Vickers machine gun firing forward and a Scarff-ring-mounted Lewis gun to protect the rear. It had been nicknamed the 'Harry Tate', a piece of rhyming slang using the name of a popular London music hall entertainer who was noted for his comedy. But there was nothing funny about the reputation the machine acquired. Many regarded it as a flying death trap — it went into a spin easily and invariably burst into flames if it crashed. Others complained about its lack of agility and difficult landing characteristics. The highest casualties suffered by the RFC in Bloody April were found among the RE8 squadrons, but, in modified form, RE8s were kept in service until the end of the war and it was on these machines that 3 Squadron AFC, managed to build its enviable record.

In any clash between an RE8 and an Albatros DVa, the odds were heavily stacked against the British aircraft. In a clash between one RE8 and six Albatros DVas there could only be one result, but Sandy and Hughes in A3816 had little choice but to engage the enemy.

Men on the ground saw the fight. They heard the rattle of machine-gun fire and saw the German planes twisting and zooming around the Australian machine. Helplessly, they waited for the inevitable to happen.

Six against one ... it could not last long. Tense minutes dragged by.

One of the planes fell away from the fight. There was no smoke or fire. As it fell closer the watchers could see that it carried black patee crosses — it was German! Still under control, the Albatros came lower and lower — it was coming in to land!

And land it did, right in the lines of the 21st Infantry Battalion, Second Australian Division. As it rolled to a stop soldiers came from all directions. There was little damage to the plane itself, but when the men reached the cockpit they saw that the pilot was wounded. He was taken prisoner and given medical attention.

Meanwhile, the uneven combat continued with the odds reduced to five to one. An artillery officer, watching from the ground, later described the fight as one of the most gallant actions he had seen. The RE8 refused to fall and it had forced down one of its attackers. The officer noticed another aeroplane joining the fight. The newcomer was another RE8. The odds were now five to two, but still very much in favour of the Germans.

As the Albatros was making its shaky landing in the Australian lines, in the second RE8 Lts A. J. Jones and K. C. Hodgson had seen the lone Australian plane under

Albatros Scout DVa, D.5390/17, the aircraft that landed in the Australian lines.(AWM)

heavy attack. They immediately went to its aid. The Albatros fighters did not break away and continued to make their determined attacks. Blazing away whenever he had a target, Hodgson fired 400 rounds in the course of the battle.

Five minutes ... six minutes ... still the unequal duel continued. Eight minutes ... still no result. Then at approximately 3.05 the remaining German aircraft broke off towards their own lines. They had seen a third British machine approaching, another RE.8 from 3 Squadron. Six sleek Albatros DVas had been chased off by the lumbering Harry Tates, and one of their number had been lostin the process.

Jones flew closer to the first RE8, noted its number, and realised that it was Sandy's machine. It did not seem to be badly damaged and was flying normally. Neither Sandy nor Hughes waved or acknowledged his presence as he flew alongside. Convinced everything was all right, Jones broke away and returned to Bailleul for more ammunition.

By 6 pm all but one of 3 Squadron's aircraft had been accounted for. Sandy and Hughes had not returned. Perhaps they had landed in another field. Concerned telephone calls were made all that night seeking any information of the two fliers. Results were negative.

Based on the combat reports of Jones and Hodgson and on information received from ground positions, both Sandy and Hughes were recommended for immediate decorations because of their courageous action. Sandy was recommended for the Military Cross and Hughes for the Distinguished Conduct Medal.

Meanwhile, Captain R. Ross and a salvage team were dispatched to the 21st Infantry Battalion to recover the downed German aircraft. That night, in spite of heavy shellfire from an enemy battery, the DVa was removed from the forward positions and transported back to 3 Squadron's aerodrome.

Morning came and went and there was still no news of Sandy and Hughes. It was as if they had vanished from the face of the earth. It was not until the evening that a telegram came from 12 Stationary Hospital at St Pol stating that the bodies of Lt Sandy and Sgt Hughes had been found in a crashed RE8 in a field three miles north-east of St Pol. This was 50 miles from where they had last been seen by Jones and Hodgson.

Captain Ross was sent to examine the crash site. His trained eye read the signs. The plane had obviously descended in a steep glide and, after hitting with one blade of the propeller, the right wing had touched the ground. Then the wind had caught the tail and swung the fuselage around in the opposite direction so that it finished facing the way it had come down. The throttle was in an open position and the fuel tank was empty. The observer's auxiliary joystick had not been used.

Meanwhile, a post-mortem was carried out on the bodies at the hospital. Medical opinion suggested that both Sandy and Hughes had been killed at the same time by the same bullet. An armour- piercing shell had been fired from directly behind, passed through the observer's left lung and then travelled on into the base of the pilot's skull.

Back at the squadron, the pieces of the puzzle were fitted together. It was obvious that Sandy and Hughes had been killed during the aerial battle at the same time as, or immediately after, the wounding of the Albatros

Predawn, an RE8 of 3 Squadron AFC prepares for take-off. Note the relative positions of the pilot and observer/gunner. Medical examination suggested that both Sandy and Hughes had been killed by the same bullet. (AWM)

pilot. After that the aircraft had flown itself. The later model RE8 was a very stable machine and, correctly trimmed, it had that capability. It had continued to fly itself in wide left-hand circles until its fuel supply ran out. Supporting this theory is the fact that the prevailing wind on 17 December was from the north-east, which would have caused the RE8 to drift south-westwards. The crash site was on a line 50 miles south-west of the area of the dogfight.

Nevertheless, there is something eerie about an aeroplane with no guiding hand carrying dead men on through the December air. The thought of it gives an uneasy feeling. They are alone in the sky and nobody knows; they are at peace in a heaven at war. Alone. The engine drones on ... and on ... and ... stops. Silence, now except for the soulful whistling of wind in the wires...

The death of Sandy and Hughes having been established, recommendations for decorations had to be withdrawn.

Albatros Scout D.5390/17, the aircraft that had landed in the Australian lines and been transported back to Bailleul was, by order of the 2nd Brigade RFC, sent to No. 1 Supply Depot at St Omer. It was afterwards

presented to the Australian government as a trophy of the war. Restored at Camden Museum of Aviation, NSW, in the late 1960s, it has been on display (though not in its original colours) in the Australian War Memorial, Canberra.

Albatros Scout DVa, D.5390/17, in the Aircraft Hall of the Australian War Memorial, Canberra. On the wall in front of it can be seen Keith Swain's painting. (Dennis Newton)

3

ALPINE EAGLE

The Australian Flying Corps created traditions and set standards of achievement which would be taken up after World War I by the Royal Australian Air Force. Altogether, the AFC consisted of four operational squadrons: 1 Squadron in the Middle East followed by 3, 2 and 4 Squadrons, all of which saw distinguished service on the Western Front. These were backed by a UK-based training wing comprised of 5, 6, 7 and 8 Squadrons. All eight squadrons were disbanded in 1919 and their personnel returned to Australia.

Not all the Australians who fought in the air were in the AFC. Many joined the flow of recruits from Canada, South Africa and New Zealand who enlisted in the British air services: the Royal Naval Air Service (RNAS) and the RFC, both of which amalgamated to form the Royal Air Force (RAF) in April 1918. Among them were Robert Little and Roderic Dallas. With at least 47 and 32 victories respectively, they were the two top Australian fighter aces of World War I (next was the AFC's top ace, Harry Cobby, with 29). Among other noteworthy Australians who flew in the British services were Charles Kingsford Smith, Bert Hinkler, Norman Brearley and Raymond Brownell. One who seemed destined for fame was Captain Cedric Ernest Howell, DSO, MC, DFC, RFC/RAF.

On 19 March 1919, the acting Australian Prime Minister, Mr W. A. Watt, made the following announcement in the House of Representatives in Melbourne:

With a view to stimulating aerial activity, the Commonwealth Government has decided to offer £10 000 for the first successful flight to Australia from Great Britain, in a machine manned by Australians. The rules and conditions governing the contest are now being drawn up and it is proposed that competitors be required to supply their own machines and to make all other necessary arrangements in connection with the flight.

This announcement drew public attention to what was to become the England-Australia Air Race of 1919, and the scheme was received with enthusiasm by Australian airmen who had been demobilised in England. One such airman was a Captain C. E. Howell, formerly of the Royal Air Force.

On 15 August, 1919, the Martinsyde Company officially entered their A1 biplane in the race. They nominated Captain Howell as pilot and teamed him with air mechanic George Fraser of Coburg, Victoria.

Cedric Ernest Howell as a pupil pilot in 1916. (National Library of Australia)

The Martinsyde A1 was powered by a single Rolls-Royce Falcon engine of 275 hp. It had a win span of 43 feet 4 inches (13.2 m) and was 27 feet 5 inches (8.4 m) long. It could house 160 gallons (727 litres) of fuel, giving it a range of around 1200 miles (1931 km). A similar plane had flown from London to Paris via Dieppe on 8 April 1919, a distance of 215 miles (346 km) in 75 minutes.

Howell and Fraser were ready to take off on 4 December. They were the sixth to go. Among those who had taken off earlier were Ross and Keith Smith, the eventual winners.

On that December day there was only a small group of people, consisting mostly of Royal Aero Club officials and members of the Martinsyde Company, who saw Howell and Fraser depart. They carried with them some mail, including a letter for the Prime Minister 'Billy' Hughes. There were also messages for a safe journey, including one from HRH Prince Albert and another from Mr Winston Churchill.

After an informal and unceremonious beginning, Howell and Fraser said their hasty farewells and finally shouted over the noise of their engines: 'Ta ta, boys, we're off!'

With that they taxied onto the field and moments later the Martinsyde was airborne. As it climbed away, Howell headed it towards the English Channel. The weather was closing in. The observers on the ground watched the biplane disappear from view. They would never see it again.

Cedric Ernest Howell was born in Adelaide, SA, on 17 June 1894. He was educated at the Church of England Grammar School in Melbourne and afterwards was employed as a draughtsman. With the outbreak of World War I, he endeavoured to enlist in the AIF but was rejected. However, at the same time, he held a commission in the Citizen Military Forces. In a bid to go overseas with the regular army, he resigned his commission and at last, early in 1915, managed to enlist as a private. He sailed to Egypt with the 16th Battalion which was to reinforce the men of the 14th Battalion.

On Gallipoli, he became familiar with the horrible slaughter which marked the infantryman's war and gained the reputation of being an expert marksman. Also, like so many others, he contracted malaria. Later he saw service as a sniper with the 46th Battalion in France during the earliest battles of the Somme.

In November 1916 he applied for and was accepted by the Royal Flying Corps, and in early 1917 received a posting to Denham for initial training. After being commissioned as a second lieutenant on the special reserve for officers on 17 March, Howell went to No. 17 Training School at Portmeadow in Oxford where, on 25 July, he was awarded his wings. From Oxford, Lieutenant Howell went to Yatesbury for final training flying DH5s. In October he was posted to 45 Squadron (Sopwith Camels) at St Marie Cappel in France.

On his arrival at 45 Squadron on the 28th, he was placed into 'A' Flight. His flight leader was Captain Norman Macmillan, the colourful Scottish pilot who later wrote the WWI aviation classics, *Into the Blue* and *Offensive Patrol*.

The commanding officer of 45 Squadron was Major A. M. Vaucour and he was not very impressed when he met Howell. In front of him was a tall, thin and dismal looking fellow, who had been given the nickname of 'Spike' as soon as he arrived. Believing the Australian's

Pilots of 45 Squadron at Grossa, Italy. Left to right: 2/Lt J.E. Child, 2/Lt C.E. Howell, 2/Lt J.P. Huins, Lt H.D. O'Neill, 2/Lt T.F. Williams, 2/Lt H.M. Moody, 2/Lt G.H. Bush, 2/Lt C.G. Catto. (Norman Macmillan via James Brown)

appearance was an indication of poor morale, Vaucour's first reaction was to declare him unsuitable and send him back to England. Meanwhile, however, Macmillan had had time to befriend the new arrival, who confided that before leaving for France he had suffered a recurrence of malaria. Macmillan interceded on Howell's behalf and it was largely through his persuasion that Vaucour allowed the Australian to stay in the squadron.

Spike Howell flew his first patrols in early November. On his first he was obliged to return early nursing a misfiring engine. On another, three German planes were attacked but results could not be assessed because of poor visibility.

Then in mid-November 1917, 45 Squadron was ordered to Italy.

Events there had taken a disastrous turn. On 24 October, the 14th German Army, under the command of General Otto von Below — a force consisting of six German and nine Austro-Hungarian divisions — divided into three attack groups of almost equal strength and launched an offensive. After four hours of gas shell bombardment and an hour of general bombardment, which completely disrupted the Italian communication system, they moved forward through drizzling rain and snow. The misty conditions were a major factor in their success because they provided cover and preserved the key element of surprise. Although the right and left wings were delayed by sturdy Italian resistance, the centre group of four divisions broke through at Caporetto and by that evening reserves were pouring through the defences.

To plug this gap, the Italians were obliged to make a general retreat. There were several critical days, especially 30 and 31 October, but by 10 November the main body of the Italian Army succeeded in reaching the Piave, where it began to reform behind the natural barrier of the river.

News of the disaster shook the Allies. The year had hitherto seen slow but real progress towards apparent victory. A pattern of ever- increasing pressure, limited advances and heavy losses against stubborn resistance had been established but now, suddenly, there was an almost overwhelming reversal. This had been completely unexpected in Italy, where the Italian Army had been attacking and making steady advances throughout August and September.

French and British reinforcements were hurriedly dispatched by rail to the Italian Front. However, they took time to organise and concentrate and during the interval before they relieved the Italians the situation remained grave. A serious attack developed in the sector between Piave and Abrenta, but after five days of heavy fighting it was successfully blocked. At the beginning of December units of the French Army under General Fayolle took over the defence of this area while the British, under Lord Plumer, relieved in the Montello sector.

The Allies also sent air units. Altogether the French sent six divisions supported by three squadrons of army contact aircraft, but they had no fighter squadrons. By the end of 1917 there were five British air units in Italy of which three were fighter squadrons. These were Nos 28, 45 and 66 all of which flew Clerget-engined Sopwith Camels.

No. 45 Squadron ceased operational flying in France on 15 November, ready for the transfer to the Italian Front. Next day the pilots flew their planes to No. 2 Aircraft Depot at Candas. Here they were dismantled, packed in cases and loaded on railway wagons, but there was a delay of over three weeks before the journey to Italy commenced because of the opening of the Battle of Cambrai on 20 November. There were two trains: the first conveyed 'A' and 'B' Flights and the second 'HQ' and 'C' Flights. The first train arrived in Padova, Italy, on 18 December. Pilots began flight testing their uncrated and reassembled Sopwiths five days later, but there was not a great deal of flying because of bad weather.

Meanwhile, a Canadian by the name of William George Barker, who would later win a Victoria Cross in France, scored the RFC's first victory on this front on 29 November.

By the end of 1917 RFC Camels in Italy had shot down fourteen enemy aircraft and destroyed two kite balloons. Two of the victories belonged to 45 Squadron, gained by it on 31 December, on its third day of operations from

No. 45 Squadron's Sopwith Camels in Italy in 1918. (IWM)

the airfield at Istrana. They both went down before the guns of Tasmanian 2/Lt Ray Brownell, who shared the second with 2/Lt Mike Moody.

The air fighting gained momentum in January and two of the kills for the month went to Howell. Then there was a lapse of three months before he scored again.

Spike Howellshot down his first enemy plane on 14 January over Cimetta. A patrol of four Camels led by Brownell attacked five Albatros DVs from out of the sun. Howell and Moody went after the same DV, which defended itself skilfully until the Australian at last managed to manoeuvre into a favourable position and pour out 50 rounds of ammunition. The German aeroplane fell in flames. Howell's second kill was another Albatros DV which crashed at Sette Casoni on the 26th.

Because of the smaller number of aircraft employed on the Italian Front, this theatre of operations did not witness the almost daily aerial battles which became a feature of the air war over France. Encounters were far less frequent. In February, 45 Squadron could claim only ten victories and the number dropped to only two in March, during which month the squadron moved to Grossa. April was also a slow month but on the 22nd Spike managed to bring down his third enemy plane, an Albatros DIII, which crashed near Levico.

The duties of the Sopwith Camels in Italy consisted mainly of long patrols behind the enemy lines, short patrols over the front lines and escort for RE8s on reconnaissance or bombing missions. In February a new duty was added. It was decided to try them at dive-bombing. Each Camel was required to carry four 20-pound Cooper bombs on racks fitted under the fuselage between the rear struts of the undercarriage. There were no bomb sights and in order to drop these bombs the pilot dived and aimed his aircraft at the target, levelled out at 200 feet (61m) and released the bomb by a toggle and wire control. There were some initial successes but, in general, the results achieved less and cost more than the usual type of bombing by the RE8s.

On 4 May 1918, six Sopwith Camels from 45 Squadron were ordered to bomb the Trentino hydroelectric power station which lay in a deep valley north of Lake Garda. The formation was led by Captain G. H. Bush, another Australian. Bush intended to dive on the station from the west in line astern formation. Unfortunately, the mountainous terrain made it impossible to fly lower than 2000 feet (600 m) over the target. Without any means of communicating a change of plan to the others, Bush decided to drop the bombs from this height in order to avoid confusion. All except Howell unloaded without scoring a hit.

Because he was last to bomb, Spike had the opportunity to observe the results and to use his own initiative to

change tactics without disrupting the others. He left formation and turned south. Then, diving into the valley, he flew upstream at a height of 100 feet (30 m). As he passed over the power station he dropped his four bombs. Two of them burst on the station to the east of its tower and a third fell onto a large building nearby. Anti-aircraft fire was light and inaccurate. In spite of the accuracy of the attack, it was obvious that the puny 20-pound bombs could do little damage to such a huge industrial target.

Since his first victories in January, Spike Howell had been gaining invaluable experience and he was beginning to demonstrate the skill and initiative of a potential flight leader.

On 13 May he led a patrol out for the first time — a flight of three Camels on a long patrol behind the enemy lines. They took off at 5.10 a.m. and just over an hour later, while flying at 12 500 feet (3800 m) ten Albatros DIII Scouts were sighted escorting two LVG two-seaters apparently on a reconnaissance mission. The enemy was flying in a scattered formation south-east over the Brenta River near Coldarco. Taking advantage of the sun to prevent being seen, Howell positioned his flight and then dived among them, splitting them into two groups. The two other Camels went for the three highest enemy scouts. Howell fired a brief burst of Vickers at one Albatros at close range and saw it stall. While it was unable to manoeuvre, he fired again and sent it down out of control.

Seconds later he attacked another Albatros with a long burst of fire and caused it to go down in a vertical dive. One of the other British pilots saw this machine crash near Coldarco. Howell then noticed one of his comrades down another Albatros, which crashed into the ground near Costa.

Meanwhile, the remaining enemy planes had been scattered all over the sky. One LVG had dived away when the fighting began, but the other, escorted by two Albatros, attempted to continue its mission. Howell turned south to intercept and overhaul them. When he was in position he began an attack on the LVG but gun trouble forced him to stop. He pulled out of the fight and watched as the other two Camels attacked the two-seater which eventually went down emitting thick smoke. As it fell it gradually broke up into debris. While this was happening Howell managed to clear his guns.

Searching the sky above he found it clear of the enemy but down below he sighted another Albatros DIII. He dived and chased it up the Brenta Valley, flying at about 500 feet (150 m). A burst of Vickers caused it to catch fire and nose dive into the river. He circled the spot where it disappeared, but the only thing he could see was a piece of debris from the tailplane floating on the water.

When the flight of Sopwiths returned home it could claim the destruction of five enemy aircraft for no loss.

Spike Howell in front of the wreckage of Tasmanian Ray Brownell's Sopwith Camel B6283 which had crashed after a cylinder had blown off the engine on 22 February 1918. Brownell was slightly injured.
(R.J. Brownell via James Brown)

Fossalunga, Italy, February 1918. Captain R.J. Brownell MC, MM, Lt Harold Bush and Lt Cedric 'Spike' Howell with 45 Squadron's mascot, 'Spud'. All three men were Australians serving in the squadron. This photograph was taken shortly after Ray Brownell's crash. (R.J. Brownell via James Brown)

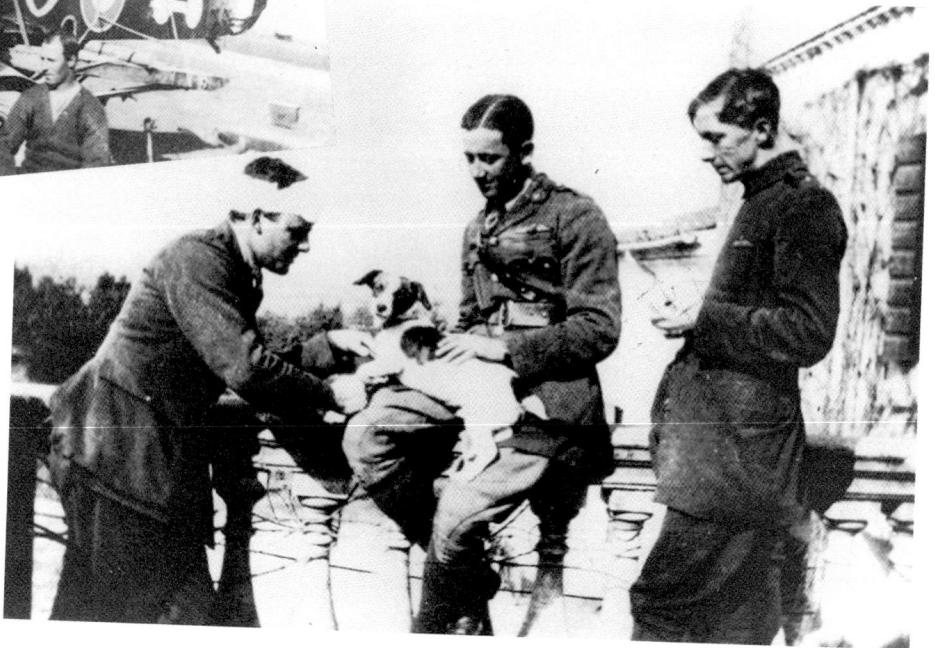

Three belonged to Spike Howell and as well he was allowed another as 'out of control'. His first patrol as flight leader had been an outstanding success. It brought his tally of confirmed victories to six and also earned him the Military Cross.

On 1 June he was promoted to the rank of captain and given command of 'C' Flight in succession to Captain H. M. Moody. June was also a successful month for him for other reasons. He scored two doubles, which brought his tally of enemy aircraft destroyed to ten, and was also recommended for the Distinguished Flying Cross which was duly awarded on 22 June.

At 3 a.m. on 15 June, the peace of the morning was shattered by a heavy artillery barrage against the whole length of the Italian front line from the Adriatic to east of the Astico. The Germans and Austrians were launching another offensive. Using smokescreens to hide their preparations for crossing the Piave, their engineers swiftly laid pontoon bridges across the river. Soon the infantry was able to cross and mass in considerable force to begin the assault. Reinforcements crowded across the bridges to support the attack.

The first news of the Austrian offensive was received from 45 Squadron's early patrol led by Spike Howell.

He landed at 11.40 a.m. with the news. Then, with the aircraft refuelled and loaded with bombs, he led them off again. 'C' Flight was to fly four missions that day. They and the rest of 45 Squadron bombed and strafed with deadly effect. One bomb hit a pontoon bridge filled with soldiers, another destroyed a boat and another hit an enemy filled trench. With their bombs gone the Camel pilots dived their planes and sprayed the enemy soldiers with machine-gun bullets. It was estimated that they caused over 100 casualties.

Soon all the RAF fighters were in action, disrupting the enemy's supply lines and bombing and strafing troops crossing the river. At night, the Austrians rebuilt the pontoon bridges and flew in supplies with their own aircraft. With the arrival of daylight the RAF squadrons again attacked as long as weather conditions permitted.

Generally, the weather was not good and, at first, the cover it provided assisted the enemy. But then the situation changed. The clouds and heavy rain which grounded the RAF soon caused the streams of the upper Piave to fill and the river began to swell. It changed into a raging torrent which rushed down onto the Austrian bridges, sweeping many of them away. By the afternoon of 18 June only two of them remained useable and they were a long way downstream of the main attack. The Austrian troops on the Allied side of the river were now isolated. Realising the opportunity, the Allies counter-attacked.

No longer required to bomb bridges, the RAF fighters returned to their patrols. Austrian and German aircraft had not been much in evidence of late but now several encounters took place. On 19 June, Spike Howell's 'C' Flight met an enemy formation of more than twice their number at 16 000 feet (4900 m) over the Asiago Plateau. Six were shot down of which the Australian claimed two.

By 22 June, the German and Austrian troops had been ordered back across the river. British and Italian aircraft reverted to bombing and strafing the now retreating enemy. Two days later the armies were back in the position they occupied before the attack had been launched. The Central Powers had suffered heavy casualties and lost much equipment as well as having some 20 000 men taken prisoner.

By the end of June, Captain Howell was well established as one of the most lethal fliers on the Italian Front. His formula for success was always to keep height above the enemy and never to allow himself or his flight to be caught by surprise from above. By adopting these tactics he always retained the initiative.

But even the most experienced airman can be tricked. On one occasion he saw an enemy aeroplane sneaking up the Asiago Plateau. He dived at it and found himself going down to the bottom of a valley, where he flew into concentrated ground fire. It was then that he noticed that the plane was in fact a dummy suspended on a cable-car system. which machine-gunners were using for firing practice. Howell had suddenly given them a real target and was lucky to escape unscathed from the unintended trap.

On 12 July, while flying at 14 000 feet (4300 m) in the vicinity of Mont Tomba, Spike Howell and another pilot saw ten enemy aircraft flying west-south-west from Feltre. There had initially been three Sopwiths but one had been forced to turn back with engine trouble. The two remaining Camels climbed up-sun. As they approached unseen they noted that the enemy formation consisted of seven Albatros DVs and three other fighters which they could not identify. They might have been Pfalz Scouts.

As the formation turned south-east, Howell dived to the attack. He swiftly closed in on the enemy leader's Albatros and fired. It immediately spun down for a distance of 500 feet (152 m) where its lower right wing fell off. Howell then turned on one of the unrecognised fighters and, after skilful manoeuvring, cut loose with his twin Vickers. The plane burst into flame and fell.

Suddenly, five Austro-Hungarian Berg Scouts came diving out of the sun and into the dogfight. One made for the other Camel but Spike noticed it and gave chase. He fired just before the Berg could open up. It went down with smoke pouring from its fuselage.

The two Camels were heavily outnumbered but continued to fight. It seemed only be a matter of time before they were overwhelmed, but help was at hand. Two SPADs and a number of Hanriot HD1s of the Italian Air Force saw the plight of the British planes and joined in.

Another Berg attacked Howell, but using the Camel's unique turning ability he quickly reversed the position. He fired and saw hits on the centre section of the enemy plane. He had no time to see what happened to the Berg because things were becoming more hectic and there were suddenly three enemy planes on his tail. (An Italian pilot coming into the battle did see Howell's victim crash.) Howell outmanoeuvred the three scouts and, sending a brief burst of Vickers at one DV, had the satisfaction of seeing it fall out of control. Then, from out of nowhere, the second Sopwith came to his aid and drove off the others.

The Italian fighters began to make their presence felt. A Hanriot shot yet another Berg off Howell's tail — it fell out of control. A SPAD sent down an Albatros which first gave off smoke and then fell to pieces. Howell next dived onto another Albatros attacking a Hanriot and fired at close range, but so furious was the fight that he had no chance to observe the result.

The battle ended as abruptly as it had started and the sky was suddenly clear of aircraft as if by magic.

The two Camels joined up again and turned homewards. Moments later they noticed two more enemy planes at 6000 feet (1800 m) above the Piave. They dived to the attack but Howell had to break off to clear a gun stoppage and his target escaped. Meanwhile the other Camel pilot dispatched his victim, another Berg D1, which Howell saw crash near Cavrera. Between the two of them, the Camel pilots obtained six confirmed victories, four of them falling to Howell.

Two days later, on a close offensive patrol, Spike Howell was leading 'C' Flight when he saw five Albatros DIIIs at 16 000 feet (4900 m). He tried to climb into the sun but his engine was running badly. Two of the enemy planes were above when he led his flight unseen onto the other three. He opened fire on one and it shot up into a climbing turn which he could not follow because of his defective engine. One of the other Camels took up the attack and the Albatros keeled over into a vertical dive, leaving a column of smoke in the sky.

Another DIII dived to assist his comrade but Howell cut it off with several well directed bursts. The enemy aircraft turned towards the Allied lines with Spike following close behind cutting off its line of retreat. He could easily have sent it crashing down but he chose not to do so. Instead he held his fire and watched as the Albatros made a wobbly landing near Tresche about 500 yards inside Allied territory. As it rolled to a halt its wheels must have struck an obstacle because it suddenly flipped over onto its back but Spike saw with satisfaction that the pilot scrambled out safely.

Howell's last battle occurred the next day, 15 July. It was another long patrol. Just after 10 a.m., he sighted two formations of enemy planes, four at 16 000 feet (4900 m) and five at 18 000 feet (5500 m). He guided the flight onto the lower group and kept watch as a number of the enemy were shot down.

Eight more enemy aircraft appeared and Howell dived among them. When six of them attempted to climb away, Howell was in position to cut them off. He chose one and fired a deflection burst which caused the enemy machine to fall in flames and crash near Costa Alta.

Another fighter manoeuvred onto his tail but he spotted it and executed a steep climbing turn and reversed the positions. Now with the advantage, he drove his adversary down, firing whenever he had the chance, until the plane finally crashed on Mount Forcellona. The remaining enemy scouts all fiercely attacked the lone Australian and the odds were too great for him to stay and fight. He managed to escape their unwelcome attention by spinning down continuously from 16 000 feet to 7000 feet (2100 m).

Spike Howell's two victories on the 15th brought his total for July to seven and his overall score to seventeen, plus two out of control. On 22 July he was awarded the DFC and then, with his tour of duty over, he left for England on 9 August. He and his Sopwith Camel had developed into a deadly combination. Whenever he found the enemy, and usually regardless of the odds, the results he achieved in combat were nothing short of spectacular.

He served at the Central Flying School at Upavon for the remainder of the war.

After the quiet take-off in the 1919 England-Australia Air Race, Howell and Fraser headed their Martinsyde A1 out across the English Channel. Their intended overnight stop was Lyons but as they flew on the weather deteriorated.

There was another setback when they reached Paris. They found that the fuel pump had to be replaced, an operation which took two hours. Their plane had to be modified and they decided to go as far as Dijon. Again they ran into bad weather and almost disaster. While flying down a valley in thick cloud they were suddenly confronted by the last ridge and almost hit a tree.

It had been too close. They'd had enough and picked the next possible landing area to put down before anything else happened. This was somewhere near Dijon and the French locals who greeted the fliers treated them well. Part of the Martinsyde's tail skid had been broken off while landing but there was no other damage.

Next morning they took off for Pisa but the weather interfered again. They ran into gale-force winds and by noon they were well off course. Approaching Toulon, conditions worsened even further so they had no choice but to land and hope that the winds would ease in a couple of hours. It was mid-afternoon before they could risk becoming airborne. They flew out over the Gulf of Genoa and landed at Pisa.

It now became necessary to carry out emergency repairs on the damaged tail skid. Fraser improvised a new skid by using a hacksaw and a pocket knife to whittle down a block of local timber. Darkness fell before he could finish. Rain and wind continued throughout the night. With the coming of daylight there was little improvement. It was not until 1 p.m. that they were able to take off from Pisa's water-soaked airfield and two and a half hours later they landed at Naples.

Poor weather continued to plague them on Sunday, 7 December, but, in spite of the rain and strong winds, they tried to reach Taranto. In the vicinity of Mount Vesuvius conditions took a dramatic turn for the worse. The flight became so rough that both airmen were sick. They progressed to Salerno but, because any attempt to land was far too hazardous and therefore out of the question, they had to turn back to Naples.

Howell and Fraser did not reach Taranto until the next day. They took off from Taranto at noon with the object of reaching Athens, a distance of 400 miles, but never made it....

There was no news of the plane until a few minutes after 8 p.m. when it was seen flying in the semi-darkness over St George's Bay, Corfu. It fell into the water about a quarter mile out to sea. Peasants on the shores of Corfu reported later that they had heard cries for help coming from the sea that night but it was too rough to attempt a rescue.

Next day, as soon as the seas moderated, a naval patrol boat was dispatched to the vicinity but it conducted a search in vain.

Eventually, the crashed Martinsyde was discovered in good condition under about twelve feet of water. Spike Howell's body was later washed ashore but George Fraser was never found. Attempts were made to salvage the plane but, before this could be achieved, rough weather and seas again intervened and it broke up.

Spike had married in England during the war. He had been one of the few married RFC/RAF pilots to serve on the Italian Front. His wife was travelling en route to Australia on the liner Orsova at the time of the race. The airmen had hoped to overtake and circle the ship at Naples.

News of Howell's death was cabled to the Orsova but it was not passed on to the widow because of her poor state of health at the time. When the ship docked at Adelaide, Howell's father boarded and broke the news.

Mystery surrounds the crash. Corfu is only 150 miles from Taranto. It has never been adequately explained how the two men could have flown for eight hours, twice the length of time necessary to reach Athens, and yet have come down where they did. Howell's father was never really satisfied that the correct report of the fatal accident was made public.

There is little doubt that Howell ditched safely. The relatively intact condition of the plane when it was found testifies to this, as does the fact that cries for help were heard during the night. What really happened beforehand will never be known.

Numerous explanations were offered. One was that Spike must have been nearing Athens when he discovered that his wallet, with all his money, had been left in Taranto. It was suggested that, since they could not go on without the cash, they turned back. As they did so, they ran into increasing headwinds and the Martinsyde's headway was considerably reduced until, finally reaching the vicinity of Corfu, it ran out of fuel and Howell was forced to land it on the water.

Another suggestion was that they had been obliged to land somewhere and make repairs. Upon taking off again, poor weather caused them to lose the way. Then, as night came on, and still unable to find a landmark, they were attracted by the lights of a village on Corfu. Not knowing where they were, they were again obliged to land where they could by using the lights as a guide.

Officials of the Martinsyde Company suggested that Howell seesawed his flight over the direct course and could not find a landmark because of the weather. Finally, with his fuel supply exhausted, he had to come down in the sea.

The body of Captain Cedric Ernest Howell, DSO, MC, DFC, was finally brought from Corfu to Australia and buried with full military honours at Heidelberg Cemetery, Victoria.

C. E. 'SPIKE' HOWELL: HONOURS AND AWARDS

London Gazette, 16 September 1918:
MILITARY CROSS
Lieutenant Cedric Ernest Howell, RAF, Special Reserve

For conspicuous gallantry and devotion to duty. He bombed an electrical power house with great skill, obtaining three direct hits from 100 feet. With two other machines he carried out a most dashing attack on a formation of twelve enemy aeroplanes. Although badly hampered by frequent jams in both of his machine-guns, he destroyed three and drove down one out of control. He is a most successful and gallant patrol leader and has destroyed six enemy aeroplanes and shot down one out of control.

Spike Howell (with pipe) in the cockpit of his Martinsyde A1, about to leave on his ill-fated flight in the England Australia Air Race, 4 December 1919. (National Library of Australia)

Sopwith Camel B6283/C of 45 Squadron RFC, one of the aircraft flown by Spike Howell's compatriot Ray Brownell. (Dennis Newton)

London Gazette, 21 September 1918:
DISTINGUISHED FLYING CROSS
Lieutenant (Temporary Captain) Cedric Ernest Howell
    On a recent occasion this officer, leading his patrol of three machines, attacked nine enemy aeroplanes, destroying six and driving down one out of control; he himself accounted for two of these. On a former occasion he destroyed three enemy aeroplanes in one flight. He is a fine fighting officer, skilful and determined.

London Gazette, 2 November 1918:
DISTINGUISHED SERVICE ORDER
Lieutenant (Temporary Captain) Cedric Ernest Howell, MC, DFC
    This officer recently attacked, in company with one other machine, an enemy formation of fifteen aeroplanes and succeeded in destroying four of them and bringing one down out of control. Two days afterwards he destroyed another enemy machine, which fell in our lines, and on the following day he led three machines against sixteen enemy scouts, destroying two of them. Captain Howell is a very gallant and determined fighter, who takes no account of the enemy's superior numbers in his battles.

London Gazette, 6 January 1919:
MENTIONED IN DESPATCHES
Lieutenant (Acting Captain) C. E. Howell, DSO, MC, DFC
(Howell was mentioned in a despatch dated 26 October 1918 from the General the Earl of Cavan, KP, KCB, MVO, Commander-in-Chief of the British Forces in Italy to the Secretary of State for War which was published in the London Gazette of 6th January, 1919. The 'mention' is for 'distinguished and gallant services and devotion to duty' during the period 26 February,

1918 to midnight on 14 September 1918. Howell left Italy on 9 August, 1918.)

C. E. HOWELL: CONFIRMED VICTORIES

Date	Type	Result	Locality
14/1/18	Albatros Scout	1 In flames	Cimetta
26/1/18	Albatros Scout	1 Crashed	Sette Casoni
22/4/18	Albatros DIII	1 Crashed	Levico
13/5/18	Albatros DIII	3 Destroyed	Coldarco, Costa & Rocca
13/5/18	Albatros DIII	1 Out of control	Coldarco
8/6/18	Scout (type unknown)	1 Crashed	Vicinity Mt Tomba
8/6/18	Berg Scout	1 Crashed	Vicinity Mt Tomba
9/6/18	Albatros DIII	1 Crashed	Camporovere
19/6/18	Albatros DV	1 Crashed	Mt Meatta
12/7/18	Albatros DV/Berg/ Scouts (type unknown)	4 Destroyed	Mt Tomatico
2/7/18	Albatros DV	1 Out of control	Mt Tomatico
14/7/18	Albatros DV	1 Crashed	Tresche
15/7/18	Scout (type unknown)	1 In flames	Costa Alta
15/7/18	Scout (type unknown)	1 Crashed	Mt Forcellona

4

MISSING OVER DUNKIRK

The Australian Air Force was born on 31 March 1921 ('Royal' Australian Air Force effective from 31 August 1921) with an initial strength of 151 personnel and 164 aircraft, of which 128 were gift aircraft plus supporting equipment from the British Government. Twenty were standard trainers (Avro 504-K), ten scouting planes (Sopwith Pups bought during the war) and six were Fairey seaplanes bought in 1921. Later, six Avro 504-Ks which were built in Australia were added. It was a diminutive air force, sustained by some £500 000 per annum, its leaders being drawn mainly from the AFC.

At the Imperial Conference of 1923, the UK proposed offering four-year short-service commissions in the RAF to RAAF officers who had just graduated from Point Cook. By this method, it was reasoned, a reserve of trained pilots would be built up which could be used to reinforce RAF

Famous pre-World War II photograph of a formation of Spitfire MkIs of 65 Squadron RAF. The picture was used extensively in wartime publications. Gordon Olive was flying FZ-A, fourth in line. With the outbreak of hostilities, 65 Squadron's identification letters were changed from FZ to YT. Olive was flying his regular aircraft, Spitfire K9903/YT-A, over Dunkirk on 28 May, 1940. (IWM)

squadrons in an emergency and the RAAF would benefit when the men returned after four years operational training at British expense. The scheme began in 1927. At the outbreak of war on 3 September 1939 there were around 450 Australians serving in the RAF in various parts of the world and most were operational pilots on short-service commissions. One such pilot was F/L Gordon Olive of 65 Squadron RAF, who first saw combat over the British evacuation from Dunkirk.

In May 1940 F/Lt Gordon Olive of 65 Squadron RAF was flying Spitfires over Dunkirk. Years later, in an interview, he described a dogfight in which he was involved on 26 May:

> Dunkirk was the first bit of action we saw and the first dogfight I got into was over Calais. One morning we were slightly off the coast making towards Calais when a formation of somewhere around twelve or fifteen 109s suddenly came out of a clear blue sky and attacked us. They swung around to repeat the attack and we finished up in a ding-dong swirling dogfight. During that I got some very good shots at quite a few of them but every time I got a working shot they dived into a layer of strata cloud which was just 500-1,000 feet below where the fun was going on.
>
> At one stage I suddenly realised they were escorts for a dozen or more Henschel dive-bombers, which were attacking Calais, so I tried to get over and get a shot at them. A couple of 109s spotted me and came after me. They drew my attention to them by shooting at me so I went after them, got some shots at them and they went down into the clouds.
>
> After we had thinned them all out, because they had gone down into the cloud, we went down under the cloud but there was nothing to be seen down there except quite a lot of strange-looking soapy blobs in the middle of the Channel. These, we subsequently learned, were the types of spots aeroplanes made when they crashed so we may have got half a dozen or more. We were passed by 54 Squadron, coming to relieve us, and they commented a couple of days later when we saw them that we must have been having quite a party because they saw six or more 109s come out of the clouds and go straight down into the sea.
>
> We apparently got quite a few of them, I don't know how many, but didn't claim any because we didn't see them crash. Perhaps we got the lot for all I know. They certainly didn't stick around and come back for any more.

Gordon's Combat Report for 26 May 1940 adds a few more details:

> Our Squadron sighted about 30 Me 109s.* A dogfight ensued when the 109s made considerable use of

cumulus cloud to avoid engaging Spitfires for more than a few seconds. On three occasions while patrolling under the cloud, Me 109s came through the clouds in a position directly in front of me. I fired short bursts at these in succession and was following one which appeared to have been hit and was diving towards the sea, when I had to break away as I noticed tracers coming from the rear and had to manoeuvre on to the tail of this 109. This one, however, climbed into cloud and disappeared. After another half hour's patrol I saw no further 109s and returned to base.

Charles Gordon Chaloner Olive was born in Bardon, Queensland, on 3 July 1916, the son of Mr and Mrs H. C. Olive of Yeerongpilly. He was educated at Brisbane Grammar School and Queensland University and then joined the RAAF, commencing training at Point Cook, in January 1936. He was awarded his Pilot's Flying Badge on 8 December 1936, but in January 1937 he sailed for England to take up a short service commission with the RAF.

On 22 May, 1937, with the rank of pilot officer, he was sent to 65 Squadron. At the time the squadron was equipped with Gloster Gauntlets but in June it converted to Gloster Gladiators. He was promoted to flying officer on 19 August 1938, and less than a year later, on 24 July 1939, he was made acting flight lieutenant. By then 65 Squadron had converted to Spitfires.

In September 1939, when war broke out, 65 Squadron formed part of the Hornchurch Wing and it flew its first scramble on the 5th without result. The squadron achieved its first kill in May 1940 when, towards the end of the month, offensive patrols began to be flown over France and the Low Countries to cover the evacuation of the battered British Expeditionary Force from Dunkirk.

The Australian's second Combat Report was filled out next day on 27 May. In another action east of Dunkirk, after first engaging Messerschmitt Bf 110s and then attacking a close formation of Dornier Do 17s, Gordon Olive noticed one of the Do 17s lagging behind.

Chasing this, at a range of 300 yards closing to 100 yards, he fired off all of his remaining ammunition, silencing the rear gunner and setting the Dornier's port engine on fire. Unfortunately he was unable to observe what happened next because there were too many other enemy aircraft in the vicinity:

> Our Squadron was on patrol over Dunkirk when we saw considerable anti-aircraft fire about ten miles on the forward starboard quarter. I formed my section in line astern and we proceeded to investigate and found about nineteen Me 110s flying singly about 500 yards apart. I attacked one head-on firing a burst of about two seconds and saw considerable return fire. I attacked

Spitfires of 65 Squadron on their way to Dunkirk. Painting by Gordon Olive.

another one from the beam and in the break-away noticed five Do 215s [Do 17s] flying in close formation with three in vic followed by two in vic about fifty yards behind. I attacked these with a quarter attack but did not notice any results.

On the break-away I saw a sixth Do 215 which had apparently been left behind the main formation of five. I fired all the remaining ammunition at a range of 300 to 100 yards, the rear gunner was silenced and flames were coming from the port engine. I did not observe the enemy aircraft crash as there were too many other enemy aircraft in the vicinity.

Fifty years later he recalled:

We used to run into individual pairs of bombers. The next day we ran into some Dorniers. I got a shot at some and got one of them I think. His engine was on fire but I had to get away, there were other fighters in the vicinity, hostile ones, and I was by myself so I had to break it off. I don't know whether I got him or not, probably did because he was reasonably well alight.

There were one or two others. I took some shots at a 110 but that was fairly inconclusive and he made for cloud and got out of the way. I got return fire from him...

I also got return fire from the Dornier I was shooting at which was the first time that I'd seen tracer coming back at me. It sort of fanned out all around me. The gunner must have been hosing it or his gun was probably bouncing in his hands. At any one time there seemed to be about a dozen tracers in the air in front of me. They looked like little ping-pong balls coming up. They came up quite slowly for a start and they went past at an incredible bloody speed.

On the 28th Gordon was listed missing 'as a result of air operations'. Up to this time he had completed 25 operational sorties totalling 35 hours flying time. No. 65 Squadron formed part of a wing of Spitfires on patrol over Dunkirk, Gordon Olive flying K9903.

A Gruppe of Messerschmitt Bf 109s suddenly swooped onto them and the three Spitfires broke formation and split up. Olive pulled up in a steep climbing turn to the right and came around behind his attackers. The Australian's wingmen both escaped into cloud and made their way independently back to Hornchurch. After landing, each reported that he had last seen Olive 'chasing a dozen Messerschmitts!'

Time passed and Olive did not return, nor was there any news of him. That evening, 65 Squadron moved back to Kirton-in-Lindsey with its Australian flight commander listed as missing.

In fact, he had not been shot down, but as je recalled many years later, it had been close ... very, very close:

We'd come into Dunkirk, a wing of Spitfires making for the patrol line which was twenty-odd miles inland from Dunkirk which cut across the approaches from the German aerodromes the other side of the Rhine. Provided we patrolled across the line we would certainly get a few interceptions and stop them before they could get to Dunkirk.

We were on our way and came in under the huge mass of black cloud which was burning from the Dunkirk ocean terminal — a square mile of tanks was on fire. It writhed up in a huge, vast tornado-like funnel which was the best part of a mile in diameter I suppose up to 7000 feet into the base of a huge sooty cloud which spread into probably a twenty-mile radius. It was spread all over the Dunkirk area but particularly inland to the west of Dunkirk and rose up to about 40 000 to 45 000 feet and blew away in a big anvil which they told me subsequently caused soot to fall out over Glasgow and Edinburgh a day or two later.

We went in under this at about 10 000 feet on our way to the Dunkirk patrol line. Looking down, we spotted a couple of greyish-looking aeroplanes, low-wing monoplanes, but they were a bit too far down below us to know exactly what they were. I was ordered by the wing leader to go and find out what they were and deal with them.

When we came into firing range I suddenly realised that they were a couple of Skuas which were doing some sort of beach patrol. The boys with me and I went up beside them, waggled our wings and waved hello and then did a U-turn to join up with our wing of 33 Spitfires.

The wing should have been by then in the patrol line. As I headed off in the direction which I estimated to be the correct one I saw through a gap in the lower clouds beside the big mushroom what appeared to be near enough to 36 aeroplanes. I thought, 'Ah? They haven't gone as far as I thought they would go', but in a very short space of time I realised they weren't going in, they were coming out, and they were heading for me. In less time than it takes to tell about it they opened fire and the leading half dozen were squirting lead at us. We were under attack!

They were in three lines of twelve, presumably squadtons in line astern formation, and I yelled to both

of my boys to break because we were being shot at. They broke to either side of me and each of them attracted a row of twelve Messerschmitt 109s. I found myself with the leader squirting at me and I dived under his attack. His tracers went over me harmlessly Then I whipped into a right hand climbing turn to get out of trouble.

This right-hand climbing turn was an old trick that an old boy from World War I, old Kanga de la Rue* sold us on when I was at Point Cook. I'd tried it a number of times in mock dogfights and found that it worked fairly well because most people invariably turned to the left. When they turned to the right they felt uncomfortable so I practised until I felt very comfortable with it.

I tried this and the leader of the squadron, the wing leader of the 109s, wheeled around and came after me going off in the right hand-climbing turn and in a very short space of time we were all committed, going round in a long snake on one side of the circle with me on the other side. I was able to turn very much tighter than the 109s and in a very short space of time got on the tail of Tail End Charlie who was flying in formation on the fellow in front of him who was flying in formation on the fellow in front of him, and so on. His attention was fairly well occupied.

I got up as close as I could to him and gave him a squirt and he disappeared as if he had evaporated. I went on to the one who was travelling immediately in front in only a matter of seconds because I was travelling a bit faster than the 109s and he was in the same position, so he got a squirt for about a second

*Messerschmitt Bf 109E Gordon Olive was last seen by his wingmen **chasing** no less than a dozen of these formidable German fighters!* (MAP)

Amid and around the swirling thick black smoke from oil fires at Dunkirk, Gordon Olive's painting depicts his vivid memories of his desperate battle. Painting by Gordon Olive.

and he disappeared. The third one flipped over and he went the other way, then the fourth, the fifth, and the sixth and so on until eventually I got up to No.9.

No. 9 didn't disappear suddenly, he just straightened out slightly. He must have been hit, I think, otherwise he would have done something fairly violent like the others. My mistake was to try and get a better shot at him when I was line astern of him.

I put myself in a perfect position for his leader and he plastered me with a blast which was only a second or two in duration but it was enough to make a hell of a mess of my aeroplane. It started with one enormous explosion which sounded as if the end of the world had come. The cockpit filled up with stinking fumes of cordite and there was a series of lesser bangs as bullets arrived after the cannon shell. Something went off with a great bang under my seat which turned out to be the compressed air bottle.

The aeroplane took off in a screaming oblique loop of its own accord and I subsequently found out that one of the slugs had damaged the elevator trimming tab and put it into a configuration which enabled the plane to fly in very tight turns or a loop but not straight and level. That saved my life because it put me up into an oblique loop and brought me out of the loop onto the tail of the plane which was No. 10 in the formation, No.3 from the leader.

When I pushed the button to give him a ration of bullets nothing happened because the compressed air bottle under my seat had been blown away. There was no compressed air and I thought that was the end of

the line for me but the bloke whose tail I was on thought it was the end of the line for him and he disappeared with the same remarkable rapidity as the others had.

This left me on the tail of the one immediately in front of him and he did the same which left me with the squadron commander or wing leader, or whatever he was. He didn't wait to see if I had bullets or not, he decided that seeing the other boys had gone he would go too. It was all over in a relatively short space of time.

That presented me with some fairly monumental problems. I suddenly felt very drowsy and dizzy, as if I was being anaesthetised and realised that the cockpit was absolutely full of fumes and I was sniffing petrol at a very dangerous rate. I managed to whip the canopy open. The Spitfire continued to go around in a giddy circle and let some fresh air in.

One of the bullets had holed the petrol tank, it subsequently turned out, around about the 20-gallon mark. At that stage I didn't know that. There was something like 60 gallons of petrol slopping around in the bottom of the Spitfire and the fumes from that had been affecting me.

Fresh air coming into the open cockpit improved things a bit and I was able to take stock of the situation. My leg had been hit but I couldn't tell how badly. I flew down to the beaches at Dunkirk and checked the petrol gauges on the way down.

By the time I arrived there the petrol had gone from 18 gallons down to 16 which was about normal consumption, so I assumed that the lowest bullet hole in the petrol tank was around the 20-gallon mark. There was just sufficient fuel, other things being equal, to get back to England if I was extremely lucky.

Next thing was that I had to check that I hadn't suffered glycol damage or other problems which would show up as I was committed to a Channel crossing... The engine was shaking like a big shaggy wet dog, trying to shake itself out of its mounting. Very nerve-racking and shattering for the confidence. I thought, well, its just not my idea of enjoying a flight across the sea so I went along the coast.

As I started off about ten miles out of Dunkirk, I suddenly flew through an air pocket which should not have been there because the air was very still. A couple of seconds later I saw a large black onion-shaped cloud appear on my starboard wingtip followed by a couple more that were just ahead of me all the time. Obviously there was an anti-aircraft battery which had got my range and height almost exactly. They were shooting a bit ahead of me, possibly because they thought I was going a bit faster than I was with my sick engine.

I pushed off out to sea and dropped a thousand feet and watched the onion-shaped, clouds follow my old track for a while. Then they suddenly popped up near me again so I had to go further out to sea and change my height. I went upstairs that time and when I looked back I could see them following my old track again and then suddenly change to more or less in line with me but falling short so I knew I was out of range.

Because of all this I'd added another ten miles to my crossing which had been finely calculated to get there, so I thought that I'd almost certainly finish up in the drink because I wouldn't have enough petrol.

A Spitfire in good condition would probably do about seven or eight miles to the gallon and I had about 80 miles to go to get back to Manston. I didn't have any petrol to spare for any diversions. The next fifteen minutes seemed more like fifteen days. Fortunately I made it. When the cliffs eventually emerged from the haze I was able to spot Manston. I was within about ten miles of it at that stage.

There was a big cloud of dust over Manston and when I got there I found that there was a squadron of Hurricanes taking off to go to Dunkirk. They were occupying most of the aerodrome and I had to try and land at some little spot where I could do so safely without disturbing their take-off or colliding with them or getting myself into any further trouble than I was already in. I had quite enough as it was.

In the landing I was aware of the fact that I didn't know whether or not my tyres had bullet holes in them. If they did I was in for cartwheels and probably fire. If I belly landed there was still so much fuel in the Spitfire that she would have caught fire anyway from the sparks and things generated.

An additional problem was that I had no flaps to slow me down in my approach so I was landing 10 mph faster than I would have with flaps and I had no brakes, so when I got wheels down on the deck and if I didn't do a somersault I still had to stop!

Anyhow, I got her down and finished up doing a very wide circle and coming back facing the heading I was on when I landed. I managed to taxi up to the tarmac where I got out and had a look at my leg. My boot seemed pretty well full of blood and there was a lot of blood running, down the back of my leg.

I fished around to see if I was hit anywhere else but found nothing. My old parachute was pretty well riddled with bits of fragments of compressed air bottle which had come through the seat and into it, fortunately not into my bottom because I was sitting on the parachute. The parachute had saved me from that.

I waited for the troops to come back from breakfast so I could scrounge a ride over to the main camp at Manston where I could then find the doctor to have a look at my leg and decide what would happen from there on. Eventually I got a week off.

When I got back to Hornchurch to report in to my Squadron I found that they had been ordered north to Kirton-on-Lindsey for a rest when they returned from the fight that I'd got into so much drama at Dunkirk. They'd gone completely, including the Intelligence Officer, so I had nobody to report my trip to. As it turned out I never did get around to writing out a combat report.

I was listed as missing-in-action for about 36 hours actually, presumably because Headquarters did not bother telling our squadron I was back. They didn't know for 36 hours and my parents out here [Australia] thought I had been shot down and lost at Dunkirk.

My fiancée had also got a message that I had been shot down that day and my great aunt whom I was in touch with in England, she lived in London, had also got the message but I wasn't aware of this. I picked up my fiancée and she was very relieved to see me.

Later, on the following day, I was talking to Alan Deere and we were comparing notes. He'd been shot down the same day at Dunkirk and he was on the beach and had seen a portion of my combat. He said that he'd seen a Spitfire, he didn't know who it was, shoot down, as far as he could see, four or five 109s and eventually hunt the rest of them off. He wasn't sure if they'd crashed or not but he hadn't seen the entire combat, only seen part of it.

Two of my sergeants were in the scrap with me... They'd avoided too much drama by both going into loops and rolling off the top. When the 109s tried to follow them they all spun off the top of their loops because they couldn't get round as well as the Spits and for all I know they might have found it too low down to pull out of their spins. I saw them spinning. I don't know.

Anyhow, when they (the sergeants) got back they reported me as being in hot pursuit of twelve Messerschmitt 109s! Actually, I thought the twelve 109s were in hot pursuit of me!!!'

After the action over Dunkirk, 65 Squadron moved to Lincolnshire to refit but a week later it was back at Hornchurch ready to play its part in the Battle of Britain. It was heavily involved in the fighting of July and August so that by the time it transferred north to Turnhouse in Scotland on 28 August, it could claim the destruction of 26 German aircraft for the loss of eleven.

Gordon Olive scored his first confirmed victory, a Bf 109, on 20 July and on 12 August he probably destroyed another. The following day he shot down two and probably a third and on the 14th he scored another probable. Two days later he damaged a Bf 109 and then attacked a lone Ju 88 which he left disappearing into cloud in an almost vertical dive with smoke pouring from both engines.

On 19 August he was promoted from acting flight lieutenant to flight lieutenant. In an action on the 24th, he probably shot down another Bf 109 and he brought his score to five on 26 August by destroying a Bf 110.

At Turnhouse, the squadron rested and was brought up to strength, taking no part in the air battles of September and October. Meanwhile, Gordon Olive received a DFC which was gazetted on 24 September. At this time two officers, Gordon Olive and F/Lt 'Sammy' Saunders, were called upon to give their impressions of the air battle over the radio. They were interviewed anonymously for the BBC and the broadcast went to air on 4 October.

It was late November before 65 Squadron went south again, this time to Tangmere. On 9 December Gordon Olive shot down a Bf 110 for what turned out to be his sixth and final official victory although he claimed a probable Ju 88 on 15 February 1941 while flying a Spitfire Mk. II, P7827. In March 1941, he was promoted to acting squadronlLeader and took up fighter controller duties at Tangmere for the next three months, during which time the aerodrome was bombed at night on at least ten occasions.

Gordon Olive in 1986, at the time he was president of the Australian Division of the Battle of Britain Fighter Association. (Dennis Newton)

LEFT F/Lt Gordon Olive, DFC, at Readiness at Tangmere in December 1940. (John Wallen)

On 20 June 1941, he was appointed to command 456 Squadron which was being formed at RAF Station Valley in the Isle of Anglesey. This was Australia's first night-fighter squadron and initial equipment consisted of sixteen Boulton Paul Defiants. After training, the squadron became operational in August but towards the end of September it began to be reequipped with Bristol Beaufighter MkIIs which necessitated retraining and conversion to twin-engined aircraft. The unit's first victory came on the night of 10 January 1942 when a Dornier Do 217 was shot down in flames.

Gordon Olive was promoted to squadron leader on 8 January 1942, and altogether he carried out 17 sorties with 456 Squadron before ill-health cut short his tour of duty. On 1 March he was posted to Station Valley, Fighter Command.

Other postings during his career with the RAF included: No. 9 Group (20 April 1942); No. 81 Group (9 July 1942); No. 55 OTU (15 July 1942); No. 58 OTU (28 October 1942); and No. 83 Group (25 May 1943). He was still with 83 Group when on 3 June 1943, he joined the Royal Australian Air Force, thus relinquishing the rank of acting wing commander he had attained on 29 December 1942. He recorded another interview on the Battle of Britain for radio which was broadcast over the BBC on 24 September.

Meanwhile, although he had joined the RAAF, he stayed with 83 Group until 20 October 1943 when he was attached to Overseas Headquarters, RAAF. Ten days later he left England for Australia.

On 12 February 1944, he went to RAAF Command where he received the rank of Acting Wing Commander on 1 April. He stayed there for the remainder of the year until he was posted to No. 101 FCU as commanding officer on December 29, but his stay was short because he was then sent to Air Defence HQ Sydney on 21 January 1945. His final wartime posting was to Air Defence HQ Morotai which he commanded from 16 July.

Altogether, W/Cdr. Gordon Olive, DFC completed four tours of operational flying involving 219 sorties, many of them of short duration during the hectic days of the Battle of Britain, and 180 hours of operational flying. He was discharged from the RAAF on 7 March 1946.

In civilian life, Olive returned to Brisbane and joined Rheem Australia in an executive position. He retired in 1972 but after a spell of farming he joined Boral Ltd, staying with this company until he retired again in 1981. In 1967 he was awarded an CBE for his work in organising the Empire Youth Movement. At one time, in the early 1970s, he dabbled in federal politics. He was appointed chairman of the board of the Queensland Fire Brigade and was also president of the Australian Division of the Battle of Britain Fighter Association. After courageously, and characteristically, fighting off a long-term illness for several years, Gordon Olive died towards the end of 1987.

5

No Real Chance

The RAF short-service commission scheme open to RAAF officers who had just graduated from Point Cook was officially suspended in Australia in July 1938, but shor-service commissions in the RAF continued to be advertised in the Australian press and intakes continued until mid-1939. Those accepted at these later dates were civilians without any formal preliminary military training. The last group of young men to depart for England left in August 1939. They were fated to be thrust, half-trained, into the cauldron of war.

> Gentlemen of the Dominions. Colonies and Territories under the Crown are invited to apply for Short Service Commissions in His Majesty's Air Force... Apply to RAAF H.Q., Melbourne.

These words appeared under the Royal Air Force crest in newspaper advertisements around Australia in the mid-1930s.

John Dallas Crossman, a sixteen-year-old former student of Newcastle Boys' High School, saw the advertisement. Although he worked in the office of an engineering firm and was studying accountancy, his heart was not in it because he wanted to join the air force. He was under age, and needed his father's written permission to enlist before the age of 21, but this was contingent upon his performing well in his final accountancy examinations. Apparently this proved to be sufficient incentive for him to top the course when he sat for his examinations at age twenty. As promised, his father gave the required permission.

Joan Bowden, John's sister, recalls:

> When I think back as a schoolkid, we had quite a way to walk to the tram to get to school. My brother always carried my school case for me. He was that sort of person. I think probably a bit theatrical, as most people in that time were. You know... the pipe was very fashionable to smoke. It was fashionable to have your

hat on one side, a bit sort of Errol Flynnish and the big coat with the collar turned up. It wasn't just John, it was all of them. You'll see photographs of John like that, you know...

John was born on the 20 March, 1919, at Mossman. My father was an engineer at Mossman and he wasn't allowed to go to war. Twice he was arrested for joining up... He was third engineer at the sugar mill. When Mum was seven months pregnant there was the worst cyclone ever in Queensland. They had built a house. Mum was ferried across the river by Dad on a mattress. He was swimming. The house was flooded and it was going. Shortly afterwards John was born in the hospital at Mosman. I was born at Port Douglas

P/O John Dallas Crossman. (Joan Bowden)

in 1922 on 15 November so I was four years and eight months younger than John and there were twins in between.

Mother's family were from Wesbaden in Germany originally. Her grandfather came out as a migrant, and settled in the Hunter Valley. [She was known as 'Mick'.] Dad was English born in Taunton on a small farm, actually the house he lived in is now a boarding school. His full name was George Edward Crossman... There were four girls in his family and he was the much-wanted son. He was at a private school in Taunton when his father died and he was sort of pitchforked into the work force. He was trained at an engineering business in Bristol and he stayed with some people there. Then he became a seaman on a boat... Dad went through the Depression when people who didn't have something behind them couldn't get jobs. My Father had 13 jobs in 11 months and was never out of work during the whole Depression but he had to chase them all over the place, Sydney, Newcastle, everywhere... He was highly qualified and then he got the job at Lysaght's as chief draftsman. Later he became chief engineer...

John was always called "Xman", not "Crossman", in fact all his friends called him 'X'. He had a tremendous group of friends. He was a boy that always had people around. Dad built a huge verandah on the back of our house at Waratah — that was before we moved to New Lambton — and we would have up to 40 people there dancing. We had a huge tabl- tennis table. Mum was the sort of person that no matter who came there was a meal, something to eat always ready. So, I always think of John with friends around him.

In response to the air force advertisement, John travelled to Sydney early in 1939 for an interview and medical examinations. His first attempt failed on medical grounds; his chest expansion was not good enough — he needed a further ten centimetres. Disappointed, but not deterred, he spent the next six months training and performing breathing exercises so he would be ready for the next intake. This time his efforts were rewarded and on 12

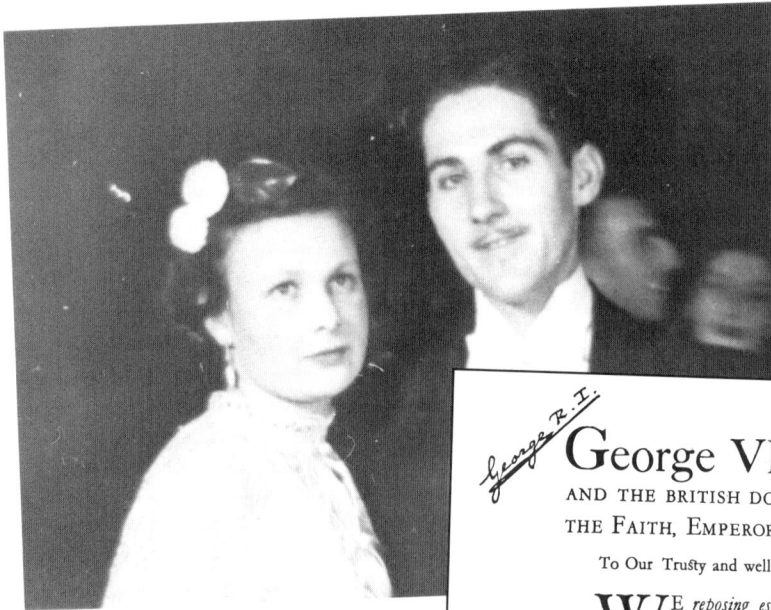

Pat Foley and John Crossman before he left for England. (Joan Bowden)

John Crossman is appointed a pilot Officer in the Royal Air Force. (Joan Bowden)

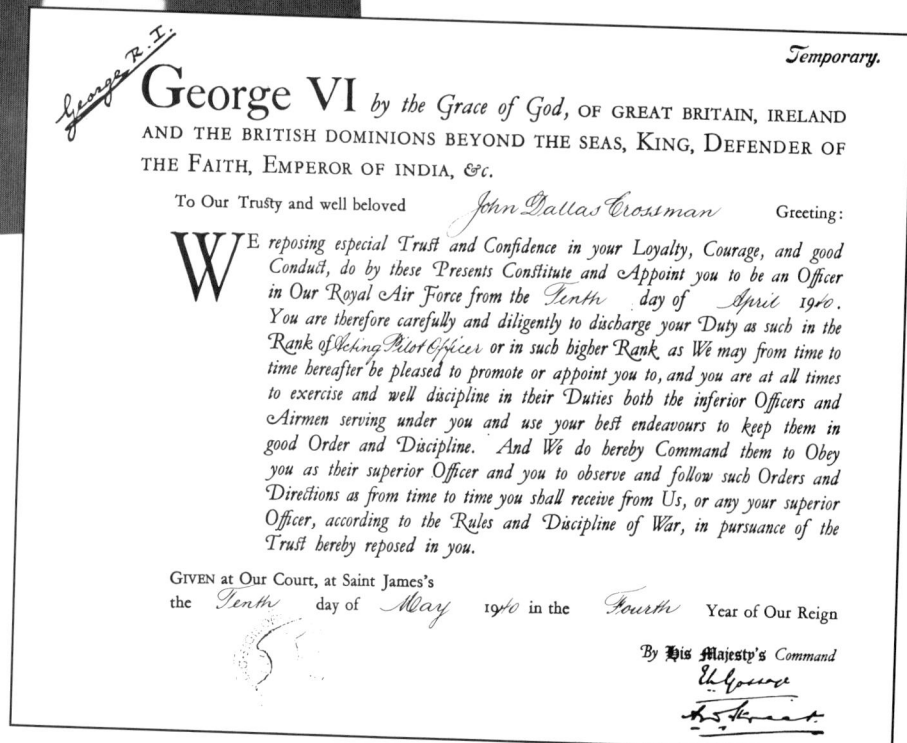

Temporary.

George VI *by the Grace of God,* OF GREAT BRITAIN, IRELAND AND THE BRITISH DOMINIONS BEYOND THE SEAS, KING, DEFENDER OF THE FAITH, EMPEROR OF INDIA, &c.

To Our Trusty and well beloved *John Dallas Crossman*   Greeting:

WE *reposing especial Trust and Confidence in your Loyalty, Courage, and good Conduct, do by these Presents Constitute and Appoint you to be an Officer in Our Royal Air Force from the Tenth day of April 1940. You are therefore carefully and diligently to discharge your Duty as such in the Rank of Acting Pilot Officer or in such higher Rank as We may from time to time hereafter be pleased to promote or appoint you to, and you are at all times to exercise and well discipline in their Duties both the inferior Officers and Airmen serving under you and use your best endeavours to keep them in good Order and Discipline. And We do hereby Command them to Obey you as their superior Officer and you to observe and follow such Orders and Directions as from time to time you shall receive from Us, or any your superior Officer, according to the Rules and Discipline of War, in pursuance of the Trust hereby reposed in you.*

GIVEN at Our Court, at Saint James's the *Tenth* day of *May* 1940 in the *Fourth* Year of Our Reign

By His Majesty's Command

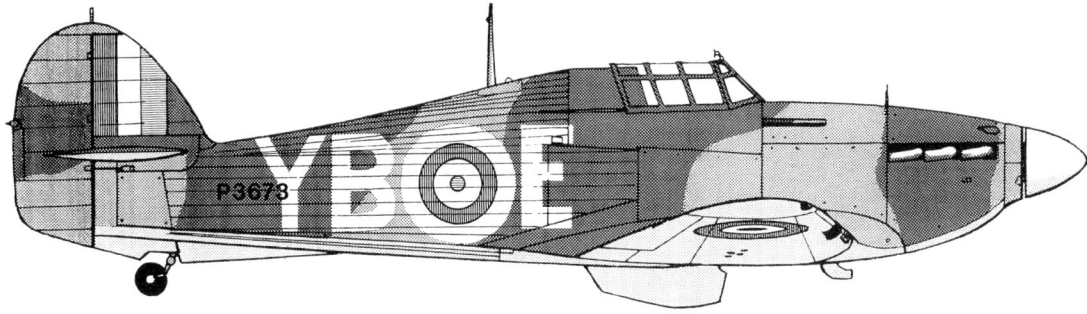

Hawker Hurricane Mk.I. Numerically, the Hurricane formed the backbone of RAF fighter Command's defence against the Luftwaffe during the Battle of Britain. (Dennis Newton)

August 1939 he boarded the SS Orama to sail to England via the Suez Canal. On board were a handful of other young men, New South Welshmen and Queenslanders, who were setting out on the same great adventure. John waved good-bye to his family and girlfriend, Pat Foley, and afterwards wrote in his diary:

August 12th 1939. To-day was the day. I really did sail for England. It was almost too good to be true. My feelings were awfully mixed and I didn't feel so good after I said goodbye to everyone and held streamers on the wharf. Mother and Pat very bright at the boat, but I guess not so bright after it sailed. Dad waved both hands and ran the wharf until I couldn't see him any more. Pat's pink feather in her hat and mother's yellow jumper showed out.

August 13th. Met one Rob Kerr yesterday, doesn't seem a bad sort. We are both at the same table No. 13. Met one Jack Burraston to-day. A fine fellow. We look like having fun together. Seas rather choppy but have not yet been sea sick so here's hoping!

John Crossman's story has been recorded in his own words in letters to his mother, father and sister back in Australia, together with notes in his diary (of which only fragments remain) and letters from his English aunts living in Buckinghamshire. They capture an image of a cheerful young man going off to a career of adventure and excitement only to be caught up in the irresistible vortex of war.

Also boarding the Orama in Sydney was John Francis Pain, who was born in Scotland but was living in Brisbane in 1939. Australian Battle of Britain veteran, Gordon Olive, also from Brisbane, remembered him well when interviewed:

John Pain was quite a character. He was the stepson of Sir Alan Mansfield who was Governor of Queensland for some time. His mother was Lady Mansfield who had previously been married to a gentleman named Pain but the marriage had broken up and as far as I know John was the only child of the marriage. He was

a fairly wild young boy, known as 'Tiger' Pain, at school and also in the Air Force, and he had a somewhat cat-like look about him . ... at least, I thought he had.

The ship steamed southwards to Melbourne and then west to Adelaide, across the Great Australian Bight and around to Fremantle. At each of these ports more young men joined the RAF contingent until its numbers rose to 22. One who joined at Fremantle was John Douglas Peterkin of Cottesloe in Perth.

Doug Peterkin had an avid interest in flying and, back in 1935, had become a member of the Western Australian Gliding Club. In September 1938, completely by chance, he had caught sight of the RAAF advertisement in an old newspaper. He saw to his horror that the closing date for entries was two days off; without much hope he sent a telegram to Melbourne requesting the necessary forms and after waiting a very long week they arrived. In due course he was granted an interview late in December in front of a panel headed by Squadron Leader Raymond James Brownell, a distinguished Australian airman of World War.I. Out of 80 Western Australian applicants only four were selected. They joined the eighteen from the other states. Doug Peterkin received his acceptance in May 1939.

After Fremantle the Orama left Australian waters. John Crossman recorded in his diary for 22 August: 'Have left Australia now and don't feel so good about it. Very hard to realize that I'm definitely gone now. However. have a very good friend in Jack.' Two days later it was his girlfriend's birthday: 'Pat's birthday to-day. Should have liked to send a cable but costs too much. We had bottled cider, sandwiches and biscuits in my cabin at night and drank her health.'

His words captured the changing mood on board, from the loneliness of leaving home to the excitement of a voyage at sea:

August 27th. To-morrow we cross the line, so the RAF fellows have all volunteered to be victims. There should be some fun.

Hawker Hurricanes on patrol. The critical shortage of fighter pilots during the Battle of Britain forced the RAF to adopt desperate methods of acquiring them. Some were stripped from the light-bomber squadrons. More serious were the drastic cuts to the training program which resulted in only partly trained young men being thrown into battle. When John Crossman reported to 32 Squadron at Biggin Hill, he had never before flown a monoplane, let alone a modern fighter like a Hurricane or a Spitfire!! (IWM)

August 28th. Crossed the line to-day. We were all duly initiated in the approved style. Pills, leather, barber etc. and it was fun. Then we did Neptune and his court.

The mood, however, was beginning to change and on 29 August he wrote: 'Have:
been travelling for two nights now without lights on deck at all. No smoking on deck etc. at night. The war scare seems very bad.' There followed a light-hearted break in Colombo but three days later, back at sea, the young Novocastrian wrote:

September 2nd. War scare very bad now. Poland is being attacked and we expect hourly to hear that England is going to have a go at Hitler. The usual blackout precautions on deck are being tightened up. We listen in to the news from London direct every night. It is broadcast all over the ship.
September 3rd. Situation becoming almost desperate now and it seems almost impossible for Britain now not to come into it. It's a very bad thing when one man can cause such a thing as this promises to be.
September 4th. WAR has been declared by Great Britain on Germany. The news came through to us at 4.15 ship's time. Should this last any time it seems unlikely that I'll ever see home again. Still I expect it can't be helped. A fellow has to realsze that.
September 5th. Awfully sorry for all back home. They must be worrying, but I can't help it. I'd give the world to be able to go back if only for an hour. I do feel so rotten when I think of them . . .

But there could be no going back.

Almost immediately, just a few days after Britain's declaration of war, some Australians already serving in the RAF were flying on operations. While both sides were settling into a period which became known as the 'phoney war', the SS Orama reached England with the last Australian volunteers. On Wednesday 11 October they sat down to their final dinner on board ship. It was a time of excitement and high spirits. Some wits had composed a series of limericks, one for each man in the group, and these were typed, copied and handed out. Amid cheers and laughter, they all acquired their own souvenirs of the occasion. Doug Peterkin collected autographs on his copy of the limericks. John Crossman kept his menu and had each man sign it, for this was a night to be cherished and remembered.

The Australians had their initial training at Jesus College, Cambridge, and then went to No. 9 Elementary Flying Training School at Ansty, Warwickshire, where they arrived on 30 October. On the last day of the month John Crossman wrote his first entry into his new RAF Pilots' Flying Log Book, recording a 35-minute flight in a Tiger Moth, N6579, with F/Sgt Webb.

At Ansty, those deemed suitable for further flying training were selected. Unfortunately, Doug Peterkin was not one of them. John Crossman, in a letter to his parents, noted:

Another one of our fellows was passed out today and will leave for Australia soon. We feel awfully sorry about it, especially as he was so very popular and such a great fellow. We will all miss Doug very much, it wasn't his fault, he just couldn't fly well enough . . .

But Doug Peterkin did not return home. He retrained as an air gunner at the Gunnery School. Stormy Down, Panthcawl, South Wales, and was then posted to 248 Squadron as a commissioned air gunner/fire controller at RAF Station North Coates. He reported for duty there on 5 March 1940. Two other Australians in the same squadron were Charles Bennett and Lewis Hamilton. The newcomer soon established himself as something of a character and he picked up the nicknames of 'Wild Man' Peterkin and 'The Big Bushman'.

On 10 April 1940, the day the Germans invaded Norway and Denmark, John Crossman received his appointment as an acting pilot officer in the Royal Air Force. He had logged 45 hours 5 minutes of dual flying, 34 hours 55 minutes solo and 8 hours 45 minutes of instrument flying. His days on Tiger Moths were over and he reported with others from his intake, including 'Tiger' Pain and Jack Burraston, to RAF College (FTS) Cranwell for advanced training.

Exactly one month later, just ten days after British forces began evacuating from Namsos in Norway and the same day that Winston Churchill became prime minister, the 'phoney war' came to an abrupt end when the Germans marched across the Ardennes plateau into neutral Belgian territory. By 18 June Winston Churchill was telling the British people:

> What General Weygand called the Battle of France is over. I expect that the Battle of Britain is about to begin . . . Let us therefore brace ourselves to our duties, and so bear ourselves that, if the British Empire and its Commonwealth last for a thousand years, men will say 'This was their finest hour'.

To be eligible for the much prized Battle of Britain Clasp to the 1939-1945 Star, an airman must have served with RAF Fighter Command (including three Coastal Command squadrons — 235, 236 and 248 — which were temporarily attached to Fighter Command) and flown at least one operational sortie between 0001 hours on 10 July and 2359 hours on 31 October 1940. There were no RAAF fighter units in England during this time but Australian airmen were sprinkled throughout all RAF commands (only one RAAF unit, 10 Squadron, operating with Sunderland flying boats, was in Coastal Command). The Roll of Honour at Westminster Abbey contains the names of 24 Australians, two of them Orama boys, who lost their lives during the Battle of Britain. Under normal circumstances, in which the usual duration of courses and proper training schedules were maintained, the Orama boys would never have reached operational squadrons during the Battle of Britain period — but these were not

normal times. Training schedules were being slashed in order to keep enough pilots flowing into Fighter Command to replace the increasing numbers lost in the aerial fighting over southern England.

Jack Burraston was the first of the Australians from the Orama to be killed, on 6 July in a tragedy at RAF College Cranwell. Burraston was the passenger in a Hawker Hind, being flown by another cadet, which stalled and crashed into the ground while performing low-level aerobatics over the airfield. When observers reached the wrecked plane Burraston was dead with a broken neck. The pilot had a fractured skull and died an hour later. Both were buried in Cranwell churchyard.

On 14 July John Pain and John Crossman were graded as pilot officers on probation. Some trainee pilots in No. 9 Course who had opted to fly single-engine aircraft received postings to operational squadrons before their traditional passing-out parade. Although he had never flown a monoplane, let alone a modern fighter like a Hurricane or a Spitfire, Crossman was posted to 32 Squadron at Biggin Hill. Pain went to No. 7 OTU.

John Crossman found his first day with 32 Squadron much more informal than the daily routine at Cranwell. During the morning he practised take-offs and landings

Dornier Do 17s on their way to bomb London. (IWM)

in Miles Magister, P2466, but after lunch the weather closed in. In the evening, he wrote to his family:

15.7.40

As you can see by the address I have finally arrived at my squadron. It is to 32 Fighter Squadron and the planes are Hurricanes so I now have all I want from the R.A.F. I haven't actually flown a Hurricane yet as I only arrived here yesterday afternoon. This morning I went up in a Magister just to get an idea how to fly a monoplane. I should have gone up in a Hurricane this afternoon had the weather been at all good, but it is rather lousy so I was just out of luck. This squadron is not very far from London as you can see by the address, but from what I'm told there is very little chance of much time off. However, when we do get away from here London will be easy to get to . . .

I must say I do like this place as everything is very free and easy and we don't have any parades and just do almost as we please. Instead of getting up at 6.30 a.m. as I did at Cranwell I rose this morning at 8. This will be o.k. of course until I get on operations. Just now I have lots to learn and so won't take part in any fighting for a week or two yet. When I do start on operations I have to be like the rest and stand by ready in flying kit in shifts through the night waiting to go up to intercept Jerry. No. 32 Squadron has a very distinguished record dating back to the last war and we have here three chaps all about my own age with D.F.C.s.

You will remember my telling you how each course at Cranwell as it passes out gives a show. The course I was in will give its show on Thursday. I am hoping

to get permission to fly a 'plane up to Cranwell for the show and come back here Friday morning. Most of the course I was in are still at Cranwell as only those who any single-engined aircraft were posted. So of course only the twins are left to put on the show.

We were nearly all posted to different places and I was sent here on my own, so I feel just a little out of things at present, although they seem a decent crowd of fellows and are all about my own age . . .

At the end of July a familiar face arrived when John Pain was posted into 32 Squadron from No. 7 OTU. Pain flew his first operational sortie on 3 August in a Hurricane, P3147, and the following day he was in a flight of six to patrol over Hawkinge. Enemy aircraft were encountered but no combat ensued. Meanwhile, because of the difficulties of training a fledgling pilot on an operational squadron at this time, John Crossman was posted away. Through no fault of his own he obviously could not be risked in combat, so he was ordered to report to No. 6 OTU Sutton Bridge on 2 August, for further training.

By the time John Crossman reported back to 32 Squadron on 28 August it was on the point of being sent north to Acklington for a rest and John Pain was gone. On 15 August the Luftwaffe had suffered its heaviest casualties of the Battle of Britain and Pain had made his contribution. Over Croydon he became embroiled with six Messerschmitt Bf 109s and claimed one destroyed. This was stated as such in both the 32 Squadron's Operations Record Book (ORB) and Pain's typed Combat Report, but apparently the claim was amended to a 'probable, this having been added in handwriting after

Hurricanes being refuelled. After the heavy engagements during the morning of 15 September, later declared Battle of Britain Day, the British fighters were quickly refuelled and rearmed for the battles in the afternoon. John Crossman, now with 46 Squadron, claimed a Dornier (afterwards allowed as a probable) in the early heavy raid. (IWM)

A dreaded sight in the rear-vision mirror, a Bf 109E closing in for the kill. (IWM)

the typed 'One ME.109' for 'Enemy casualties' in the Combat Report. During a battle over Biggin Hill next day he had shot down a Ju 88 according to the ORB but again, handwritten at the bottom of his Combat Report is the statement '1 Ju 88 probable'. On 18 August he was shot down and injured but he had managed to bale out safely. Pain's injuries were serious enough to keep him in hospital for the best part of two months and he did not rejoin the squadron until 31 October.

John Crossman's stay with 32 Squadron was again brief and a fortnight later he was sent south to No. 46 Squadron at Stapleford Tawney. With this unit, his first engagement with the enemy took place on 14 September. On the 15th, later declared Battle of Britain Day, he was involved in the heavy fighting over London. He claimed a Dornier Do 215 (afterwards allowed as a probable) in the early heavy raid. (The latest research suggests that this was actually Dornier 17, No. 2361, of III Gruppe/ Geschwader 76, piloted by FW Heitsch. This machine was apparently damaged initially by Sgt Holmes of 504 Squadron and then finished off by attacks from P/O Lawson of 19 Squadron, John Crossman of 46 Squadron and P/O Mortimer of 257 Squadron. It crash-landed near Sevenoaks at about 12.20 p.m. One of the crew was killed and three captured.)

In the afternoon, Crossman closely pursued a second Dornier but it escaped into cloud.

For the rest of the month, John was involved in numerous patrols and there were some brief clashes with an elusive enemy which had given up heavy daylight bombing and switched to night assaults and fighter-bomber raids. John's

last letter, written to his family on 22 September, conveys a feeling of pride and a sense of achievement: 'I hope I will never have to leave the R.A.F. There's something about the service that gets into one's blood and these days I get a very satisfied feeling . . .'

His wish would be granted.

On Monday, 30 September, the weather was generally fair with some clouds and light winds. At Holly Cottage, Forest Row, Sussex, Edmund Wimperis decided to spend his day painting watercolour scenes of the English countryside and, after breakfast, he set up his easel in the grounds of Tablehurst Farm. He was enchanted by the peace and beauty which surrounded him. The war seemed a long way off.

After a morning patrol, John Crossman landed back at Stapleford Tawney and pencilled into his Log Book: 'Large formation Me 109s passed us but we did not attack — were looking for bombers'. It was his last entry.

That afternoon the Hurricanes of 46 Squadron, together with those of 249 Squadron, were up again and this time they found what seemed to be hundreds of Bf 109s above them. The Germans were too high and well out of reach. A tense situation developed. As the Hurricanes continued to patrol, looking for the bombers, they were shadowed by the enemy fighters. Seizing a brief chance, a few Bf 109s made a swift hit-and-run attack on 46 Squadron. Further back, at least one pilot of 249 Squadron, P/O George Barclay, saw a Hurricane falling in flames, plunging down towards the village of Forest Row.

Edmund Wimperis was now working on his second

watercolour but from time to time his attention had been caught by the sound of aero engines and sometimes by firing in the distance. Suddenly, the howl of a diving aircraft shattered the tranquillity. It hurtled out of the sky and crashed directly in front of him, right into the middle of the scene he was painting! The burning wreckage was what remained of Hurricane V6748, John Crossman's aircraft. John had not bailed out.

Wimperis afterwards finished his painting and in it he added the trail of wreckage left by the burning Hurricane, showing it almost submerged in the seemingly unchanged peacefulness of the English countryside. He called it 'The Last Flight'. The other he named 'The Journey's End'. Later, Wimperis found out the identity of the pilot and sent these paintings to John's parents in Newcastle. He also sent a third painting of the scene to Pat Foley, John's girlfriend in Australia.

What happened to the Orama? John Crossman mentioned her in a letter home on 12 June: ' Did you hear in the news that the Orama had been sunk off Norway? I have known now for some time that the old tub has been a troop carrier. It was such a tub that I don't know that I'm sorry they sunk her, but still, it was British.'. .

John Crossman, 22 years of age, formerly of 46 Squadron, was buried at Chalfont St. Giles Churchyard, Buckinghamshire, on Friday, 4 October 1940, beside the grave of one of his English aunts. His other aunts, Mabel and Anne, wrote to his parents in Australia. Anne's poignant letter is quoted here:

Friday
October 4th, 1940
My Dear Ted & Mick: All the words in the world could not tell you of our sorrow. Three weeks ago to-day he was here — to-day he is here again, but in our little churchyard beside Flo, and Flo would feel very proud I shall tell you all I can of this sad week. The first we heard of it was on Tuesday night at eight— a wire 'Request details of funeral arrangements you desire to be made etc.' It was signed 'Aeros. Epping.' Will tried to wire at once but a raid was on from 8.30 p.m. until 5.30 a.m. next day. He was trying to get through but everywhere there was disconnection. He sent a telegram, then a telegram letter. No reply. He went everywhere trying to find someone to take him over but private people had no petrol and garage people

On 30 September 1940, as artist Edmund Wimperis was painting a watercolour picture of the English countryside near Forest Row, Sussex, a burning Hurricane crashed out of the sky into the very scene he was painting. He included the wreckage in his picture and thereby recorded forever the last moments of John Dallas Crossman. (David Bowden)

not enough for so long a journey (50 miles). At last he got a man to take him over yesterday morning. No telegrams had been received. They must have been sent elsewhere but he saw the Commanding Officer and the Adjutant. In the meantime he had made arrangements for him to be brought here Everyone spoke most highly of him — said he was so keen they could not keep him out of the air and he was popular with everyone. Everything was then arranged. There are no military funerals now, but one of his fellow officers would come and six bearers from a nearer aerodrome, but in the end they could not be spared, but the officer came in time for lunch with us and these are the details. His name is Patulla, and I think he may write you. He was Formation Leader and John one of his formation. John shot down a Messherschmitt a few days before, and on Monday his Squadron got into contact with the enemy but he did not return to the base. He had been shot while at the controls evidently or he would have baled out. He came down at Forest Row in Sussex. This officers aid that if he had been 25 000 feet up it would have been all over in 40 seconds. He said that John was entirely fearless and controlled — a wonderful pilot and was constantly scouting about for the enemy, and sort of went off the DEEP end, as we say, when he missed one. A letter of mine is on the way saying that John brought his surplus luggage here and slept one night — three weeks ago to-day. The rest of his personal effects will be sent here and you must say what I am to do with them. I don't think there is much in the way of clothing, and should presume

you would rather that did not come back. When he was here I said 'Leave me a key of your bags, so that if you ever want anything I can send it'. He did so, but of course I shall open nothing until I hear from you. One case is very heavy and contains mostly books, so now you will see why all the delay was caused. He was brought here to-day from Forest Row by road. We met him at the Church. The young pilot brought a very beautiful wreath from the Squadron. Mabe is trying to take a photograph so you shall see we have thought and cared for you. We ordered a lovely cross from you and Mick and Ted laurel leaves, white chrysanthemums and red carnations. We sent one of bronze chrysanthemums, and I made two beautiful sprays — white and pink Michaelmas daisies from Joan and white and mauve from Pat, and several of our dear friends sent flowers too, our neighbours, the schoolmaster and his wife and they were present at the funeral. All our little village was shocked. He is the first soldier of this war to find rest here. Even the kiddies Mabe looks after sent a beautiful spray of carnations. I hope we shall get a photo He was enclosed in a plain oak coffin with

Pilot-Officer John Dallas Crossman
Died September 30th

on the plate, and a large Union Jack was used as a pall. Three weeks ago to-day he was admiring the growing flowers, and carried armfuls into the little Church for the Harvest Festival. Our eyes have scarcely been dry because of the tragedy and of our thoughts

The telegram informing John Crossman's parents of his death. (Joan Bowden)

for you, but over and over again it has come into my mind 'Jesus called him o'er the tumult' for indeed these are dreadful days and on Tuesday night it came into my mind to wonder if we ever may be alive to see him laid at rest For this terrible thing is more like colossal murder than war. Places without the least military or any other significance are bombed indiscriminately and all night long it goes on and on, and often as not does no damage that counts.

What can I say that can ease your burden? One thing he was never meant to plough, and perhaps Ted that was what you did not understand, because we have all had to plough so hard. I wrote to Nell after seeing him the second time that he seemed as though his feet were not planted on earth and all the officers say 'You couldn't keep him out of the air' He said here last time 'I don't care about anything so long as I can fly.' There are some things to be grateful for I said I would rather this than have his beautiful body crippled or brought down on enemy soil. I think in a way that he died as he would have wished — but a little sooner than he hoped. But who shall say whether 'tis best so to live out long days each facing slow decay of age. He has been very happy over her e—- said the last time that no-one could be kinder than all the folk he had met and he worshipped you Mick and said he saw your point of view plainer, Ted. He never spoke an unkind word of anyone — confessed to hate being thwarted. When he came here it was the day he went down to Stapleford. He said that a nice fellow came forward and asked if he could show him round They palled up at once and it was he who came to-day. He was shot down two days before John — petrol tank shot away, face very cut and glass in it, still he managed to land safely.

We thought you would rather he laid here than among strangers and I hope we did rightly. I think you are very wonderful Mick to be doing so much for England, but she is worth it and don't relax those efforts Mick You are blessed among women because you gave to the world a hero. Always bear in mind that he did the thing he wished. He is with his friend again and I am confident that they who have gone for a while can be very near We all send our very fondest love. We did all we could for him, but youth seeks youth and we are understanding He said last time 'Don't worry if you don't hear from me. You would get a telegram if anything were amiss.'

Yours affectionately,
Anne

Joan Bowden, John's sister recalls:

I was just reading back when John was killed he was the first boy killed from Newcastle in any of the forces on active service. John was actually killed on the last day of the Battle of Britain... Dad said he could go, you see. If Dad didn't sign the papers you couldn't go in those days because he wasn't 21. Anyhow he said to his father: 'I'm going to try to see if I can get in. I'm not going to wait until I'm 21. I'm 20. I'll be 21 in a few months time.' They only took intakes twice a year so he went and Dad signed the papers. But Dad, 'til the day he died, never forgave himself because if he had let him go two years earlier John would have been more experienced. He would have had more chance. That's silly of course, you just never know...

Of the 22 carefree young men who set out on their great adventure on the Orama in August 1939, half did not survive the war and most of these were killed before the end of 1940.

6

COMBAT DIARY NORTH AFRICA 1940-43

On 10 June 1940, as the victorious Germans were about to enter Paris, Italy declared war on France and Britain. The surrender of France days later not only led to the Battle of Britain, it also created a serious military situation for the British in the Mediterranean. French leaders accepted the German armistice terms and left Britain to face the Italians alone. Italy's aim of dominating the Mediterranean seemed likely to become a reality. The pitifully ill-equipped Royal Air Force had the task of defending Egypt, the Suez Canal and communications through the Red Sea. The RAF commander, Sydney-born Sir Arthur Longmore, nevertheless decided to take the initiative and use his small force quickly and offensively. His bold action had the effect of putting the Italian Air Force on the defensive from the very start.

Numerous Australians were with the RAF in the Middle East, even during this early difficult stage. Their numbers mushroomed as the campaigns continued and more and more reinforcements arrived. They served in both RAF and RAAF units. This diary outlines many of their achievements.

1940

June 10: Italy declares war on Britain and France.

June 11: Determined to strike first in North Africa, 26 RAF Blenheims attack Italian aircraft on the ground at El Adem. This is followed by another raid later in the day. eighteen aircraft are claimed destroyed or damaged for two Blenheims lost and two which force-land, one bursting into flames.

June 19: Because the collapse of France has interrupted civil air routes between Britain and the Middle East, Africa, India and Australia, the 'horseshoe' Route is introduced linking South Africa and Australia to Cairo. The route between Cairo and Britain is another 'horseshoe', trans-Sahara, around to Oran via Luxor, Wadi Halfa, Khartoum, Fort. Lamy and Gao, and the UK. Qantas Empire Airways will operate between Sydney and Singapore travelling via Brisbane, Gladstone, Townsville, Karumba, Groote Eylandt, Darwin, Koepang, Surabaya and Batavia.

Gloster Gladiator II. When Italy declared war on 10 June 1940, the RAF had only five Bristol Blenheim bomber squadrons and three fighter squadrons in North Africa. All of the latter were equipped with Gladiators, plus one only Hawker Hurricane Mk 1 which had been sent out for test flying. Gladiator K8008 belonged to 112 Squadron RAF, the unit which later displayed the famous 'shark's mouth' insignia on its Kittyhawks. (Dennis Newton)

Savoia-Marchetti SM79 Sparviero (Hawk) bomber of the Regia Aeronautica. It was a robust and reliable aircraft, faster in level flight than the RAF Gladiators, and used by the Italians extensively throughout the war. (MAP)

The Fiat BR 20M Cicogna bomber was used successfully by Italian 'volunteers' during the Spanish Civil War and in World War II by the Regia Aeronautica in operations over Yugoslavia, Greece, the Mediterranean and Africa. (MAP)

June 21: HMAS *Sydney* bombards Italian positions in Bardia. Her Supermarine Seagull V, A2-21, used for spotting, is attacked by three aircraft thought to be Italian CR 42s. F/Lt Thomas Price nurses his crippled plane to British territory and force lands at Matruh. The Seagull is a write-off. He learns afterwards that his attackers had been RAF Gloster Gladiators!

June 28: Because of the collapse of France, British civil aircraft flights across French colonial territory are banned, thus severing the trans-Sahara route to Cairo and cutting Britain off from the empire air routes.

July 4: During a day of successful combats for British fighters, Gladiators of 80 Squadron intercept ten Savoia SM 79s north of Alexandria. F/O Greg 'Shorty' Graham and another pilot shoot down one bomber, but the rest outdistance them. Graham is the first Australian fighter pilot to score in North Africa.

July 15: Australia. The officers and men of 3 Squadron RAAF sail from Sydney on the Orontes, bound for the Middle East.

August 23: Personnel of 3 Squadron arrive at Port Tewfik, Egypt.

September 1: 3 Squadron commences training at Ismailia with borrowed Lysanders.

September 16: 3 Squadron is ordered to Helwan. Two flights are to be be equipped with Gladiators and one with Lysanders plus four Gauntlets. It is to be a close-support squadron rather than an army co-op unit.

October 9: Flying a Gladiator on a lone patrol south of Sidi Barrani, F/O Richard 'Ape' Cullen from Newcastle, NSW, encounters six Italian Breda 65 bombers and attacks, probably destroying one. Cullen is a new member of 80 Squadron.

October 31: Gladiators from 112 Squadron encounter Italian SM.79 bombers escorted by CR 42s. P/O B. Duff of Randwick, NSW, attacks ten bombers but is set upon by no less than six CR 42s and obliged to bail out.

November 2: 3 Squadron's two flights of Gladiators arrive at Gerawla in preparation.

November 3: 3 Squadron's Gauntlets join the Gladiators at Gerawla but its flight of Lysanders remains at Helwan to act as a reinforcement pool. It will transfer to Ikingi Maryut on the 21st.

November 13: 3 Squadron flies its first tactical reconnaissance mission, a sortie between Sofafi and Nibeiwa.

November 19: 3 Squadron has its first combat. F/Lt Blake Pelly, with an escort of three other Gladiators, is on a reconnaissance mission east of Rabia when they are attacked by eighteen CR 42s. Pelly, F/O Alan Rawlinson and F/O A. H. Boyd each shoot one down; a fourth is probably destroyed and a fifth is damaged but 3 Squadron's CO, S/Ldr P. Heath of Muswellbrook, NSW, is killed in action.

December 9: General R. N. O'Connor, commander of the Western Desert Force, launches a 'reconnaissance in force' against the Italians. He has two divisions, 7th Armoured and 4th Indian, supported by Matilda tanks of the Royal Tank Regiment. Ahead are seven Italian divisions under General Graziani entrenched in fortified camps and positions. The obsolete Gloster Gauntlets of 3 Squadron carry out their first close support dive-bombing attacks.

December 10: While flying a lone early morning reconnaissance mission F/Lt C. B. Gaden of 3 Squadron in a Gladiator encounters and destroys an Italian IMAM Ro 37. Later, four Gladiators catch twelve CR 42s strafing advancing British troops near Tummer and drive them off, claiming three destroyed without loss. Scorers are S/Ldr Ian McLachlan, F/Lt Gordon Steege and F/O A. Gatward.

The British capture Sidi Barrani. O'Connor's 'reconnaissance in force' has so far taken 20 000 prisoners.

December 12: Just after noon, five Gladiators of 3 Squadron intercept seventeen CR 42s north-west of Sofafi. Most of the Italians climb away, circle once and

The remains of a Fiat CR 42. Although highly manoeuvrable and in wide use, these Italian biplanes were outclassed by the faster British monoplane fighters. (Trevor Mear)

then leave, but of the six or seven which stay and fight three are shot down without loss. They fall to F/Os A. Gatward, A. H. Boyd and Wilfred Arthur. No. 3 Squadron's tired old Gauntlets are withdrawn from active service. They have suffered no losses, but keeping them serviceable has become impossible.

By now five of the seven Italian divisions have been destroyed but, because his 4th Indian Division is to be sent to the Sedan, General Wavell, C-in-C Middle East, must limit O'Connor's pursuit of the enemy.

December 13: A black day for 3 Squadron. Near Sollum in the early morning, six Gladiators intercept five SM.79s attacking British troops. One bomber is shot down and another damaged, but before the Australians can reform they are bounced by eight escorting CR 42s. Two are destroyed but five Gladiators fall too. F/Lt Gaden from Windsor, Victoria, is killed, F/Os Arthur and L. D'A. Winten bail out and F/Os Gatward and Boyd crash-land. Damage to Boyd's machine is slight. After quick repairs he flies it back to base, carrying Gatward as a passenger. Meanwhile the squadron is ordered forward to Bir Malla to be air cover for advanced army units. One Gladiator crashes while landing. With five Gladiators lost and two damaged, 3 Squadron's serviceability is drastically reduced. It has little chance of carrying out its allotted task.

December 14: 3 Squadron can only muster a single Gladiator to fly two sorties.

December 15: 3 Squadron is temporarily withdrawn from operations.

December 17: Sidi Omar and Sollum fall to the British. No. 3 Squadron resumes limited operations with four repaired Gladiators plus four others from the almost exhausted stocks available in the Middle East.

December 26: While waiting to escort an RAF artillery reconnaissance Lysander, eight Gladiators of 3 Squadron encounter ten SM.79s escorted by 24 Fiat CR 42s. Two of the escorts are shot down into the sea and five damaged, one so badly it is counted probably destroyed. Three Gladiators are slightly damaged.

1941

January 3: The 6th Division AIF assaults Bardia. By midday it has 6000 prisoners.

January 5: Bardia is taken. Over 40 000 prisoners have been captured plus about 500 guns, 115 light tanks, 12

A Hawker Hurricane Mk I of 3 Squadron RAAF. The type was used very successfully by the Australians after they handed over their Gladiators in February 1941. (RAAF)

medium tanks and 708 motor vehicles. Australian losses are 130 killed and 326 wounded.

January 21: The 6th Division AIF launches its assault on Tobruk.

January 22: Tobruk surrenders. Twenty-five thousand prisoners and 208 field and medium guns have been taken. Australian casualties are 49 dead and 306 wounded.

January 25: Near Mechili, 3 Squadron encounters Fiat G 50s for the first time. Attacking from height, the radial-engined monoplanes prove superior, except for manoeuvrability, to the Australian Gladiators. The Italians claim four Gladiators destroyed but only F/O J. Campbell of Charleville, Queensland, is shot down and killed. F/O Peter Turnbull damages one G 50.

January 29: 3 Squadron receives its first Hawker Hurricanes.

January 30: The 19th Australian Brigade takes Derna.

February 3-14: Prime Minister Menzies inspects Australian forces. In spite of several meetings with the C-in-C Middle East, General Archibald Wavell, and senior British military leaders he is not briefed on the Greek situation and the probable commitment of Australian troops.

February 6: The Australians take Benghazi.

February 8: 3 Squadron turns its remaining Gladiators over to 274 Squadron which is being rested. In return, it receives 274 Squadron's Hurricanes.

February 9: The British advance halts at El Agheila, despite little Italian resistance. General Wavell has been informed that a portion of his troops are to be ready to go to Greece.

February 12: General Erwin Rommel arrives in Tripoli two days ahead of advanced units of the German Africa Corps.

February 15: F/O J. Saunders of 3 Squadron shoots down a Ju 88 after a long chase out to sea. The crew is rescued by a minesweeper. It is the squadron's first meeting with a German aircraft.

February 16: 450 Squadron RAAF is formed at Williamtown, NSW. Nos 450 and 451 Squadrons are the first Australian units to be created under Article XV of the Empire Air Training Scheme (EATS) program.

February 17: 3 Squadron moves to Tobruk to operate with 73 Squadron RAF.

February 18: Three Hurricanes from 3 Squadron bounce twelve Ju 87 Stukas attacking British positions near Mersa

Brega. F/Lt Gordon Steege claims three destroyed, F/O John Jackson three and F/O J. Saunders two.

February 19: Luftwaffe scores its first victory in the desert. While escorting Ju 7 Stukas, Bf 10s of III/ZG 26 clash with three Hurricanes of 3 Squadron. P/O A.Gatward of Mittagong,NSW, is shot down and killed. F/Lt John Perrin destroys a Stuka and a Bf 110 before crash-landing his burning aircraft. The Hurricane is strafed but Perrin, suffering from burns and injured in one eye, manages to escape. Afterwards, a British patrol finds and transports him to hospital in Tobruk.

March 30: Believing British forces have been overstretched, Rommel moves forward from El Agheila towards Mersa Brega.

March 31: A fierce battle develops between British and German forces at Mersa Brega.

April 1: British forces withdraw from Mersa Brega.

April 2: The German advance gathers momentum, splitting into three columns towards Msus, Mechili and Benghazi.

April 3: 3 Squadron withdraws from Benina to Sceleidima and then to Gut es Sultan. During the afternoon, seven Hurricanes with four more from 73 Squadron RAF bounce eight Stukas escorted by Bf 110s. P/O Peter Turnbull claims four of the escorts and F/Lt Gordon Steege one. Of the Stukas, F/Lt Alan Rawlinson shoots down two and F/O Smith one. Three are claimed as probables.

April 4: Italian and German forces retake Benghazi.

April 5: During three patrols over the Barce Pass covering the withdrawal of the Australian 9th Division, 3 Squadron,

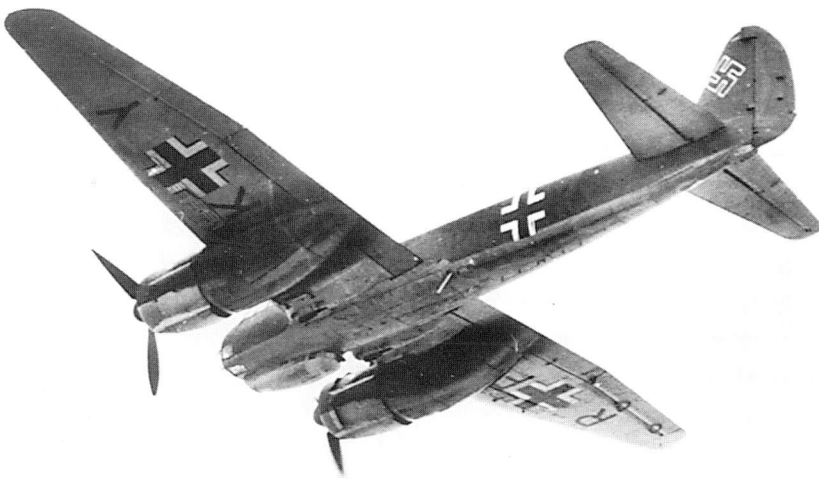

Junkers Ju 88, the first German type to be shot down by 3 Squadron. It was a machine of II/LG shot down on 15 February 1941. The successful pilot was F/O John Saunders in Hurricane V5476. Saunders went on to score a total of six destroyed and two damaged before he was killed in action on 22 November 1941. (MAP)

Hurricane Mk I, V7670, had a chequered career. It was used in the defence of Malta by 261 Squadron RAF where Queenslander P/O John 'Tiger' Pain flew it on several occasions. In it on 25 February 1941 he claimed a Bf 110 damaged. When 261 Squadron was disbanded in May, its surviving planes were flown to North Africa for re-allocation to another unit. V7670 was evidently abandoned on a Cyrenaican airfield and captured by the Germans. It was painted in Luftwaffe insignia, only to be recaptured by the British in good condition at Gambut during Operation Crusader in November 1941. (Dennis Newton)

operating from Maraua with 73 Squadron, has another highly successful day. Out of fourteen kills the Australians score 10, all Stukas. F/Lt John 'Jock' Perrin 3; F/O John Jackson 2; F/Os Ellerton, Kloster and Jewell 1 each. The remaining two are credited to lost pilots, Victorian F/Lt A. Edwards, who is picked up by the British 2nd Armoured Division but later captured, and S/Ldr D. Campbell who is KIA. Afterwards, the Hurricanes fly to their new base at Martuba.

April 6: The Australian 9th Division begins to pull back from Derna to Tobruk.

April 7: 3 Squadron strafes near Mechilli destroying two Ju 52 on the ground. F/O E. Knowles force lands behind Allied lines because of engine failure.

April 8: The 9th Division completes its withdrawal into Tobruk. No. 3 Squadron flies offensive patrols over Mechili during the day. F/O W. Jewell force lands because of engine failure. The squadron is then ordered back into Egypt to protect Salum, with the additional duty of reinforcing 73 Squadron by providing air cover for Tobruk when required.

April 10: Tobruk is now under siege but the defences have been well prepared. Inside is the Australian 9th Division, supported by a British infantry brigade, an anti-aircraft regiment and a tank regiment all commanded by General Leslie Morshead.

April 11: Rommel makes a violent but unsuccessful attack against Tobruk.

April 14: Near Tobruk, F/O Wilfred Arthur and Lt A. Tennant, a South African flying with 3 Squadron, are attacked by three Bf 110s. Each man claims a probable. German records admit to losing one Messerschmitt.

April 15: The new CO of 3 Squadron, S/Ldr Peter Jeffrey, surprises four unescorted Ju 52s. He shoots one down and, finding the others have landed, strafes and leaves them all in flames.

April 20: 3 Squadron is ordered to hand over all its Hurricanes to 274 Squadron RAF and go on leave to Aboukir before re-equipping with Curtiss P-40 Tomahawks. During its first tour of duty it has destroyed 47 enemy aircraft, probably destroyed 10 and damaged 13 for the loss 12 aircraft and 6 pilots.

April 30: Bound for the Middle East are 64 ground staff for 3 Squadron, 279 for 450 Squadron, 270 for 451 Squadron, and 25 for No. 1 Ambulance Unit. In the last three weeks German aircraft have launched 677 sorties against Tobruk. Approximately 70 aircraft have been claimed destroyed by defending fighters and anti-aircraft batteries. At dusk, after heavy shelling, the Germans launch another major attack.

May 1: Rommel's attack on Tobruk continues but his assaults are contained.

May 2: Rommel's efforts to widen the Tobruk salient continue to be frustrated by stubborn resistance.

May 3: The ground staffs of 450 and 451 Squadrons disembark in Egypt but they are without pilots and aircraft. They have arrived at a critical time, with Libya and Greece now in enemy hands, Tobruk under heavy attack, Crete threatened and all established squadrons desperately short of planes. Because of the need to move reinforcements into action as quickly as possible, the

Hurricanes and Blenheims on their way for delivery to the Desert Air Force. (MAP)

A Junkers Ju 52 being strafed on the ground. On 15 April 1941, S/Ldr Peter Jeffrey, the new CO of 3 Squadron, surprised four unescorted Ju 52s, shot one down and, finding that the others had landed, strafed and left them all in flames. Before he returned to Australia for service in the Pacific at the end of December, Peter Jeffrey had been promoted to wing commander, led 324 Wing RAF, destroyed five enemy aircraft and shared in another and collected a DSO and DFC. He did not claim his share in destroying a Bf 110 with another pilot on 30 March, nor did he include the three strafed Ju 52s in his total. His other exploits included being shot down and walking back to Allied lines on foot, and landing in the desert to pick up a fellow pilot who had been shot down. (Bryan Philpott)

decision will be taken to blend 450 Squadron ground crew with the pilots and Hurricanes of 260 Squadron RAF to form a single unit. The amalgamated squadron will be taken over by the newly promoted S/Ldr Harry Steege, formerly of 3 Squadron.

Meanwhile, many EATS-trained RAAF pilots and aircrew are coming from OTUs in England, posted mainly to the Wellington squadrons of 257 Wing and scattered among RAF personnel. Others have been arriving since April direct from Australian flying training schools at the rate of 30 pilots, 30 observers and 45 WAGs per month for the Middle East aircrew pool. By the month's end there will be about 50 of these in Wellington squadrons, fifteen in W/Cdr Alan McDonald Bowman's No. 39

(Maryland) reconnaissance Squadron and fewer numbers in all Blenheim units. To keep pace with operational wastage, Australian fighter pilots will go to RAF units too — mainly to 112 and the newly forming 250 Squadron — and soon will comprise approximately 45 per cent of the strength of each. Some will also be posted to 3 Squadron which at the moment is re-equipping with Curtiss P-40 Tomahawks.

May 4: The German and Italian attack on Tobruk is abandoned.

June 8: At 2 a.m., the British invade Syria. The force includes the 7th Australian Division (less one brigade which

Curtiss Tomahawk IIB (P-40C). Considered to have an inferior performance and therefore unsuitable for operations from Britiain over Europe, the type was nevertheless widely used in the Middle East. (MAP)

is in Tobruk), 4th Indian Brigade, the Free French Division and some composite motorised units. They will be fighting numerically superior Vichy French defenders consisting of 45 000 men. Air cover consists of 70 aircraft: 3 Squadron (Tomahawks); 80 Squadron RAF (Hurricanes); 208 Squadron RAF army co-op. (Lysanders and one of flight Hurricanes); 'X' Flight (Gladiators); and 815 Squadron FAA (Swordfish) operating from Cyprus. Limited numbers of Blenheims from Iraq and Wellingtons from Egypt can be called in for support if needed.

In its first raid of the campaign 3 Squadron strafes six Morane 406 fighters on the ground at Rayak. That evening four Tomahawks escort Blenheims bombing oil tanks at Beirut. No opposition.

June 13: Syria. The Australians attack Sidon.

June 14: While covering British naval units off Tyre and Sidon, eight 3 Squadron Tomahawks intercept eight Ju 88s in Italian markings. Three bombers are destroyed, one each by S/Ldr Peter Jeffrey, F/Lt John Perrin and F/O J. Saunders.

June 15: Operation Battleaxe, a major British offensive to relieve Axis pressure on Tobruk, begins. In spite of some initial success at Capuzzo, by the end of the day heavy tank losses leave the attackers at a serious disadvantage. Vichy French counter- attacks in Syria. No. 3 Squadron Tomahawks successfully attack twelve tanks and 30 vehicles near Sheikh Meskine. S/Ldr Jeffrey and F/O Peter Turnbull each destroy a Vichy Glenn Martin bomber.

June 17: In Syria, Australian troops capture Jezzine, just inland of Sidon. In North Africa, after confused fighting, the British withdraw to avoid being surrounded and cut off by Rommel's tanks. By the afternoon the situation on the Libyan/Egyptian front is as it had been two days ago. Battleaxe has failed.

Valton William James Crook from Orange, NSW, was working in New Zealand when war broke out so he enlisted in the RNZAF. He joined 37 Squadron RAF as a gunner at Shallufa, Egypt, in April 1941. This unit operated Vickers Wellington ICs and was engaged in night-bombing raids on enemy ports and bases in Libya. In May it took part in suppressing the Iraqi uprising but its main work was concentrated upon Libya and the Desert. On the night of 6/7 June 1941, five aircraft from 37 Squadron were detailed to attack enemy stores and vehicles in Benghazi and it was from this raid that Bill Crook's Wellington, N2917, failed to return. After bombing the port's docks, heavy flak was encountered and the Wellington crashed into the sea. Bill Crook and the others, although shaken up, were able to take to the dinghy. They were not found for 38 hours, after a harrowing two days of exposure, when a seaplane picked them up. Crook's experience was typical of those had by many aircrew from both sides who were shot down into the sea. (Kenneth Wynn)

Curtiss P-40 Tomahawk AK354, one of five 3 Squadron aircraft which initiated operations against the Vichy French in Syria on 8 June 1941. (Dennis Newton)

June 19: After an uneventful mission escorting Blenheims, Tomahawks of 3 Squadron intercept and disperse Vichy Glenn Martin 167 bombers trying to bomb Australian troops near Sidon.

June 20: While the Indian brigade assaults Damascus, Tomahawks of 3 Squadron make low-level attacks on Vichy French troops retiring towards Beirut.

June 21: 3 Squadron Tomahawks continue to strafe retreating Vichy French troops on the road to Beirut. Ground fire damages three aircraft. Damascus is captured. An independent British force, 'Habforce', under the command of Lt-General John Laverack of Melbourne, begins to move from Iraq against Palmyra. Aerial reinforcements include 45 Squadron RAF (Blenheims) and 260/450 Squadron (Hurricanes).

June 26: Between Tobruk and Capuzzo Tomahawks of 250 Squadron RAF encounter 30 enemy aircraft while escorting bombers to Gazala. In the dogfight, P/O Clive Caldwell of Rose Bay, NSW, and Sgt G. Coward of North Ipswitch, Queensland, both destroy Bf 109s. P/O Jim Kent from Edgecliff, NSW, heavily damages a Bf 109, shoots down a Fiat G 50 and strafes a staff car on the escarpment near Sollum. One Australian, Sgt David Gale, is lost. In Syria, eight 3 Squadron Tomahawks encounter four Vichy LEO 45s south-west of Palmyra and shoot down at least three.

June 28: Nine 3 Squadron Tomahawks intercept six Glenn Martin bombers attacking Habforce units near Palmyra. All are shot down. F/Lt Alan Rawlinson claims three; F/O Peter Turnbull two; and Sgt Rex Wilson one.

June 29: In a strafing attack on the airfield at Kuseir, 3 Squadron damages numerous trucks, destroys petrol and ammunition dumps and leaves a hangar on fire. P/O L. Knowles of Canberra shoots down a Glenn Martin 167. Since the 22nd, when airfield attacks began again, the squadron has destroyed seven aircraft on the ground and damaged thirteen others.

June 30: Nine Tomahawks of 250 squadron intercept 20 Stukas and 30 escorting fighters while covering a Tobruk bound-convoy. Clive Caldwell accounts for two Ju 87s and shares a probable Bf 110 with Sgt Robert Whittle. P/O Jim Kent fails to return.

July 1: General Claude Auchinleck is appointed C-in-C Middle East. General Wavell, out of favour with Churchill since the failure of the Battleaxe offensive, takes Auchinleck's old post as C-in-C India.

Tobruk remains besieged but the defenders have not stayed docile. General Morshead's program of maintaining constant outward pressure on the perimeter through vigorous night patrols and skirmishes is paying dividends. The line around the Salient forced by the Germans at the end of April has been advanced by around 2000 yards, leaving it about 3000 yards deep in the middle.

The only method of supplying the fortress and the port of Mersa Matruh is by sea. Carrying out this duty are the gallant vessels of the 'Scrap Iron Flotilla' which, while maintaining this lifeline — the 'Tobruk Ferry Service' — often came under heavy air attack. Just two days ago destroyer HMAS Waterhen had been crippled by Stukas. A tow had been attempted but at 1.50 a.m. she tipped over and sank, becoming the first RAN ship to be lost by enemy action in World War II.

July 7: 250 Squadron RAF, together with several other units, carry out a large-scale fighter sweep over Bardia. P/O Clive Caldwell becomes separated from the others. Near El Adem he encounters two G 50s and shoots one down. While returning to base he strafes a variety of targets along the way. One of the Australian fighter pilots beginning to make a reputation for himself over North Africa at this time, Caldwell possesses that rare combination of outstanding flying skill, aggression and deadly marksmanship which makes an ace. He will soon earn the grim title of 'Killer' and eventually be credited with 28½ victories to become the highest scoring Australian of the war.

July 9: Clive Caldwell of 250 Squadron destroys a Bf 109. Meanwhile, in Syria, Australian troops take Damour opening, the way to Beirut.

July 10: Five Vichy Dewoitine D.520s succeed in shooting down three Blenheims of 45 Squadron RAF before they are all destroyed by Tomahawks of 3 Squadron RAAF. Scorers are F/O Peter Turnbull (2), F/O John Jackson (1), P/O E. Lane (1) and Sgt G. Hiller (1).

July 11: 3 Squadron and 260/450 Squadron attack airfields in the Aleppo-Hama area. In aerial combat, F/O Frank Fischer's Tomahawk is shot up by a Dewoitine but he manages to crash-land safely. F/O R. (Bobby) Gibbes of 450 Squadron destroys the French fighter immediately afterwards. Meanwhile, Fischer escapes capture by hiding in an Arab village and later returns to his unit. The Vichy commander, General Dentz, accepts the armistice terms dictated by the Allies. The cease-fire begins at 2100 hours and all Syrian operations are suspended after midnight. The campaign has cost the Vichy French 3500 casualties

A Hurricane sheltering in shade under the wing of a captured Fiat G 12 military transport. Tactical reconnaissance Hurricanes of 451 Squadron RAAF were active in finding and reporting concentrations of enemy tanks and armoured vehicles, particularly around Tobruk.
(Trevor Mear)

and the Allies 2500. Of these, some 1600 are Australian including 416 killed.

July 14: A Wellington of 38 Squadron flown by Sgt F. Clowry of Canberra fails to return from an experimental minelaying sortie against Benghazi.

July 29: S/Ldr J. G. MacDonald, CO of No. 1 Air Ambulance Unit RAAF, flies a DH-86 from Heliopolis to Gaza to open the unit's first base close to the 1st Australian Field Hospital.

August 9: First mission of No. 451 RAAF tactical reconnaissance Squadron (Hurricanes).

August 10: P/O Ray Hudson scores 451 Squadron's first success when, on a reconnaissance sortie near Bardia, he shoots down an Hs 126. His victim is Oblt. Heymer, CO of the Luftwaffe's 2/H14 reconnaissance unit.

August 22/23: Responding to pressure from the Australian Government to have AIF troops relieved in Tobruk, it has been organised for 5000 Australian soldiers to be withdrawn in a series of night operations. They are to be replaced by 6000 troops of the Polish Brigade. On this night they are taken aboard the RN destroyer HMS Jervis and other vessels including HMS Kimberley, Hasty and the fast minelayer Abdiel. The convoy leaves Tobruk Harbour but with the coming of daylight is subjected to air attack. Upon reaching Alexandria, the ships form line ahead and proceed up the harbour to a tumultuous welcome from the assembled ships, to honour the now famous 'Rats of Tobruk'.

August 24: F/Lt J. Saunders of 3 Squadron damages a Ju 88 near Alexandria in the unit's first action since its recent

return from Syria. There are now four operational P-40 Tomahawk squadrons in this theatre, the others being 112 and 250 RAF, each containing a large Australian content, and 2 Squadron South African Air Force (SAAF).

August 29: North-west of Sidi Barrani, 250 Squadron is attacked by Bf 109s while on a shipping patrol. Acting as weaver, P/O Clive Caldwell is wounded in the back, left shoulder, leg and neck when his Tomahawk is shot up and begins to burn. The German pilot, Lt. Werner Schroer of I/JG 27, who will be credited with 61 of his 114 victories in North Africa and be second only to the legendary Hans-Joachim Marseille, returns to base and claims a kill. He does not see what happens next. As Caldwell prepares to bail out the fire dies out, so he sits down back into his cockpit. Then, despite his injuries, the Australian ace attacks and shoots down a Bf 109 in flames before flying home.

September 3: Two Tac.R Hurricanes of 451 Squadron are intercepted over Sollum by three Bf 110s of III/ZG 26. Sgt Leslie Readett of Sydney is shot down and posted as missing. (His family will subsequently be informed that he has been KIA. Later, notification will come from the RAAF that he has been overpaid by £1 19s 1d, ie., $3.91, which will be written off!) The other Hurricane has to break away when its guns jam.

September 11: A Tac.R Hurricane of 451 Squadron reports concentrations of enemy tanks and armoured vehicles near Acroma. A new German thrust seems imminent.

September 13: Now operating from airfield LG 102, the pilots of 3 Squadron begin practising a new 'fluid pairs' formation contrived to counter the diving attacks of Bf 109s.

Tac.R Hurricanes from 451 Squadron RAAF continue to monitor the German build-up near Acroma. One aircraft flown by F/Lt Byers is shot down by the German ace Lt Hans-Joachim Marseille. Byers is captured.

Since the beginning of August, 451 Squadron has been carrying out highly successful photographic reconnaissance sorties of the enemy's positions around Tobruk. On each occasion the film has been rushed back to HQ Desforce at Bagush, developed and then immediately flown back to Tobruk. There, after making a slow wheels-down approach from the sea, the Hurricane pilot would drop his valuable cargo on the landing ground and return to base. Now a proposal is made to base two of the squadron's aircraft at Tobruk itself for this purpose until such time as the siege can be raised. (The scheme will be put into action and the first to fly recce sorties from Tobruk will be 451 Squadron's F/O Geoff Morley-Mower, RAF. The next two pilots selected, Ray Hudson and Ed Kirkham, will be delivered to Tobruk by HMS Abdul early in October. Unfortunately, the two Hurricanes they are expected to fly will never become serviceable. F/O Ron Achilles and Colin Robinson are more fortunate and between 25 October and 2 December they will fly 26 searches around the perimeter. The two Hurricanes are hidden in underground shelters and will not be discovered by the enemy, despite the fact that air raids and reconnaissance are carried out almost daily. Dummy aircraft dispersed round the landing ground attract the attention of German and Italian pilots.)

September 14: The German forces which have concentrated near Acroma move eastward in two strong columns. Lighter British forces on the Lybian front avoid contact and withdraw, acting upon information from 451 Squadron's Hurricanes which continue to fly sortie after sortie watching the enemy's progress. By nightfall the Germans reach Rabia, seemingly in a position to threaten Sidi Barrani, but then they unexpectedly withdraw and return to their starting point. If the plan has been for a surprise attack, it has been frustrated by the vigilance of 451 Squadron, the only army co-op unit in the forward area, which has made 50 covering reconnaissance flights since the 11th. During the day, two Hurricanes of 451 Squadron are bounced by six Bf 109s of JG 27. F/O W. D. Hutley force-lands and is afterwards rescued by an armoured patrol. Sgt Harry Rowlands is involved in a high- speed, low-level chase almost all the way home. Despite being severely wounded in the legs, he lands his shot-up aircraft safely at Bir el Tholata.

No. 3 Squadron suffers too when five Tomahawks on a strafing mission to Gambut are intercepted by four Bf 109s and a Bf 110. F/O Burbury and P/O Lees are shot down. Lees force lands 30 miles east of Gambut and walks until he meets a patrol near Sollum. He returns to 3 Squadron on the 18th. Meanwhile, Luftwaffe records show that a Ju 87 of Stab/St.G 3 is shot down by an unidentified fighter while landing at Gambut. It may have been Burbury's victim.

September 24: F/Lt J. Saunders of 3 Squadron RAAF shoots a lone Ju 88 down in flames but is bounced immediately afterwards by six Bf 109s. He has to force land and his Tomahawk is strafed and destroyed. Saunders is slightly wounded.

September 27: F/O Graeme-Evans of 451 Squadron is shot down over Bardia by six Bf 109s. An escorting Hurricane from 33 Squadron is also lost for one Messerschmitt. Tomahawks from 3 and 250 Squadrons escort Marylands of 21 Squadron SAAF to Bardia. South of Buq Buq the force is attacked by Bf 109s. A Maryland and a Tomahawk of 250 Squadron are lost while three Messerschmitts are claimed destroyed, one by P/O Clive 'Killer' Caldwell.

September 28: Bardia is attacked again by Marylands escorted by a mixed escort of Hurricanes, Tomahawks and RNFS Grumman Martlets. 'Killer' Caldwell claims a Bf 109 probable and an Italian G 50 falls to a naval pilot.

October 1: To facilitate the development of adequate air support for future land operations, No. 1 (Australian) Air Support Control under the command of Major A. D. Malloy AIF is formed during the month. It will work closely with 451 Squadron and No.200 Air Intelligence Liaison Section.

One of the Australian fighter pilots making a reputation for himself over North Africa in mid-1941 was P/O Clive Caldwell of 250 Squadron RAF. Possessing that rare combination of outstanding flying skill, aggression and deadly marksmanship, Caldwell soon earned the grim title of 'Killer' and would eventually be credited with 28.5 victories to become the highest scoring Australian ace of World War II. He flew Curtiss Tomahawk AK498/LD-C in the latter half of 1941. (Dennis Newton)

October 3: Near Baq Baq seven Bf 109s bounce a 451 Squadron Tac.R Hurricane escorted by six Hurricanes of 33 Squadron RAF. One of the escorts is shot up and Sgt Ranger Lowry of Turramurra, NSW, has to bail out as his aircraft bursts into flames. Lowry will spend the next three months in hospital.

October 12: It is not a good day for the Australians. Operating with 2 Squadron SAAF near Bir Sheferzen, 3 Squadron becomes involved in a bitter dogfight with Bf 109s. F/O Roberts crash-lands in Allied lines, Sgt Scott crash-lands at Sidi Haneish and Sgt Parker manages to bail out of his blazing Tomahawk but is severely wounded, dying before his parachute reaches the ground. Sgt 'Tiny' Cameron claims a Bf 109 and F/O W. Jewell a probable. The South Africans lose one Tomahawk and another force lands.

In a later battle, ten 112 Squadron Tomahawks encounter fifteen Bf 109s and ten G 50s. P/O R. Jeffries of Mosman Park, WA, shoots down a Bf 109F but other Australians in the squadron suffer. Sgt W. E. Carson is wounded, Sgt Rudolf Leu and P/O Parker are shot down and Sgt McWilliam's aircraft is badly shot up but he manages to reach home. Both Parker and Leu are found slightly injured during the night by the Coldstream Guards. In two days they will be back with their squadron.

October 22: All Australian soldiers of the 9th Division, except for the men of the 2/13th Battalion, have now been evacuated from Tobruk. The 'Tobruk Ferry Service' relief convoy on its way to the fortress had been obliged to turn back because of air attack, stranding the unit. General Morshead hands over his command to the officer commanding 70th British Division. The 2/13th will remain at Tobruk until the siege ends.

October 23: On the Benghazi 'Mail Run', the almost nightly RAF attacks on Axis supplies coming into Benghazi harbour, Wellington 1C/T2832 of 108 Squadron RAF is hit by flak. On board is Queenslander P/O Allan Simpson for experience acting as substitute navigator. He is on his first 'Mail Run' op, having arrived in the Middle East 30 days earlier and joined the squadron only five days ago. Losing height, the Wellington limps towards LG 104, its advanced landing ground in Egypt, but south of Sollum, over 'no man's land', Simpson and the others have to bail out. Just after dawn they are found by a staff car occupied by South African war correspondents who are on an 'unofficial, unauthorized inspection' ahead of the forward British positions! Two nights later, Simpson is in another Wellington back on the Benghazi 'Mail Run', this time with his own crew.

October 29: 94 (Hurricane) Squadron RAF, commanded by Australian Battle of Britain veteran S/Ldr Clive Mayers, DFC, arrives at LG 103 after serving as night fighters in the Canal Zone.

October 30: Ever trying to evolve tactics to combat the high-flying Messerschmitts, British and Commonwealth fighter squadrons now usually fly in pairs. To avoid their individual weavers falling victim to the German fighters, each whole squadron weaves. Nos. 238 and 250 Squadrons carry out a sweep over Gambut and Bardia. In a clash with Bf 109Fs, Sgt Robert Whittle of 250 Squadron claims one out of two shot down. Sgt C. Cornall has to bail out of his Tomahawk fifteen miles west of Bardia and 238 Squadron loses a Hurricane and its pilot.

November 12: P/O Whalley and Lt. Thomas of 451 Squadron fail to return from a Tac.R. mission.

November 17: Everything stands ready for Operation Crusader, the second British Libyan offensive. No. 1 Air Ambulance Unit, now operating three DH-86s and a Lodestar attached from the SAAF, is awaiting orders. In the past week 3 Squadron has flown only 36 sorties without meeting air opposition while 451 has made only three reconnaissance sorties during the last three days. Things are about to change dramatically.

November 18: Operation Crusader is launched. It is the largest assault in the desert so far and the air fighting increases accordingly. Lt. W. Andrew, a South African member of 451 Squadron, is shot down while on a Tac.R. mission. He will return safely on foot next day.

November 19: Four Bf 109s strafe LG 132, 20 miles north of Maddelena, damaging three of 451's Hurricanes. F/O Frank Fischer is on a sweep with 3 Squadron when his Tomahawk's engine starts having oil trouble. Returning alone to LG 110, he spots the strafing Bf 109s, and attacks, shooting one down. The others force him to crash-land south of Sidi Omar. Fischer, slightly wounded by shrapnel, scrambles out of his aircraft before it is strafed and destroyed.

November 20: 3 Squadron escorts bombers early and later joins 112 Squadron RAF in a sweep over the 7th Armoured Division. Each squadron claims two Bf 110s destroyed. Sgt Ron Simes one plus one shared between the rest of 3 Squadron while 112's Sgt. K. Carson claims one and Sgt Rudolf Leu shares the second with two others.

November 21: 112 Squadron, patrolling near El Adem, destroy two Italian CR 42s. Sgt Leu one, and after a chase, P/O R. Jeffries, Sgt Carson and another pilot dispose of the other. No. 451 Squadron loses Lt. Smith, who crashes in flames on a Tac.R. mission.

November 22: After a confused tank battle around Sidi Rezegh the Germans now hold the initiative, having more than 170 tanks left and the British fewer than 150. It is also a bad day for 3 Squadron.. During an early escort mission, 45 Squadron loses four Blenheims and for 3 Squadron P/O Lane, F/Lt Saunders and F/O Watson fail to return. Later in the day, there is another violent battle with Bf 109s and this time F/Lt Knowles, F/O Roberts, F/O Kloster and P/O Lees do not return. Both W/Cdr Jeffrey and Sgt. Simes are shot down, picked up by friendly troops and later return. Although there are several probables, only two kills are confirmed, one to S/Ldr Rawlinson and the other to the squadron as a whole. Having lost nine aircraft in two engagements, 3 Squadron will be unable to operate again until the 24th.

Of the Australians in 112 Squadron, P/O Bartle destroys a Messerschmitt but Sgt H. Burney force-lands and, evading capture, walks 30 miles across the desert before reaching the 4th Indian Division.

November 23: By the evening Operation Crusader has gone astray and all hope of quick success against the German armour has gone.

November 24: Nine Hurricanes of 80 Squadron strafe an enemy column near Sidi Rezegh. They are intercepted by twelve Bf 110s. Sgt Russell Foskett of Sydney causes one to crash-land and is surprised to see no less than four people clamber out of it!

November 25: 3 Squadron strafes German concentrations near Sidi Omar but encounter accurate ground fire. F/O Bothwell is KIA and F/Lt Manford has to crash-land, he will later escape with the personnel of 451 Squadron evacuating Sidi Omar airfield. F/O Jewell is shot down between two columns of enemy transport and captured. When asked the way to Sidi Omar, he gives his captors wrong directions, and they drive straight into a New Zealand patrol. Jewell leaps to freedom as the Germans speed off. In a later action over Tobruk, 3 Squadron is highly successful against a force of 60 enemy aircraft. Scorers are: Sgt Rex Wilson (Bf110 and two Fi 156s), Sgt F. Reid (Bf110), Sgt. Baillie (two G50s), W/Cdr Peter Jeffrey (Bf 110) and F/O John Jackson (probable Bf 110). F/O Evans fails to return.

Rommel collects his armour and advances along the Trigh el Abd to the Egyptian frontier. This 'dash to the wire' or 'Matruh Stakes' will create some panic in the Eighth Army's rear but it is really a tactical error. The Germans will take losses and, more significantly, it will allow British tank units to regroup. During the afternoon Hurricanes of 451 Squadron, reporting the column's movement, fly nine sorties.

New Zealand infantry continues moving towards Tobruk.

General Cunningham is relieved of Eighth Army command. Auchinleck's Chief of Staff, General Ritchie takes over.

November 26: At Sidi Azeiz, 451 Squadron's advanced party is taken into an armed camp established by the 5th New Zealand Brigade, the pilots sleeping beside their machines.

November 27: In the early hours, north-east of Tobruk, HMAS Parramatta is struck amidships by a torpedo fired from a shadowing U-boat. Within a few minutes she rolls to starboard and goes under. Only 24 ratings from her crew of 160 survive.

At Sidi Azeiz, part of 451 Squadron's maintenance party is overrun and captured, but the four Hurricanes take off in the dark without a flare path. Those captured will be taken to Bardia. Major A. Molloy and Captain A. Flemming of No.1 (Australian) Air Support Control manage to escape several days later.

Units of the 4th and 6th NZ Brigades link with forces from the Tobruk garrison at El Duda.

November 30: After renewed heavy fighting around Sidi Rezegh for the past two days, the hard-fought-for link between the NZ infantry and the Tobruk garrison is under serious threat and likely to be severed once more. In a spectacular success against fifteen Ju 87s escorted by 25 Italian and German fighters about to attack the New Zealanders at Sidi Rezegh, 3 Squadron claims eight enemy machines destroyed and twelve damaged while 112 Squadron destroys three Italian fighters, Sgt Leu shooting down a G 50. No. 3 Squadron's initial tally is: S/Ldr Alan Rawlinson one Mc 200, F/O T. Trimble two Mc 200s, F/O Bobby Gibbes one G 50, Sgt Walter Mailey two Mc 200s, Sgt D. Scott a G 50 and a Ju 87, Sgt Allan Cameron a G 50. 'Tiny' Cameron's Tomahawk is shot up and he bales out, but is picked up and flown back to base by W/Cdr Jeffrey, quite an achievement as Cameron is undoubtedly the biggest man in the squadron. F/Lt Wilfred 'Woof' Arthur fails to return but he arrives back safely shortly afterwards, having force-landed due to a faulty distributor. He has a personal bag of four, a G 50, a Mc 200 and two Ju 87s, bringing the squadron tally up to twelve confirmed, and an overall total score of 106.

December 1: Two Tomahawks of 3 Squadron intercept a reconnaissance Ju 88, which Sgt Wilson shoots down.

December 4: Hurricane reconnaissance sorties of 451 Squadron report German preparations to attack Ed Duda. These flights greatly aid XIII Corps in deploying its forces within the 43-mile (69 km) long Tobruk perimeter.

December 5: During a 'Stuka party' when Tomahawks of 250 and 112 Squadrons meet 40 escorted Ju 87s south of El Adem, F/Lt. 'Killer' Caldwell, leading 250 Squadron, destroys five Stukas. Other Australian scorers are Sgt Whittle (2), Sgt Cable (2) and P/O Creighton (1). No. 112 Squadron is also successful, destroying eight, including P/O Bartle a G 50 and a Ju 87.

December 9: Nine Tomahawks of 250 Squadron with RNFS Hurricanes sweep the Adem-El Gobi area. They encounter five Bf 110s and ten Bf 109s. P/O John Waddy shares a Bf 110 in flames.

Later, south of El Adem, Tomahawks of 3 Squadron and ten of 112 Squadrons are bounced by six Bf 109s. The Australian Tomahawks suffer badly, Sgt Wilson being killed, Sgt 'Tiny' Cameron force- landing and F/O Rutter failing to return. W/Cdr Jeffrey force- lands at Tobruk, while Sgt Carson of 112 Squadron is badly shot- up. Sgt Mailey of 3 Squadron shoots down one Messerschmitt and damages a second. Cameron will return to 3 Squadron on the 12th. Rex Wilson from Glen Osmond, SA, had destroyed eight enemy aircraft and had just been recommended for a DFM.

December 12: Tomahawks of 112 Squadron RAF and 3 Squadron attack a large formation of Axis aircraft over Tmimi. F/O Barr destroys a Bf 110 but two Tomahawks collide, that flown by P/O Fred Eggleston crashing. No.

112 Squadron loses three pilots but on the credit side P/O Bartle claims a Bf 109.

December 13: Ten Tomahawks of 3 Squadron on a sweep spot eight Ju 87s with eight escorting Bf 109s west of Tmimi. F/O Barr destroys a Bf 109, while Sgt Cameron also claims one and shares another with F/O Briggs. F/O Trimble is shot down, but will return safely on the 20th. While returning to base, Barr destroys a lone Ju 88 south of Galzala.

December 14: Six Tomahawks of 3 Squadron on a 'rhubarb' over Martuba meet seven Ju 87s covered by Bf 109s and claim one Stuka but F/O Knight and Sgt Scott are shot down.

December 17: 3 Squadron hands four of its remaining Tomahawks to 112 Squadron RAF, two each to 2 and 4 Squadrons SAAF, and then collect the first of their new Curtiss Kittyhawks. It is hoped this type will perform better than the Tomahawk against the Bf 109F.

December 22: Sunderland T9071 of 230 Squadron is intercepted by two Bf 110s 50 miles north-east of Benghazi. Sgt. Jacques Dupont RAAF claims a probable after two gunners have been wounded, but the badly damaged Sunderland force-lands on the sea. The starboard float is smashed while landing and the crew has to spread themselves on the undamaged wing to keep the remaining float in the water. The aircraft drifts tail-first until striking a reef just off Ras Amt and begins to break up. Dupont helps a mortally wounded gunner into a dinghy and swims alongside but it capsizes. The Australian holds his

Ju 87 Stukas. During a 'Stuka party' on 5 December 1941, Tomahawks of 250 and 112 Squadrons met 40 Ju 87s south of El Adem. 'Killer' Caldwell, leading 250 Squadron, destroyed no less than five Stukas — the largest number of enemy aircraft shot down in a single sortie by an Australian fighter pilot. (MAP)

Curtiss P-40E Kittyhawk. More powerful and better armed than Tomahawks, it was hoped that Kittyhawks would perform better against the high-flying Messerschmitt Bf 109Fs. No. 3 Squadron was the first unit to be equipped with this type in North Africa, flying the first mission on 28 December 1941. (MAP)

companion up and after two hours, along with the others, he struggles ashore. Here, a group of Italian soldiers approach and surrender to them! More Italians then arrive and take the party prisoner, taking them to a Senussi village where the wounded gunner dies and is buried. Next day, not knowing whether or not the British have taken Benghazi, the parties split up. The Sunderland group finally reaches British lines after collecting 130 voluntary Italian prisoners along the way! Sgt Dupont is awarded a DFM.

Allied aircraft raid Magrun airfield. In one attack, six Tomahawks of 112 Squadron with seven of 250 Squadron, covered by 2 and 4 Squadrons SAAF, find 24 enemy aircraft on the airfield, some landing and some taking off. Sgt Frank 'Mac' Twemlow of 250 Squadron shoots down a Stuka which is about to land. Sgt Carson, who destroys a Ju 52 on the ground, shares in probably destroying a Bf 109. P/O Bartle shares a Ju 87.

December 23: Axis forces evacuate Benghazi.

December 28: 3 Squadron flies its first Kittyhawk mission accompanied by the Tomahawks of 112 and 250 Squadrons.

1942

January 1: Nine Kittyhawks of 3 Squadron encounter sixteen Ju87s and six Bf 1O9s about to attack Allied troops fifteenmiles east of Agedabia. In their first Kittyhawk combat, F/O Spence destroys a Ju 87, F/O Barr a Ju 87 and a probable, F/O Fischer a Ju 87, and Sgt Cameron a Bf 109 and a Ju 87 but S/Ldr Chapman is shot down, possibly by a Stuka gunner. In a separate battle, 238 Squadron's Sgt W. Metherall, slightly wounded, force-lands his Hurricane two miles west of Solluch.

January 2: The Axis garrison of Bardia surrenders after holding out since almost the start of the Crusader offensive.

January 8: 3 Squadron meets a large force of Axis aircraft about to strafe British troops south-east of Agedabia. Seven enemy planes are destroyed and four probably destroyed. F/Lt Jackson claims an Mc 200, Sgt Simes a CR 42 and two Mc 200s, Sgt Pfeiffer two Mc 200s, F/O Schaeffer a CR 42 and an Mc 200 probable, F/O Jones a Bf 109 probable, and F/O Hart a CR 42 probable. F/O Baster fails to return. John Jackson has now brought his tally to eight before returning to Australia.

January 9: While escorting seven Marylands to bomb Marsa Brega, a lone diving Bf 109 surprises 3 Squadron and shoots down two Kittyhawks: F/O G. Chinchen, who crash-lands at Msus, and Sgt Ron Simes who had just yesterday brought his score to six. Simes, from Tenterfield, NSW, is KIA.

January 11: While Kittyhawks of 3 RAAF and 112 Squadrons are escorting Blenheims on a raid, the top cover is jumped by three Bf 109s. F/O R. F. Jones of Peppermint Grove, WA, and Sgt Allan 'Tiny' Cameron, DFM, are shot down and captured. For Cameron this is the third time. F/O H. Pace claims a Bf 109 probable. Meanwhile, F/O Barr destroys a G 50 and a 109 before attempting to land and pick up one of the downed Australians. He is bounced by two more 109s and, with his wheels half retracted, shoots one down before crash-landing himself and being strafed and wounded. On his return to the squadron on 14th, 'Nicky' Barr is awarded an immediate DFC, having brought his score to seven in only two weeks of combat.

January 12: Rommel plans a surprise counter-offensive against the British. Even while retreating during Operation

Crusader, the Germans had been receiving new supplies of tanks and more had arrived on 5 January. The British forces will be weakened by the diversion of reinforcements to the Far East and the loss of two Australian divisions withdrawn to face the Japanese.

January 13: Seven Kittyhawks of 3 Squadron are bounced by four Bf 109s. F/O Schaeffer force-lands at Msus where he is able to repair the damage and return to Antelat next day.

January 14: During a pre-dawn patrol over Tobruk, Sgt. Foskett of 80 (Hurricane) Squadron intercepts a Ju 88 but just before he attacks it is blown to pieces by AA fire from the port. No. 112 Squadron receives a new CO, S/Ldr C. R. 'Killer' Caldwell, DFC and Bar, being promoted from 250 Squadron.

January 16: Sgt Foskett shoots a Bf 110 into the sea. Making use of a period of poor weather, 3 Squadron is rested for a week.

January 17: F/O Jones and Sgt. Cameron, who had been shot down, captured and taken to Tripoli on the 11th, escape and begin walking eastwards. Twice before Cameron has managed to rejoin 3 Squadron after being shot down.

January 21: Rommel's second offensive begins. Cautious German advances quickly reveal faulty British dispositions. The German attacks take the British by surprise.

January 22: The luck of F/O Jones and Sgt. Cameron, who had escaped from Tripoli on the 17th, runs out. They are betrayed by Arabs and recaptured. They will be transferred to Italy but their escape attempts will continue. Jones will eventually be successful, make his way into Switzerland, and, in July 1944, cross into France to join the French Forces.

Twelve Kittyhawks of 3 Squadron meet 30 Ju 87s escorted by G 50s, Mc 200s and Bf 109s. F/O Gibbes destroys a Ju 87 and damages two G 50s while F/O Hart and P/O P. Giddy each destroy an Mc200. On the return flight, two Bf 109s bounce them, shooting down F/O Bradbury and F/O McIntosh. Bradbury returns on 25th, suffering from shell-shock.

January 24: An advance party of 450 Squadron is sent to El Adam but only reaches Mersa Matruh, where its trucks are requisitioned to ferry petrol to elements of the retreating 8th Army.

January 25: 3 Squadron Kittyhawks carry out a strafing attack, setting four troop-carriers and a petrol tanker on fire ten miles north of Agedabia. Sgts Reid and Curtiss shoot down a Bf 110. Later, Sgt Leu of 112 Squadron claims a Bf 109.

January 26: Tomahawks of 250 Squadron strafe the Msus area and P/O Waddy shoots down an Mc 200.

January 29: Rommel retakes Benghazi.

February 7: Rommel's forces stop their advance near Gazala. They have recovered nearly all of the ground won by the British at the end of 1941.

February 8: Kittyhawks of 3 RAAF and 112 Squadrons with Hurricanes from 73 Squadron escort Blenheims to Derna. While waiting over El Adem to rendezvous, four RAAF aircraft abort with engine trouble and are attacked by Bf 109s. Sgt Curtiss crash-lands back at Gambut but F/O Threlkeld bales out and is picked up by the army. The battle is joined again over Derna, where a Hurricane is damaged and eventually obliged to crash-land ten miles from its base. On the way back, 112 Squadron loses three but claims three Bf 109s, Sgt Burney accounting for one and sharing another.

February 10: 459 Squadron RAAF, equipped with two Hudsons and four Blenheims, is formed in the Middle East as an extra flight of 203 Squadron RAF.

February 14: The ground staff of 450 Squadron move to Gambut, and the pilots and aircraft follow two days later. Here the squadron suffers its first fatality when A/C A. McKee (RAF) is killed by a delayed action bomb.

In the air the Kittyhawks of 3 RAAF and 112 Squadron have what the Americans would call a 'turkey shoot' when they meet 32 Axis aircraft and shoot down 20 without loss. The destroyed claims for 3 Squadron are: Sgt Mailey 2 Bf 109s; Sgt Thompson 1 Mc 200 shared; F/O Pace 1 Mc 200 shared; Sgt C. H. White 1 Bf 109; F/O Giddy 2 Mc 200s; Sgt Reid 1 Mc 200 and 1 Mc 200 shared; and F/O Spence 1 Bf 109. The destroyed claims for Australians in 112 Squadron are: F/O Bartle 1 probable Mc 200; Sgt Leu 2 Mc 200s; and Sgt Burney 1 Mc200. Ten more are claimed damaged.

February 15: Two Kittyhawks of 3 Squadron piloted by F/O Briggs and Sgt F. Reid, while taking off to intercept a raid, are bounced by a Bf 109 as they are climbing. Reid, from Artarmon, NSW, crashes and is killed instantly but Briggs, although wounded, manages to bale out at 300 feet. They are both victims of the German ace Marseille of I/JG 27.

February 16: Six Bf 109s attack five Kittyhawks of 3 Squadron head on. One Messerschmitt is damaged but F/O T. Threlkeld from Parramatta, NSW is killed, crashing in flames 20 miles south of El Adem.

February 17: 458 (Wellington) Squadron RAAF had been formed in Yorkshire on 1 September 1941, but now, en route to the Middle East via Gibraltar and Malta, its aircraft are scattered by sudden gales near Sardinia, the worst since the beginning of the war. Also, Wellington AD539 flown by 458's CO, W/Cdr N. G. Mulholland, DFC, is intercepted by a Ju 88C night fighter and shot down into the sea 30 miles from Malta. Thus 458 Squadron arrives in Egypt with no CO, no leaders in gunnery, signals, bombing, etc., and no ground staff. The aircraft and crews are quickly assigned to other units and for a time 458 Squadron ceases to exist.

February 19: 450 Squadron, flying Kittyhawks, carries out its first operation, a fighter sweep west of Tobruk.

February 21: After several days of rain and sandstorms six Bf 109s of I/JG 27 spot eleven Kittyhawks of 112 Squadron led by S/Ldr 'Killer' Caldwell and begin climbing to get above them. In a practical demonstration of excellent flying and marksmanship, Caldwell suddenly pulls up vertically, fires, and sends a 109 spinning down to crash-land in no-man's land. The German pilot, ace Lt Hans-Arnold Stahlschmidt, is uninjured and recovered by an Axis patrol. Meanwhile, 112 Squadron loses two Kittyhawks and another crash-lands at El Adem. Sgt Carson shoots down another Bf 109.

February 22: Sgt R. Shaw destroys a Ju8 8 south-east of Gazala giving 450 Squadron its first victory.

February 23: 450 Squadron's first full combat while escorting Bostons to bomb transport between Tmimi and Martuba accompanied by 3 Squadron. F/O C. K. Thompson, one of two brothers in the unit, is shot down and becomes a POW. Sgt K. M. McBride crashes while attempting to force-land his burning plane. He is thrown clear but is mortally injured. Sgts Young and Nursey each claim a Bf 109.

March 8: Six Kittyhawks each from 450 and 3 Squadrons, led by F/Lt Barr, intercept Ju 87s closely escorted by nine Mc 200s and 202s and two Bf 109s over Tobruk. The Italian fighters are slaughtered, P/O Curtiss, F/O Pace, P/O Giddy and F/Lt Barr of 3 RAAF, and Sgts Beste, McBurnie and Shaw of 450 Squadron shooting down one each. Probables are claimed by Barr and Sgt Dyson of 450. Curtiss and Giddy each claim a

Kittyhawks about to take off across a rough desert airstrip. No. 450 Squadron, soon to become known as 'The Desert Harassers', flew its first mission on 19 February 1942. Coincidentally, the first German type to be shot down by 450 Squadron was a Junkers Ju 88 south-east of Gazala three days later, as was 3 Squadron's first victory over a German aircraft just over a year earlier. Sgt R. Shaw was 450's successful pilot. Shaw was killed in action on 29 May 1942, shot down by Bf 109s. (Bryan Philpott)

Messerschmitt Bf 109E under attack. It has suffered so much damage that its port undercarriage has dropped. The superior performance of the Messerschmitt, particularly the later 'F' model, gave it a distinctive edge over Allied fighters in North Africa until the Spitfire was introduced late in 1942. (AWM)

Stuka. The survivors of this battle soon afterwards encounter 112 Squadron which claims a further Mc 200 and Ju 87. After this disaster the Italians demand closer cooperation between their own fighters and those of the Germans.

March 10: S/Ldr Caldwell of 112 Squadron makes the first test drop of a 250-pound bomb from a Kittyhawk, prefacing a new style of future operations.

March 14: 450 and 3 Squadrons escort twelve Bostons to bomb Martuba and are attacked by Mc 202s and Bf 109s. Sgt Packer and F/O Chinchen of 3 Squadron share a Bf 109 while F/Lt Hart and Sgt Kildey each claim a probable Macchi. No. 112 Squadron joins the fight. S/Ldr Caldwell destroys a Mc 202 and shares a Bf 109 but two Kittyhawks are lost.

March 21: 3 Squadron, their Kittyhawks fitted with long-range fuel tanks, spends the day flying patrols over a Malta-bound convoy.

March 25: 3 Squadron is withdrawn for rest and retraining. Earlier in the month, 451 Squadron had been withdrawn to Rayak in Syria to protect nearby shipping lanes.

April 5: 450 Squadron loses two new pilots in unexplained circumstances. Six Kittyhawks are patrolling over Gambut when P/O J. Evatt spins out of control, followed minutes later by P/O G. Macpherson for no reason which can be found.

Sgt Ted Oakley takes off in Kittyhawk OK-G amid a cloud of dust. Oakley joined 450 Squadron in April 1942 and during the air fighting around El Alamein he claimed one destroyed and one probable, both Bf 109s. He was later awarded a Mentioned in Despatches. (Trevor Mear)

April 7: 450 Squadron's Kittyhawks, escorting Bostons, are attacked by Bf 109s. Sgt W. Metherall bales out due to engine failure and F/O E. Thompson jumps when his aircraft's tail is shot off. Both return next day and, following air force custom, each donates £1 to the parachute section.

April 20: South-west of Bir Hakeim, P/O Russell Foskett and another pilot of 80 (Hurricane) Squadron shoot down a lone Bf 109E on reconnaissance. In Tunisia, long-range PR Spitfire IV, BP907, en route from Gibraltar to Egypt via Malta, force-lands near Djedeida. Sgt Clifton, RAAF, sets fire to his aircraft before being interned.

April 26: 3 Squadron moves to Gambut joining 112 and 250 Squadrons RAF in 239 Wing. Battle of Britain veteran, W/Cdr Clive Mayers, is appointed wing Leader.

April 29: No. 1 Air Ambulance Unit, which has been beset by delays and misfortunes, resumes operations again. A DH-86 ambulance flies its first sortie since mid-February.

May 7: Six Kittyhawks of 3 Squadron and six of 112 Squadron are scrambled over Tobruk. While returning they are attacked by two Bf 109s. S/Ldr Gibbes, the Australian CO, and a pilot of 112 Squadron claim one each.

May 12: At this time, Luftwaffe Ju 52 transports are regularly flying between Crete and North Africa with reinforcements. An attempt is made to intercept one of these missions by six Beaufighters of 252 Squadron covered by ten Kittyhawks of 250 Squadron, the whole formation being led by W/Cdr Clive Mayers, with F/Lt John Waddy leading the top cover. A large formation of transports is intercepted. 250 Squadron claims ten Ju 52s and two Bf 110s, Mayers scoring two Junkers and Waddy another two plus two escorting Bf 110s. 252 Squadron claims five more Ju 52s for the loss of one Beaufighter.

May 13: 3 RAAF Squadron is bounced over Gazala by two Bf 109s, one flown by the German ace Marseille, who shoots down two Kittyhawks. Sgt McDiarmid bales out slightly wounded but F/O Pace is KIA. F/O Chinchen damages one Messerschmitt.

May 16: In deadly form, Marseille again punishes the Australian Kittyhawks, shooting down Sgt Teade of 3 Squadron and P/O Parker of 450 Squadron, whose falling aircraft strikes that of Sgt Metherall, who crashes. Parker returns to his unit next day.

Living conditions in the desert. Tents were near the aircraft but often it was necessary to sleep in slit trenches. There was often a shortage of water and fresh food. (Trevor Mear)

May 19: Marseille causes two 450 Squadron Kittyhawks to force-land. Sgt Young is picked up by the army.

May 22: Kittyhawks of 239 Wing escort SAAF Bostons bombing Martuba. Bf 109s shoot down Sgt Quirk and Sgt Williams of 450 Squadron while F/Lt Rose scores a probable 109. S/Ldr Gibbes and F/Lt Barr of 3 Squadron and F/O Waddy of 250 Squadron each claim a Messerschmitt.

May 24: S/Ldr Clive 'Killer' Caldwell, DFC and Bar, is posted to the UK to convert to Spitfires before leading the first wing of these to Australia to fight the Japanese. His score of 20½ German and Italian aircraft will remain the highest gained by any Allied pilot in the Western Desert.

May 26: Rommel attacks the Gazala Line. No. 3 Squadron intercepts Ju 88s and Bf 109s over El Adem. Sgt Clabburn damages a Ju 88, and S/Ldr Gibbes claims a probable 109 before return fire from a Ju 88 causes him to bale out injured. Later, F/O Waddy, now flying with 260 Squadron, claims a Bf 109 probable.

May 27: Amid numerous fighter-bomber sorties, 3 Squadron loses three Kittyhawks to Bf 109s. Sgt Thomas, who crash-lands on fire south of Gambut, returns next day; Sgt Clabburn also returns next day but Sgt Norman becomes a POW.

May 29: 450 Squadron's Kittyhawks have a brutal fight with Bf 109s and Ju 87s over Gazala. Sgts McBurnie and Jenkins share one Ju 87, Sgt Nursey claims a second and McBurnie also shoots down a 109. Sgts Dean, Packer and Shaw fail to return.

May 30: A day of heavy combat with massive attacks by fighter-bombers and Bostons on German armour. F/Lt Barr and Sgt McDiarmid of 3 Squadron go missing, Barr returning two days later. From 450 Squadron, Sgt Nursey is KIA and Sgt McBurnie crash-lands injured south of Gambut.

June 1: Kittyhawks of 112 Squadron and 3 Squadron RAAF meet four Ju 88s and four Bf 110s escorted by Bf 109s. For 3 Squadron, Sgt. Alderson is slightly wounded and his aircraft damaged, while F/Lt Barr, P/O Coward and Sgt Neill each claim a 109.

No. 459 (Hudson) Squadron RAAF, formed as an additional flight of 203 Squadron RAF in February, commences operations independently from LG 40. Before the arrival of its Hudsons on 31 May, only seven anti-submarine patrols had been flown, using borrowed Blenheims. For a week it will conduct patrols over coastal shipping between Mersa Matruh and Sidi Barrani, and then be held in readiness for the Operation Vigorous Malta convoy.

June 4: Over Bir Hacheim, which is being held stubbornly by the Free French, 260 Squadron's F/O John Waddy claims a CR 42.

June 5: Bir Hacheim falls to Axis attack.

June 6: P/O Carson of 112 Squadron shares a Bf 109.

June 8: After escorting fighter-bombers, 450 Squadron strafes ground targets on their flight back to base, but Sgt J. James does not return.

A Kittyhawk of 450 Squadron undergoing an engine change. Living and working conditions for the ground crews were primitive to say the least. Maintenance was carried out in the open and both men and machines were subjected to searing heat, sand storms and chilling cold at night. (Trevor Mear)

June 12: Kittyhawks of 3 Squadron carry out a fighter-bomber mission near El Adem. Sgt Gray is shot down in flames by flak. No. 450 Squadron, on their fourth mission of the day, provide five Kittyhawks as top cover to a fighter sweep, Sgt House force-lands. Later, another Kittyhawk on reconnaissance fails to return, P/O I. Young is killed in action. No. 260 Squadron, returning from an escort mission, runs into a dogfight, F/O Waddy claiming one Mc 202, but the squadron loses two Kittyhawks.

June 13: Six Kittyhawks of 450 Squadron covering eight Kittyhawks of 112 Squadron are attacked out of the sun over El Adem by Bf 109s. From 450, Sgts W. Halliday and R. Stone are killed. They are probably two of the four kills claimed by German ace Marseille during this fight.

June 14: Twelve Kittyhawks of 3 Squadron, escorted by 112 and 450 Squadrons, carry out a strafing mission. F/Lt Chinchen is shot down by flak and becomes a POW.

June 15: F/O A. Duffield flying No. 1 Air Ambulance Unit's only DH-86 ambulance, has made daily trips to Gambut, removing 114 wounded since the enemy's offensive began on May 27.

June 16: RAF fighters carry out numerous sorties in defence of Gambut. In 3 Squadron, F/Lt Barr flies a record six sorties, F/O Spence five, and Sgt Kildey four. Sgt Biden crash-lands at Gambut when his engine stops but is killed when the bomb still attached to his aircraft explodes. Sgt Ryan fails to return. No. 112 Squadron also flies fighter-bomber sorties losing two, including P/O K. Carson.

June 17: During a day of heavy fighting, Sgt A. Glancy of 450 Squadron and Sgt Hooke of 3 Squadron are shot down by Bf 109s, one Kittyhawk being seen to crash and burst into flames. Hooke will return later on foot. W/Cdr Mayers leads 239 Wing (112, 250, 450 and 3 RAAF Squadrons) to Gazala where the Germans fighters are now established and thoroughly strafes fifteen Bf 109s on the ground without loss. Meanwhile, German ace Marseille brings his score to 101, and he is immediately ordered to Berlin to be awarded the Swords to his Knights' Cross with Oak Leaves.

June 18: No. 1 Air Ambulance Unit obtains a second DH-86 ambulance but it crashes on its first take-off. Amid the confusion of retreat the unit will have to withdraw to Wadi Natrun and then Heliopolis before the month closes.

Two Kittyhawks of 450 Squadron on reconnaissance are attacked over Gambut by a lone Bf 109, which F/Lt Williams destroys. An hour later, two 109s attack six more Kittyhawks, three being damaged. Sgt Dyson claims a Messerschmitt.

June 20: Rommel attacks Tobruk. Kesselring brings in every bomber available in the Mediterranean to support. The garrison, although well supplied, is not as well led by the South African General Klopper, as the Australians had been during the earlier siege. In a combat with Bf 109s, P/O T. Jones of 450 Squadron is KIA.

June 21: Tobruk surrenders to the Germans and Italians. Thirty thousand prisoners and huge stores of munitions, rations and fuel are taken. German soldiers even send home parcels of Australian bully beef. Rommel wishes to drive on to Egypt, but Kesselring prefers to carry out Operation Herkules against Malta. Rommel has his way and is promoted Field Marshal by Hitler.

Eight Kittyhawks of 112 Squadron bomb Sidi Aziez airfield. Australian ace, F/Lt Rudolf Leu, DFC, force-lands. Another Kittyhawk tries to pick him up, but enemy fire forces it to take off again. Leu, with his score standing at seven, now becomes a POW.

June 24: Rommel's armoured columns cross into Egypt but they are losing momentum. General Auchinleck takes over the 8th Army from General Ritchie. Despite the loss of 60 000 men, it begins forming a line at El Alamein, the narrowest point between the coast and the impassable Qattara Depression. Even while the Axis has been advancing its attacks have been broken up again and again by the Desert Air Force. Five Kittyhawks of 3 Squadron on reconnaissance meet six Bf 109s and four G 50s near Maddelena. S/Ldr Barr claims a G 50, Sgt Boardman a Bf 109 and Sgt Kildey a Bf 109 probable but Sgt Fox is last seen with a G 50 on his tail.

June 25/26: Fourteen Wellingtons of 70 Squadron bomb and strafe an enemy column advancing between Sidi Barrani and Mersa Matruh. Wellington DV564/L is badly damaged by a Ju 88 night fighter. Navigator, P/O Tom Howes, assists the wounded second pilot and wireless operator, extinguishes a fire and extricates the badly wounded Canadian rear gunner, whose leg is severed and clothing ablaze, from his shattered turret. Howes will be awarded an immediate DFC. There are nearly 200 RAAF aircrew scattered throughout RAF Wellington squadrons in the Middle East.

June 26: A day of heavy air fighting. While escorting Bostons, 3 Squadron's CO, S/Ldr 'Nicky' Barr is attacked by Bf 109s. Pouring flames, his Kittyhawk dives steeply but, although badly burnt, he bales out at 4000 feet (1220 m) and is captured. In six months he has become one of the leading Allied pilots in the Desert, with twelve kills plus several probables, and awards of a DFC and Bar. Likewise, 450 Squadron, escorting Bostons west of Matruh, lose P/O M. Jones to Bf 109s and later, during their sixth mission of the day, another escort, also P/O K. Murdoch. Both become POWs.

July 1: Rommel begins his assault on the new El Alamein line. Kittyhawks of 3 and 450 Squadrons escorting Bostons to Deir el Shein, fight a running battle with Bf 109s, Sgt George O'Neil's aircraft falling about a mile out to sea east of Alamein. He bales out, jettisoning his revolver, helmet, gloves and boots on the way down, and the rest of his clothing when he is in the water. An hour later, wearing only a wrist watch, he struggles ashore. South African troops clothe and feed him and return him to the squadron. Later, on a similar mission, 3 Squadron loses P/O Ritchie. He too bales out and returns safely.

July 3: Eight Kittyhawks of 3 Squadron bomb and strafe south of Mikheisin. P/O Pfeiffer's aircraft is hit by flak, causing him to crash-land. Elsewhere, in a violent dogfight over El Alamein, F/O John Pain of 73 (Hurricane) Squadron claims a Bf 109. Pain is a veteran of the Battle of Britain and the fighting over Malta.

July 4: Kittyhawks of 450 and 3 Squadrons bomb landing grounds west of Daba. On the return flight 450 strafe vehicles, and Sgt McBurnie shoots the tail off a reconnaissance Bf 110.

July 5: The British 8th Army at El Alamein is reinforced by the Australian 9th Division which takes positions east of Ruweisat Ridge. They will launch a heavy attack from it in two days. Sgts F. Beste (captured) and S. Simpson (KIA) of 450 Squadron fail to return from a bombing mission.

July 8: 3 Squadron, flying top cover to Kittybombers, claims one Bf 109 probably destroyed by Sgt Donald. In the same battle, W/Cdr Mayers, leading 250 Squadron, destroys a Bf 109 over LG 21.

July 10: During patrols over the El Alamein line, P/O Foskett of 80 Squadron destroys a Bf 109 and F/O John Pain of 73 Squadron damages a CR4 2 but F/O Osborne of 450 Squadron is shot down and captured. Rommel attacks in the south just as the 26th Australian Brigade attacks in the north, taking 1000 Italians prisoner.

July 11: Australian troops storm Tel el Eisa Ridge and capture 500 exhausted Germans without losing a single man.

Sgt George O'Neil, in sunglasses, preparing for take-off. O'Neil faced a harrowing experience on 1 July 1942 during a running battle with Bf 109s when he baled out of his Kittyhawk about a mile out to sea east of El Alamein. On 13 January 1943, during a strafing attack in Tunisia, he failed to return when his aircraft was crippled by AA fire but he arrived back at his base on foot two days later. For his exploits, O'Neil was awarded an MM and later, after receiving a commission, followed up with a DFC. (Trevor Mear)

July 14: Nine Kittyhawks of 3 Squadron bomb in the Bir Makhkad area. A lone Bf 109 is shot down by Sgt Neill.

July 15: Four Kittyhawks of 3 Squadron, in company with 450 Squadron, carry out a bombing reconnaissance west of El Alamein from which P/O Dougall fails to return.

July 19: On a mission to strafe LG 21, 450 Squadron Kittyhawks meet four Ju 52s and a Ju 87 coming in to land, and shoot them all down while still carrying their bombs. Scorers: S/Ldr Ferguson one Ju 87 and one Ju 52 shared with F/Lt Parker who gets a second; Sgt Dyson and Sgt Brown share a Ju 52; and Sgt Lindsay one Ju 52. The squadron then strafes five Ju 87s, three Bf 109s and a Ju 88 on the ground.

July 20: Heavy raids on Fuka and Daba. No. 450 Squadron's eight Kitty-bombers carry out their attack but over the target a Bf 109 shoots down Sgt Brown. W/Cdr Clive Mayers, DFC, the 239 Wing Leader, also fails to return. Originally from Melbourne, Mayers has a personal score of over eleven and has been recommended for a DSO, shortly to be gazetted. Searching Spitfires find his Kittyhawk, crash-landed with little obvious damage, but with its cockpit empty. (It is believed that he was captured but killed later when a Ju 52 in which he was being transported to Sicily was shot down over the Mediterranean by a Spitfire.)

July 22: At Fuka, Sgt Keith Kildey of 3 Squadron drops the unit's thousandth bomb since 26 May — a period of nine weeks, and a record for a Middle East fighter-bomber squadron. On the ground, because of unnecessary losses, Australian and New Zealand infantry are growing increasingly critical of the failure of supporting British armour to back up their advances. Meanwhile, Rommel, his supply lines stretched to the limit, decides that the drain on his strength has been too much for further attacks. Both sides now pause to rest and regroup.

July 25: Sgt George O'Neal's engine fails but he manages to belly-land his Kittyhawk among forward British troops. For the second time this month he needs transportation back to 450 Squadron.

July 27: Ten Kittyhawks of 3 Squadron bomb enemy motor transport north-west of Mukheisin. Sgt Cashmore becomes separated and is attacked by two Bf 109s, one of which he probably destroys. Later, 3 Squadron provides top cover for 450 Squadron bombing in the Deir el Dhib area. P/O T. Forsyth of 450 Squadron is shot down by Bf 109s, his Kittyhawk spinning into the ground and bursting into flames. Sgts Kildey and Churchill of 3 Squadron each damage a Messerschmitt.

July 28: 459 Squadron begins attacking German F-boats using the Tobruk-Mersa Matruh route. These vessels are tank-landing craft, armed with one 75 mm and two 20 mm guns plus machine-guns. In this initial engagement, one F-boat is damaged (and later found beached) for the loss of one Hudson to flak and another damaged. After this, 459's crews exchange their depth charges for ten 100-pound bombs and, in a 17 day period, will fly 85 sorties and account for twelve of the sixteen F-boats sunk.

August 10: After scoring direct bomb hits on an F-boat, P/O V. O'Brien of 459 Squadron finds his port engine on fire, his aerial shot away, and his Hudson badly holed. His crew extinguishes the fire but everything movable has to be jettisoned for the aircraft to keep height as he nurses the Hudson 250 miles home.

August 13: General Montgomery assumes command of the 8th Army and General Alexander replaces Auchinleck as C-in-C Middle East.

August 17: Eight Kittyhawks of 3 Squadron top-cover 450 Squadron bombing motor transport near Deir el Qattara. Sgt Stevens is shot down by Bf 109s. He bales out, slightly burned, and is back with his unit by 5 p.m.

August 29: The 8th Army has taken up defensive positions in expectation of a German attack. Between 20 and 30 August, Kittyhawks of 239 Wing have been largely held in reserve and 3 and 450 Squadrons fly only 169 sorties, of which 127 are low-level bombing attacks. Today, four Kittybombers of 450 Squadron are attacked by Bf 109s. P/O N. Shillabeer (KIA) and Sgt A. Markle are shot down. Markle is picked up next day, wounded in his head, arms and legs. In hospital, an armour-piercing

General Bernard Montgomery, the new British general facing Rommel at El Alamein. (Trevor Mear)

The battle to cut off Rommel's supplies. Enemy trucks are caught in the open and strafed. (Brian Philpott)

Curtiss P-40E Kittyhawk AL171/CV-A of 3 Squadron, one of the aircraft flown regularly mid-1942 by Tasmanian Sgt Keith Kildey. Besides being in the forefront of bombing and strafing attacks, Kildey scored a string of probable kills and damaged between March and November 1942 and was at last rewarded with a confirmed victory over a Bf 109 on 9 November. (Dennis Newton)

bullet is removed from the base of his skull. He will survive and eventually rejoin the squadron.

August 30-31: Rommel begins an attack designed to clear the British out of Egypt.

September 1: Heavy fighting as Axis armour runs into well-prepared defences. In various air combats, 450 Squadron's S/Ldr Ferguson destroys a Bf 109; Sgts McFarlane and Lindsay each claim a probable. S/Ldr Gibbes and Sgt Stewart of 3 Squadron each destroy a Bf 109. Total Allied losses today are 20 single-engined fighters (plus two Beaufighters) against a Luftwaffe claim of 26, no less than 17 being credited to just one man, the German ace, Marseille.

September 2: The German assault is weakening with one Panzer Division out of fuel. Rommel orders withdrawal.

September 3: Six Kittyhawks of 3 RAAF and five of 450 Squadron escorting 18 Baltimores to Deir el Ragil are attacked by sixteen Bf 109s and Mc 202s. Sgt Thomas of 3 Squadron is severely wounded and he crash-lands at home. Sgts Dyson and Hannaford of 450 Squadron each claim a Bf 109 probable, but Hannaford is wounded and he too crash-lands at base.

September 5: Bf 109s badly damage a Kittyhawk of 450 Squadron piloted by Sgt Oakley. The 66th US Fighter Squadron is attached to 239 Wing with 112, 250, 450 and 3 Squadrons. Nine Halifax bombers, including four from 76/462 Squadron, raid Heraklion, Crete, in daylight. One is shot down by Bf 109s, and another damaged.

September 6: With the battle of Alam Halfa over and the Germans withdrawn to their original positions, Montgomery's 8thArmy begins building up and training for an offensive.

September 7: 10/227 and 76/462 Squadrons are amalgamated, becoming 462 Squadron RAAF, the first fully established Halifax (Mk IIs) squadron in the Middle East.

September 8: Kittyhawks and Spitfires of 239 Wing intercept 20 Ju 87s escorted by Bf 109s and Mc 202s. Sgt Neill of 3 RAAF claims a Stuka, a 109, a probable Bf 109 and a damaged, Sgt Scribner a Bf 109, a damaged and an Mc 202 damaged, and Sgt. Boardman a Bf 109 probable and a damaged. Sgt Freer crash-lands, slightly wounded. Sgt Taylor of 450 claims a probable. One Spitfire is lost.

September 12: 239 Wing Kittyhawks intercept Ju 87s and Bf 109s over El Alamein. For 450 Squadron F/Lt Williams claims a Ju 87 probable and a damaged, and Sgt Oakley destroys a Bf 109.

September 13: 239 Wing Kittyhawks intercept Bf 109s bombing in the Alamein area. F/O Glendinning and Sgt Boardman of 3 Squadron each claim a probable.

September 13/14: After heavy aerial attack, the British raid Tobruk by land and sea to destroy depots and installations. A similar operation is launched against Benghazi. Both fail with heavy losses. New CO of 104 Squadron, W/Cdr Don Saville and crew, in Wellington 'X for X-Ray', bomb gun positions near the Tobruk- Derna road.

September 14: Eight Kittyhawks of 3 Squadron bounce six Bf 109s west of Qattara. F/Lt Coward and Sgt Jones share one destroyed.

September 15: 239 Wing Kittyhawks intercept another Stuka raid. P/O Clabburn of 3 Squadron claims a probable 109, and others are damaged but P/O Donald and Sgt Scribner fail to return. P/O Kildey and Sgt Bee (slightly wounded) each have their aircraft badly damaged. F/O Marting of 450 Squadron destroys a Messerschmitt and Sgt Gleeson claims a probable but Sgt Ewing bales out and is captured.

September 16: 239 Wing again intercepts a Stuka attack. No. 3 Squadron's Sgt Woods is shot up and wounded but he manages to return to base.

September 20: Stukas and Bf 109s are intercepted by Kittyhawks of 4 Squadron SAAF. F/O John Waddy, now with the South Africans, destroys a Bf 109.

September 27: 450 Squadron receives new Kittyhawk IIIs, their Mk Is being divided up between 112, 250 and 3 Squadron.

September 30: The German 'Star of Africa', Hpt Hans-Joachim Marseille, is flying a new Bf 109G when it catches fire. He bales out but hits the tailplane as he falls, and his parachute fails to open. His confirmed claims total an incredible 158 (151 scored over the Desert).

October 1: The Desert Air Force (DAF) maintains constant pressure on Rommel's supply routes. Vehicles and equipment unloaded at Benghazi and Tobruk are attacked by long-range Beaufighters while making the long journey to the front. In typical sorties, Sgt R. Swift of 272 Squadron strafes six lorries, setting two alight and forcing the others off the road; F/O G. Pattearson strafes a dozen trucks and then a small camp, causing a huge explosion; and yesterday two Beaufighters intercepted four bombers over the Sollum-Sidi Barrani road, F/O E. 'Ted' Coate destroying an He 111.

October 2: Scrambled over Alamein, ten Kittyhawks of 3 Squadron meet a lone Bf 109 and F/Lt Plinston shoots it down. In a later combat, Sgt Neill claims a probable. No. 450 Squadron moves temporarily to LG 124 at Mena as part of Cairo's defences.

October 7: Kittyhawk pilots of 3 Squadron report being attacked by an aircraft with yellow cowling and wingtips, possibly an Fw190. One of several 450 Squadron pilots attached to 1 (ME) Training School, RAF, at El Ballah on the Suez Canal, Sgt. R. Downes, is killed when his Hurricane crashes while taking off. His death is not recorded on 450 Squadron's memorial but his name is on the roll of those killed while serving with the RAF. The squadron is still flying sorties over the Front.

October 9: The 'Daba Prang'. Reconnaissance discovers Daba airfields underwater, and Fuka almost unusable,

due to recent rain. Seizing the opportunity, the DAF mounts an all-out effort to destroy Axis aircraft on the ground. Altogether, 500 sorties are flown. No. 450 Squadron strafes four Bf 109s, a Ju 87, a Ju 88 and a Ju 52, but Sgt. Holloway fails to return. Twelve Kittyhawks of 3 Squadron covering 450 Squadron are attacked from the sun by five Bf 109s. P/O Ritchie shoots the tail off one, which falls into the sea.

October 19: Beaufighters of 272 Squadron on a long-range patrol over the sea intercept 32 Ju 52s with six towed gliders escorted by Bf 110s. Sgt Pattearson claims a Ju 52.

Sgt J. K. Wood, RAAF, of Hornsby, NSW, and Canadian W/ O R. S.Spence, RCAF, part of the crew of a Wellington of 40 Squadron RAF who evaded capture when their Wellington caught fire while circling Tobruk after an attack on 8/9 October 1942. The aircraft was forced down near Fort Capuzzo. With limited supplies they walked for over three weeks towards Allied lines, via the Qattara Depression, covering a distance of 350 miles. Despite frugal and determined rationing, their food and nearly all their water were consumed by the twentieth day, but fortunately they met several parties of Bedouin camel drivers from whom they secured a few dates and some rice. They had no knowledge of the fierce battle which was then raging at El Alamein. On 2 November (their twenty-fourth day), near El Maghra, they heard a motor lorry in the distance. Heading northwards, they met elements of an armoured unit. It was British. They were safe at last. (AWM)

October 20: Heavy fighter-bomber and light bomber raids on Axis landing grounds begin as a prelude to the forthcoming Battle of El Alamein. Kittyhawks of 3 and 450 Squadrons cover Baltimores and B-25s. Over Fuka Mc 202s attack 450, F/O 'Tex' Marting, shooting one down. The aircraft of F/Lt Clarke and Sgt Gregory are damaged. During another escort mission, 3 Squadron spots a twin-engined Italian bomber, which P/Os G. Neill, Ritchie and Taylor attack. Hit many times, it lands near Abu Haggag. Meantime, intercepting fighters shoot down P/O E. Alderson and Sgt Wood.

October 22: Eighteen B-25s escorted by six Kittyhawks of 450 Squadron as close cover, ten of 3 Squadron as medium cover and 250 Squadron as top cover, attack LG 104. There is heavy flak over the target, one Mitchell being shot down apparently by flak. No. 3 Squadron pilots also see a Kittyhawk receive a double flak hit, and the pilot bale out. Bf 109s attack after the bombing, and P/O Neill goes down streaming glycol. Sgts J. 'Curley' Evans and G. 'Blondy' Lindsay of 450 Squadron also fail to return. Both are captured. During a wing sweep by Spitfires of 92 Squadron and Kittyhawks of 260 Squadron, F/O Waddy, DFC, having just joined 92 Squadron, claims a Bf 109.

October 23: Kittyhawks of 450 Squadron with others of 3 Squadron strike at Daba. From this mission F/O 'Tex' Marting fails to return, and Sgt Prowse crash-lands due to engine failure. No. 450 has better luck later when six Kittyhawks are intercepted by eight Bf 109s, F/Lt F. Schaaf and Sgt J. Gleeson each destroying a Messerschmitt. At 2140 hours, more than 1000 British guns commence the greatest barrage since World War I, firing on the narrow front between the Qattara Depression and the Mediterranean. Twenty minutes later the infantry moves forward. The Battle of El Alamein has begun.

October 25: Four enemy fighters attack 3 Squadron Kittyhawks escorting bombers. Sgt Richardson is shot down, but P/O Harris damages a Mc 202. During an attack by Beauforts and Bisleys on a small Axis convoy making for Tobruk, eight escorting Beaufighters of 272 Squadron intercept 35 Ju 52s with six Bf 110s. F/O Rankin damages a Messerschmitt (later confirmed) and four transports are shot down for the loss of one Beaufighter. On the ground, attempts by the British to break through at El Alamein are repulsed with heavy losses. Only the 9th Australian Division, attacking in the north, achieves some success.

October 26: Twelve Kittyhawks of 3 Squadron, escorting 450 Squadron on an early raid, are jumped by nine Bf 109s over Alamein. Sgt J. Bullwinkel bales out, breaking his leg. Sgt W. Cashmore claims a Bf 109 probable. Later, F/O Waddy of 92 Squadron destroys a 109 to bring his score to 14+; six Kittyhawks of 450 Squadron cause a Ju 88 to force-land; and while escorting bombers, F/Lt Bill Cundy of 260 Squadron claims a Bf 109.

October 27: Amid other activity, four Spitfires of 92 Squadron bounce nine Bf 109s of II/JG 27. Two Messerschmitts are claimed destroyed and F/0 Waddy claims one damaged. In fact, three 109s are shot down in the encounter and all belly-land in Axis territory south of Alamein. Later, while flying top cover to eighteen Baltimores, Sgt Stevens of 3 Squadron sends an Mc 202 down in flames.

October 28: Rommel, realising that the Australian attack in the north is the decisive area, moves all German forces from the south, leaving the Italians to hold the quieter sectors. Six Kittyhawks of 3 Squadron fly top cover above Baltimores and B-25s attacking LG 20. The bombers badly damage five Bf 109s on the ground. Afterwards, S/Ldr Bobby Gibbes, attacks a Bf 109 north of Ras el Shaqiq and shoots it down into the sea. This is credited as 3 Squadron's two-hundredth confirmed victory. The unit has achieved its second century in just under eleven months, the first hundred having been reached on 30 November 1941. It is the highest scoring Allied squadron in North Africa.

October 29: Near Alamein, 92 Squadron Spitfires meet a formation of Ju 87s escorted by 33 Bf 109s. Three of the escorts are shot down, F/O Waddy claiming one.

October 30: Kittyhawks of 450 Squadron concentrate on ground attack, strafing three Bf 109Fs, a Bf 109E and a Ju 52. P/O Crouch and Sgts. Markle, Jenkins and Reid, shoot down a hapless Ju 52. In the evening, 3 Squadron fittingly celebrates its two-hundredth victory after the Adjutant, F/Lt 'Col' Greeves, brings up beer from Alexandria and food from Pastroudi's famous restaurant. Included in the revelry is the sacrificial removal of half of Sergeant J. Hooke's much-loved walrus moustache '... for a noble cause'. While the antics continue, Australian infantry attacks the German strong point at Thompson's Post, breaking through to the coast road.

October 31: German counter-attacks on the Australians make no headway and the cost to both sides is high. The 2/24th and 2/48th Battalions, 1300 strong at the beginning of the battle, have been reduced to 95 officers and men. In the air, 260 Squadron's F/Lt Cundy destroys a Bf 109 and shares a second. No. 450 Squadron is bounced by 109s. Sgt H. Reid is KIA and the CO S/Ldr J. Williams

Kittyhawk nose art symbolising the work of the 'Desert Harassers'. The two men in the picture are identified as 'Tom and Linz'. (Trevor Mear)

is shot down and captured. (He will be murdered by the Gestapo after the mass escape from Stalag Luft III in March 1944.) No. 112 Squadron Kittyhawks, with 3 Squadron as top cover, scramble to bomb and strafe around Daba and Fuka. They meet Ju 87s escorted by Bf 109s. During the mêlée, P/O Ritchie of 3 RAAF claims a Stuka probable.

November 1: Kittyhawks of 112 Squadron with the P-40Fs of the 66th US Squadron meet 30 Ju 87s escorted by Bf 109s over Alamein. The Stukas are forced to jettison their bombs on their own troops; South Australian Sgt R. Wild destroys one in flames. In the evening, 458 Squadron returns to operations, the first being a seven-hour sortie carried out by P/O Prior and crew against shipping north-west of Tobruk. No. 458 had been reconstituted at Shallufa under W/Cdr Johnston, training with a mixture of Wellington Ics and VIIIs for torpedo-bomber work.

November 2: Ten Kittyhawks of 3 Squadron escort eighteen Baltimores and B-25s to bomb the Rahman track. Bf 109s attack after the bombing and Sgt Holder has to force-land.

November 3: 80 Squadron RAF Hurricanes claim seven Stukas destroyed, nine probables and three damaged. Of these F/Lt. Foskett claims two probables (later confirmed) but has to force-land with an oil pipe fracture., Bf 109s attack six Kittyhawks of 3 Squadron flying top cover to B-25s, shooting down Sgt A. Jones. Hitler orders Rommel to stand firm and fight for every inch of ground.

November 4: Axis forces at El Alamein crack. In the north the British 1st Armoured Division breaks through, as do the New Zealanders and the 7th Armoured Division further south. Throughout the day, DAF Hurricanes, Kittyhawks, Tomahawks, P-40Fs, Spitfires, Beaufighters, Bostons, Baltimores and Mitchells continually bomb and strafe the mass of Afrika Korps vehicles retreating along the coast road. Hairpin bends along the coastal escarpment at Fuka and Mersa Matruh become death-traps. When twelve Kittyhawks of 260 Squadron escort South African Kittybombers attacking motor transport near Galal, a Ju 88 is spotted and shot down by F/Lt Cundy.

November 5: DAF squadrons begin moving forward after the retreating Germans and Italians as the pace of the advance quickens. The movements of 450 Squadron's 'A' Flight are typical. On the 5th to El Daba; 7th to Sidi Heneish; 9th to Qasaba; 11th to Mischifa (LG 76); 12th to Gambut; 15th to Martuba. All through, attacks against the enemy do not slacken and during the month over 600 sorties are flown, bombing and strafing motor transport, enemy camps and airfields.

November 8: Operation Torch, the Allied invasion of French North Africa, begins. Meanwhile, near Gambut, Sgt Al Markle of 450 Squadron is shot down while strafing and taken prisoner by the Italians. Telling them he is a pilot officer, he will spend captivity as an officer (unpaid)!

November 9: German rearguard action at Sidi Barrani. Thirteen Kittyhawks of 3 Squadron bomb vehicles on the Halfaya Pass. Two Bf 109s attack, F/Lt Kildey destroying one and S/Ldr Gibbes damaging the other. No. 450 Squadron escorts Bostons and Baltimores bombing the Sidi Barrani-Sollum road. Intercepted by Bf 109s, Sgt Borthwick's aircraft crashes in flames. F/Lt Clarke claims a probable and a damaged, and Sgt Oakley a probable. Dave Borthwick, although wounded in both legs, manages to bale out but lands deep in the desert. He crawls on hands and knees for four days behind the lines until he is finally picked up by the advancing army.

November 10: Axis forces are now forced to fight on two fronts along the North African coast, in the west against the US-British invasion and in the east against Montgomery's 8th Army. Malta is being used more and more as a supporting offensive base. Nine Beaufighters from one of Malta's strike units, 272 Squadron, attack Axis aircraft on the ground at El Aouina, Tunisia. Nine aircraft and a large glider are destroyed in flames, with fifteen others and one large glider damaged. F/Os Ron Rankin and Ted Coate claim two each.

November 10/11: A Halifax of 462 Squadron RAAF is shot down by flak over Tobruk. No. 462 is unique in that it contains English and Dominion air and ground crews but not one Australian! Although nominally and officially a unit of the RAAF it is Australian 'on paper only' and will remain so until early 1943 when the supply of personnel from Australia will at last begin catching up with demand.

November 11: Advanced units of the 8th Army reach Halfaya Pass, move into Libya and take Bardia unopposed. F/Lt Cundy of 260 Squadron spots an Fi 156 and shoots it down. Six Beaufighters of Malta-based 272 Squadron on patrol in the Cap Bon-Trapani area destroy a hapless He 115 floatplane, F/Os Rankin and Coate having shares.

November 12: Twelve Kittyhawks of 450 Squadron, covering 3 Squadron strafing the road between Gazala and Tobruk, meet four Bf 109s. F/Lt Schaaf claims one probably destroyed. Seven 272 Squadron Beaufighters patrolling the Tunis-- intercept sixteen Ju52 and thirty S.81 troop carriers off Tunisia claiming six destroyed and six probables for one loss. P/O R. Willis is hit in the ankle by return fire, and has to break off, flying back to Malta where he makes a safe landing.

November 14: Two 450 Squadron fitters, Allan Sherwood and Eddie Meakins, with P/O Gough and F/Lt Clarke, salvage a Henschel 126. After quick repairs, painting with squadron markings, it becomes 450's 'hack'.

Off Cap Bon, Tunisia, F/O Rankin of 272 Squadron, leading a section from Malta, shoots down a Cant Z.506B floatplane. Shortly afterwards, attacking Aouina, he burns a Ju 52 before evading two Bf 109s. One Beaufighter is lost.

November 17: Nine Kittyhawks of 3 Squadron and twelve of 112 Squadrons are attacked by three Bf 109s over the Magrun-Benghazi road. P/O Upward of 3 Squadron and a Bf 109 (Fw. Buter of II/JG27) collide and go down. S/Ldr Gibbes and F/Lt Smith of 112 share a Bf 109. Three hours later 450 Squadron strafes the area.

November 18: Six Kittyhawks of 3 Squadron attack Magrun airfield. P/O Ritchie and P/O Dent destroy a Ju 52 as it is taking off and S/Ldr Gibbes strafes a Bf 109. Two He 111s are also strafed. Later, six more 3 Squadron Kittyhawks return, F/Lt Boardman burning a Ju 52 and a Bf 109, and P/O Taylor a Ju 52 and an unidentified aircraft and two more Bf 109s are strafed. Meanwhile, 450 Squadron flies escort to a convoy of 25 vessels bound for Malta. Sgt Keith Marrows is shot down over land. When a German armoured car endeavours to capture him, it is strafed by F/Lt Schaaf. Marrows escapes and eventually rejoins the squadron.

November 19: F/O John Waddy, DFC, leaves 92 Squadron RAF to return to Australia. Credited with 15½ confirmed victories, he is one of the leading Allied pilots of the North African campaign.

November 21: Tunisia. During a reconnaissance over Sousse, Sfax and Gabes, the 272 Squadron Beaufighter flown by F/Lt Rankin is hit by flak and crash-lands on returning to Malta.

November 22: Six Kittyhawks of 450 Squadron on convoy patrol met a Ju 88 which is shot down by F/Lt Schaaf and P/O Winn. While returning through a heavy rainstorm, Sgt R. Payne, RNZAF, disappears without trace.

An abandoned Stuka at Gambut. (Brian Philpott)

Trevor Mear of 450 Squadron ground crew leaning on the tail of a wrecked Stuka at Gambut. (Trevor Mear)

November 23: Tunisia. North of Sfax, F/O Coate of 272 Squadron claims a Cant Z.508 four-engined transport floatplane.

November 24: Tunisia. North from Linosa, F/O Coate destroys a massive six-engined Blohm und Voss Bv222 flying boat. It is the first of its type to be lost in action. Just afterwards, Coate damages a Do 24 before being chased off by three Bf 109s.

November 25: Tunisia. Leading a Spitfire patrol over the front, G/Capt Ron Lees, CO of 324 Wing, destroys a Savoia bomber, poor weather and heavy cloud making exact identification difficult.

November 28: Tunisia. Amid heavy flak during strafing attacks, the Beaufighter of P/O G. G. Pattearson and Sgt. G. J. W. Simister of 272 Squadron is last seen near the Mersa Kaiba seaplane base. Two other patrolling Beaufighters of 272 Squadron attack an SM 79, F/Lt Rankin sending it blazing into the sea.

November 29/30: A detachment of 458 Squadron Wellingtons at Berka begin anti-submarine patrols and mine-laying in the Gulf of Sirte.

December 1: Tunisia. A German counter-attack near Tebourba is beaten off after the Allies take heavy casualties. The German build-up is now 15 000 strong and the Italians have shipped 90 000 tons of supplies to Tunisia since Operation Torch began. The German air-transport fleet is very active. Allied attacks are taking an increasing toll of these shipments.

December 3: Tunisia. Flying from Malta, six Beaufighters of 272 Squadron patrol over Tripoli, Zuara and Kirkenna. F/Lt Ron Rankin and F/O Ted Coate share in destroying a Ju 88. Djedeida and Tebourba are captured by German troops.

December 4/5: Tunisia. After dark 89 Squadron Beaufighters shoot down three He 111s, one being claimed by F/O Arthur Spurgin and Sgt Norris.

December 9: Tunisia. Four 272 Squadron Beaufighters, covering the Lampedusa-Gulf of Hammamet area at low level, attack 30-plus Ju 52s escorted by two Bf 110s and two Ju 88s. F/O Coate destroys a Ju52 in flames, damages another and then leaves a Ju 88 with smoke pouring from its port engine.

December 11: Tunisia. From Malta six Beaufighters of 272 Squadron, escorted by eight Spitfires sight 32 Ju 52s, with an escort of three Bf 110s and two Ju 88s, near Lampion. The Beaufighters go for the transports while the Spitfires attack the escorts. F/O Coate crashes a Ju 52 in flames and another blows up as it tries to crash-land at Lampedusa. He attacks others, damaging one, but return fire damages his own aircraft. At night, 89 Squadron's Detachment claims two Ju 88s, one falling to the Beaufighter of F/O Spurgin and Sgt Norris.

December 12: Tunisia. Four Beaufighters of 272 Squadron from Malta sweep between Pantellaria and Trapani. North-east of Pantellaria, S/Ldr Ron Rankin shares in causing a Ju 88 to force-land on the sea, four men being seen to clamber into a dinghy.

December 12/13: F/O Mervyn Shipard, with 89 Squadron's Gambut Detachment, shoots down two Ju 88s over Tripoli.

December 13: Ten Kittyhawks of 3 Squadron flying an armed reconnaissance over the Marble Arch-Nofilia area, are attacked by eight Bf 109s and an Mc 202. Sgt W. Cashmore is wounded in both arms and crash-lands.

December 17: Tunisia. S/Ldr Rankin of 272 Squadron shares a Ju 88 east of Cape Passero.

December 18: Tragedy at Marble Arch for 3 Squadron when an airman of the unit's advance ground party sets off an 'S' mine. Killed instantly are LACs Maurice Thompson, Tommy Waugh and Les Horne. LAC Gates dies in an aircraft carrying him to a hospital, LAC George Barsch dies later in hospital while LACs Guerney and Kelly are badly wounded. The injuries of LAC Mellows are less serious. This unexpected disaster is a great shock to the squadron.

December 19: Kittyhawks of 450 Squadron strafing near Sultan are attacked by two Bf 109s which slightly damaged Sgt K. Marrows's aircraft. F/O G. Norton damages one attacker.

December 21: Twelve Kittyhawks of 3 Squadron escorting two Tac.R. Hurricanes are attacked south-east of Sirte by Bf 109s. P/O W. Finlayson is shot down. Later, six 3 Squadron Kittyhawks strafe the airfield at Hun. Two Ju 52s, two SM 79s or 81s, a Ju 88, a Ju 87, a Bf 110, a CR 42, an Hs 126 and two gliders are seen, and seven are set alight, two Savoias by S/Ldr Gibbes, the Ju 88 by F/Lt Watt, the Bf 110 by P/O Taylor and the Ju 87 by P/O Austin, who also damages the Hs 126. P/O Bayley destroys one of the Ju 52s and damages the other, and Sgt Bee ignites a glider and damages the CR 42. Bayley and Bee are both shot down by ground fire, but in a courageous rescue, S/Ldr Gibbes lands and picks Bayley up safely.

December 22/23: Tunisia. F/O Spurgin and F/O Norris of 89 Squadron's Detachment claim the first interception and kill of a four-engined Piaggo P-108B. However, it may have actually been a German four-engined transport type.

December 30: North Africa. Eight Kittyhawks from 450 Squadron patrolling the forward area are attacked six miles east of Bir el Zidan by four Bf 109s. P/O Winn damages one. Meanwhile, 3 Squadron's Sgt I. Roediger intercepts an He 111 at 26 000 feet (7930 m)and chases it to ground level. Unfortunately, his reflector sight fuses and he can only damage it. Later, seven Kittyhawks from 3 Squadron patrolling over Bir el Zidan, are attacked by fifteen Bf 109s of II JG 77, but the Australians are also lucky, F/Lt Watt, F/Lt Boardman and Sgt. Righetti each shooting down one fighter, Watt claiming another as probable.

December 3: During 1942 Allied Air Operations British bomber targets in Germany include Frankfurt, Duisburg and Munich. In France, American attacks are made on Abbeville and Rouen as well as other joint British and American raids with lighter forces. RAF bombers from bases in Britain attack Turin on three occasions while targets raided by the British and American forces from North Africa include Naples (five times), Palermo and Taranto. RAF Bomber Command drops 3000 tons in these operations and the US Eighth Air Force 300.

1943

January 8: Tunisia. From Hamraiet, five 92 Squadron Spitfires plus three others scramble towards Tamet and engage Bf 109s. An army unit reports seeing one of four Spitfires turn back, attack six Bf 109s and fight them off two recce Hurricanes for fifteen minutes before spinning into the ground. P/O Geoffrey Rose from Dalgety, NSW, fails to return.

January 8/9: Over Libya, the 89 Squadron detachment at Benina destroys three German aircraft, F/O Shipard with F/Sgt Oxby claiming a Ju 88 and a He 111. The Ju 88 falls north of Tobruk.

January 13: Tunisia. 239 Wing DAF strafes Churgia landing ground, damaging a Bf 109 and a Fi 156. Sgt G.

An Italian four-engined Piaggo P-108 in German markings. On the night of 22/23 December 1942, Australian night-fighter ace, F/O Arthur Spurgin of Brisbane and his English radar operator, F/Sgt D. A. Norris of 89 (Beaufighter) Squadron's Detachment, covering the Anglo-American forces in Algeria, claimed their fifth victory, the first interception and shooting down of a huge Piaggo P-108B. All five of their kills were made within a month of hectic activity and their last claim was for damage to a He 111 near Tripoli on 7/8 February 1943. Subsequent examination of enemy records suggests, however, that the 'P-108' may have actually been a German four-engined transport type or a Cant Z.1007 which was lost near Bone that night. (MAP)

Spitfire VC BR580/QJ-B of 92 Squadron RAF flown by P/O Geoffrey Rose from Dalgety, NSW, before he was killed in action on 8 January 1943 over Tunisia. Rose sacrificed himself when, alone, he took on six Bf 109s that were attacking two reconnaissance Hurricanes. Army officers on the ground who saw the action reported that Rose fought the six enemy aircraft for ten minutes, allowing the reconnaissance aircraft to escape, before his aircraft went into a spin and crashed about fifteen miles south-west of Burerat. He was buried by the side of his aircraft but, after the war, his body was recovered and now lies in the Tripoli War Cemetery. Australians were scattered liberally in most RAF units which fought in North Africa and at least four others served in 92 Squadron. These were Alfred Glendenning; Ted Sly; John Waddy (with 15.5 victories, second only to 'Killer' Caldwell in the Desert War); and Paul Brickhill. (Dennis Newton)

O'Neil of 450 Squadron is lost but will arrive back at base on foot in two days.

January 14: Tunisia. 239 Wing, escorting a raid by 18 Bostons to attack Bir Dufan airfield, is heavily attacked by twenty Bf 109s and Mc 202s. 3 Squadron Kittyhawks are hit hard, S/Ldr. Gibbes, F/O W. Diehm, P/O A. Tonkin, P/O L. Weatherburn and Sgt. N. Caldwell all failing to return. F/Sgt. A. Nicholson and Sgts. L. Frost, G. Cameron and M. Harrison of 450 Squadron are also shot down. Frost returns on the 18th, Nicholson and Gibbes on 20th. F/Sgt McFarlane of 450 claims a Bf 109, F/Sgt.Stevens and Sgt.Hooke of 3 Squadron each claim Bf 109 probables. Later, 3 Squadron flies an armed reconnaissance over the Gheddahia area, again meeting Bf 109s. P/O Bayley claims a Bf 109 but P/O Austin fails to return.

January 16: Tunisia. Four Beaufighters of 272 Squadron from Malta sweep between the island Lampedusa and the coast. F/Lt Coate shoots down a Ju 88. Further west over Tobruk during the night, F/O Shipard with F/Sgt.Oxby of 89 Squadron destroy two Ju 88s.

January 18: Tunisia. 450 Squadron Kittyhawks on an armed reconnaissance over Tarhuna attack motor transport but Sgt A. Gregory is lost. (He returns on foot on the 22nd.) On a similar mission, Sgt R. Prowse is shot down by Bf 109s.

January 19: Tunisia. Flak over the Tarhuna area causes F/Sgt Taylor of 450 Squadron to force-land his damaged Kittyhawk in no man's land.

January 21: Tunisia. Eleven Kittyhawks of 3 RAAF Squadron cover 450 Squadron attacking the Zuara-Tripoli road, but flak damages Sgt Goulder's aircraft and he has to belly-land. Later, 450 Squadron strafes Castel Benito, leaving three aircraft in flames and seven damaged.

January 22: Tunisia. Twenty-four Kittyhawks from 450 and 3 Squadrons encounter 11 Mc 202s escorting three SM 79s. F/Lt Clabburn and P/O Knox of 3 Squadron each damage an SM 79 while F/Sgt Hankey and S/Ldr Gibbes destroy a Macchi each. P/O Winn of 450 Squadron also shoots down a Macchi and F/Lt McQueen damages one bomber. Sgt J Stanley of 450 Squadron, crash-lands (he will return in two days.) Sgts Willis and Jones of 3 Squadron collide, Willis spinning into the ground, but Jones manages to return to base. On a later mission, the two Australian squadrons strafe the coast road near Zuara. Four Bf 109s attack 3 Squadron's Sgt Righetti, who is lagging. He bales out, and F/O Russell is slightly wounded. During a third mission near Zuara, five Bf 109s are bounced by 450 Squadron. F/Lt Schaaf claims one destroyed and a second shared with Sgt Minchin. F/Lt Glendinning and F/Lt Johns share a third.

January 24: Egypt. No.454 Squadron is re-established at Gianaclis. Its surviving Blenheims have been left in Iraq and in February it will begin training with Baltimore IIIs for reconnaissance duties.

Tunisia. 239 Wing bomb and strafe Ben Gardane landing ground. At least four Bf 109s are badly damaged. After leaving the target a stray Ju 88 is shot down by F/Lt Glendinning and F/Sgt McQueen of 450 Squadron.

January 27: Tunisia. During a clash with Bf 109s near Ben Gardane, F/Lt Watt of 3 Squadron fails to return.

February 16: Tunisia. Axis forces push towards Kasserine. Montgomery's 8th Army arrives at Medenine, a few miles south of Rommel's 'Mareth Line'.

February 18: Tunisia. Units of the British 8th Army enter Ben Gardane and Medenine. Kittyhawks of 3 and 450 Squadron attack defences on Medenine West landing ground in support of the advancing ground troops. Six Bf 109s and three Mc 202s attack. Sgt K. Marrows of 450 probably destroys a Messerschmitt.

February 25: Tunisia. The battle of Kasserine ends with the city's occupation by the Allies. The Axis attack has caused 10 000 Allied casualties, more than half Americans, against 2000 Axis dead.

February 26: Tunisia. 239 Wing bombs Bordj-Touaz (Gabes South) airfield. 3 Squadron engages Bf 109s. Wing Leader, W/Cdr.'Billy' Burton, crashes one, while W/O Reg Stevens claims a second and badly damages a third. F/Lt Ron Susans probably destroys a fourth. Sgt Jackie Beer force-lands (and will return safely next day). The top cover does not engage the Messerschmitts but F/Lt Alfred Glendenning of 450 Squadron dives on one and destroys it.

February 27: Tunisia. Twelve bomb-carrying Kittyhawks from 450 Squadron attack targets around El Hamma. After bombing, they spot four Bf 109s and attack. F/O G. Norton destroys one in flames. Sgt F. Sanders' aircraft is badly damaged.

March 4: F/O Bailey and crew fly 454 Squadron's first Baltimore sortie, an uneventful anti-submarine patrol over the Mediterranean..

March 7: Tunisia. Six Kittyhawks from 3 Squadron on an armed recce west of Medenine encounter nine Axis fighters. Sgt Goulder destroys a Bf 109. W/O Nash claims a probable. Others are claimed damaged. Three 92 Squadron Spitfires scramble and encounter 20 Bf 109s near Neffatia. F/O Ted Sly claims a probable.

March 17: Tunisia. Spitfires from 92 Squadron intercept twelve Bf 109 Jabos, escorted by six Bf 109s and three Mc 202s. P/O Paul Brickhill's aircraft is hit and he bales out. (After the war, Brickhill will write the classics The Dam Busters and Reach For The Sky.)

Sgt Vince McFarlane, one of 450 Squadron's most experienced fighter-bomber pilots, destroyed a Bf-109 over Tunisia on 14 January 1943. McFarlane was awarded a DFM in March 1943 and later earned a DFC. (Trevor Mear)

March 20: Tunisia. The New Zealand Corps reaches the Tebaga Gap. During the night the main attack on the Mareth Line begins.

March 23: Tunisia. No. 450 Squadron covers Kittyhawks of 260 and 3 RAAF Squadrons strafing guns south-west of El Hamma. Sgt R. Rowe is hit by heavy flak and force-lands. (He is picked up by Arabs and returned safely.)

March 24: Tunisia. Twelve Kittyhawks from 450 Squadron strafe vehicles in the El Hamma region. Fighters flown by S/Ldr Bartle and Sgt Day are hit by flak and make belly-landings.

April 3: Tunisia. Axis forces withdraw northwards on the so-called Enfidaville line.

Reflecting both better landing and take-off conditions and the upturn in Allied fortunes, Kittyhawks taxi along a freshly laid steel mesh runway. (Trevor Mear)

April 5: Tunisia. Allied air forces begin Operation 'Flax', to eliminate the huge Axis airlift between Sicily and Tunisia. During the next fortnight formations of Ju 52s, SM 82s and giant Me 323s are intercepted, mainly by USAAF units, and slaughtered, culminating on 18 April, Palm Sunday, in a massacre of 75 aircraft. These losses suffered by Axis transport units so soon after Stalingrad are crippling.

April 6: Tunisia. Twelve Kittyhawks of 3 Squadron bomb German troops massing for a counter-attack at Wadi Akarit. F/Lt Ron Susans destroys an Mc 202 but Sgt W. Ward's aircraft is seen to crash and burn.

April 7: Tunisia. The British 8th Army links with the American 1st Army near Graiha.

April 8: Tunisia. Kittyhawks from 3 Squadron strafe motor transport north-west of Sfax. Sgt Thomas' aircraft is hit by fire from a tank and he force-lands on a beach in Allied territory.

April 11: Mediterranean. Axis forces trapped in Tunisia now only have a tenuous air and sea supply link with Sicily. No. 458 Squadron continues to take a toll of shipping. F/O Hailstone makes a successful torpedo attack on a 3000 ton vessel which blows up. In a few days time, a 458 Wellington will spot two enemy destroyers which will be promptly sunk by the Royal Navy. Also, new Wellington XIIIs begin arriving to replace the earlier marks.

April 12: Tunisia. Axis troops dig in on the Enfidaville line. 8th Army attacks continue, and the Allies occupy Sousse. Now only Enfidaville separates the 8th Army from Tunis.

April 19: Tunisia. During 239 Wing's second sortie of the day, twelve Kittyhawks of 450 Squadron find a hapless lone Ju 88 and shoot it down into the sea in flames. Shortly afterwards, F/Sgt Devon Minchin destroys a Bf 109.

April 20: Tunisia. Montgomery launches a series of attacks on the Axis positions near Enfidaville, but they fail with heavy casualties. Twelve Spitfires of 92 Squadron covering Kittyhawks over Cap Bon bounce three Mc 202s, F/O Ted Sly claiming one out of two destroyed.

April 21: Tunisia. W/O George Downton, in 1437 Strategical Reconnaissance Flight, is detailed as air gunner on a recce to Cape Bon. His aircraft, Baltimore AG766, is attacked by ten Bf 109s. After 20 minutes, it crash-lands on fire. Downton scrambles out slightly wounded then, regardless of the flames, he goes back and helps extricate the mortally injured observer. His courageous effort to recover the rear gunner is defeated by heat. Downton and the only other survivor are captured. He will receive the CGM.

April 23: Mediterranean. The first CGM awarded in the RAF's anti-submarine war is gained by navigator Sgt Arthur Blackwell, RAAF, serving with 500 Squadron, Coastal Command, in a detachment at Blida, North Africa. In Hudson 'N' they spot a U-boat on the surface and attack but the submarine opens fire with cannon, killing the pilot. After closing the bomb doors, Blackwell takes over and flies the Hudson back to base. Unsure of landing safely, he orders the crew to bale out and then heads out to sea before baling out himself.

Baltimores of 454 Squadron continue to fly anti-submarine patrols and convoy escorts plus leaflet and bombing raids over Crete. Aircraft AG869 fails to return from Crete.

Tunisia. P/O R. 'Rusty' Kierath of 450 Squadron is shot down and taken prisoner. He will be one of fifty Air Force officers murdered by the Gestapo following the 'Great Escape' from Stalag Luft III in March 1944.

April 24: During a typical convoy patrol by 451 Squadron from Cyprus, the engine of P/O Ray Hudson's Hurricane catches fire over the vessels and he has to ditch. He is rescued by a ship but suffers burns and other injuries.

April 25: Tunisia. West of Cap Bon, F/Sgt. Goulder of 3 Squadron shares in destroying a Bf 110.

April 27: Tunisia. The British take Djebel Bou Aoukaz after a vicious battle. At night, a Wellington of 458 Squadron from Malta fails to return from a shipping search, possibly the victim of night fighters. It is one of three crews lost late in the month.

April 28-29: Tunisia. Heavy fighting around Djebel Bou Aoukaz.

May 4: Mediterranean. Baltimores of 454 Squadron begin a series of anti-shipping sweeps off the coasts of Greece and Crete, searching for small caiques used to resupply German garrisons on the Aegean islands.

May 6: Tunisia. Covered by a tremendous artillery barrage, the British 1st Army begins its final assault on Tunis.

May 7: Tunisia. British forces enter Tunis, the US 2nd Corps enters Bizerta. Further south, French troops with the 1st Army enter Pont du Fahs. A Halifax of 462 Squadron which had taken off at 2250 from Gardabia Main on the 6th, en route to a target in Tunisia, is last heard from at 0430 reporting that its engines have failed. It ditches and the crew take to their dinghy. After ten days and nights they drift ashore safely between Homs and Tripoli. Flight engineer, Sgt C. Curnow, is awarded a DFM for his efforts in maintaining crew morale and welfare.

May 8: Tunisia. The Allied advance to the sea continues, while the Axis troops withdraw into the Cape Bon peninsula. An Axis convoy of three steamships succeeds in reaching Tunisia, but are then attacked by Kittyhawks of 239 Wing, including 3 Squadron, and sunk before they can unload. Axis units are paralysed for lack of fuel.

May 10/11: Tunisia. At night, 73 Squadron Hurricanes patrol over Cap Bon. P/O Bruce Bretherton destroys a Ju 52 as it comes in to land at El Haouaria.

May 12: Tunisia. General von Arnim, commander of German troops in Africa, surrenders to the Allies.

May 13: Tunisia. Field-Marshal Messe surrenders to the British 8th Army. Some 250 000 Germans and Italians lay down their arms. General Alexander sends the following to Churchill: 'It is my duty to report that the Tunis campaign is over. All enemy resistance has ceased. We are masters of the North African shores.' Top scoring squadron for the campaigns in North Africa is 3 Squadron. At the end of World War II, it will be credited with 212 enemy aircraft destroyed, 63 probables and 136 damaged.

No. 3 has covered every lap of the 'Desert Stakes' and is the only squadron to have fought in the first Army push of the Nile and to be with the victorious 8th Army at the end of the North African campaign.

AUSTRALIANS WHO BECAME ACES (FIVE VICTORIES) IN THE WESTERN DESERT

Name	Squadrons	Desert score	Final total
C. R. Caldwell	250 RAF, 112 RAF	20.5	28.5
J. L. Waddy	250 RAF, 260 RAF, 4 SAAF, 92 RAF	15.5	15.5
A. W. Barr	3 RAAF	12.5	12.5
R. H. M. Gibbes	3 RAAF	10.25	10.25
P. StG. B. Turnbull	3 RAAF	9	12
G. H. Steege	3 RAAF, 450 RAAF	8	8
R. K. Wilson	3 RAAF	8	8
R. M. Leu	112 RAF	7	7
A. C. Cameron	3 RAAF	6.5	6.5
W. S. Arthur	3 RAAF	6+	10
J. F. Jackson	3 RAAF	6	8
W. H. Mailey	3 RAAF	6	6
R. G. Foskett	80 RAF	5.5	6.5
D. H. McBurnie	450 RAF	5	5
R. J. C. Whittle	250 RAF	5	7
J. P. Bartle	112 RAF	5	5
P. R. Giddy	3 RAAF	5	5
J. R. Perrin	3 RAAF	5+	8
A. C. Rawlinson	3 RAAF	5	8

7

THE BATTLE FOR MILNE BAY
FROM THE OTHER SIDE...

On 7 December 1941, Japanese aircraft bombed the American Fleet at Pearl Harbor turning the war into a truly global conflict. Totally outclassing and outfighting the reeling Allies, the forces of Japan rapidly pushed their way into the Far East and southwards into the Pacific to New Guinea gaining swift and dramatic victories as they went. Although the Battle of the Coral Sea in early May 1942 frustrated Japanese plans to take Port Moresby from the sea, they were still determined to capture this important base. From it they could isolate Australia and secure their own Pacific defensive perimeter. Little more than two months later, they initiated a bold attempt to take Port Moresby by an overland route, striking across the island from the north.

On the night of 21/22 July 1942 elements of General Horii's XVIII Army landed at Buna and Gona and advanced inland up the narrow Kokoda Trail into the rugged Owen Stanley Mountains. Pushing back light Australian opposition, Horii seized the key passes over the range by 12 Augus tand continued to advance towards Moresby but against increasingly stiff resistance. In coordination with this overland advance by way of Kokoda, the Japanese plan envisaged using Major-General Kawaguchi's 124th Infantry Regiment group in a seaborne assault on Milne Bay from where a flanking attack could be then launched on Port Moresby by sea.

Milne Bay, at the south-eastern tip of Papua New Guinea, lies between two rugged peninsulas formed by parallel mountain chains rising to elevations of 900 to 1200 metres. Numerous reefs and small islands along the eastern or open end of the bay make it a protected anchorage. The bay, about 30 kilometres long and from 8-16 kilometres wide, has a deep channel, China Strait, running toward the south-east, and East Channel leading directly out toward the east. Deep water exists close to the shores and mountains rise abruptly behind narrow coastal plains. About a quarter of the coastal area at the head of the bay had been cleared for coconut plantations

prior to World War II, while the remainder was still sago swamps and dense tropical jungle. Within the boundaries of this difficult terrain, exposed to an annual rainfall of about 5000 mm, only the plantation area lent itself to the speedy establishment of military facilities.

The Allied build-up began there in mid-June 1942 with instructions for immediate construction of a fighter airstrip and subsequent development of a bomber airfield. By 25 June, engineers were unloading at Milne Bay to repair roads and bridges for transporting heavy equipment to the site of the proposed aerodrome. Preliminary construction at Airstrip No. 1 was initiated on 30 June, and the runway was sufficiently advanced by 19 July, two days before the Japanese landings at Buna, to permit the landing of RAAF Kittyhawks. By 6 August, 1500 x 24 metres of the planned 1828 x 30 metre runway was covered with steel mat. This was in operational use and work had been started on Airstrip No. 2, located about 5 kilometres west of Airstrip No. 1. Clearing, the runway partially graded, but other sites were considered more favourable and work on Airstrip No. 2 was discontinued. Work on Airstrip No. 3, several kilometres east of Airstrip No. 1, was beginning.

Reports from reconnaissance planes showed the Japanese that the Allies were building an airfield at the head of Milne Bay near Gili Gili, but low-lying rain clouds usually covered it from aerial observation and little was known for certain about the area.. On 4 August, four A6M2 Zero fighters and an Aichi Type 99 (Val) dive-bomber making an armed reconnaissance of the area encountered eight Australian Kittyhawk P-40s on patrol and the dive-bomber was shot down into the jungle. The Zeros strafed and destroyed one P-40 on the airfield. [*The Japanese had run into a standing patrol of 76 Squadron Kittyhawks. F/Lt P. Ash recorded 76's first victory when he shot down the dive-bomber.*]

An air strike against the air base at Rabi (Milne Bay) by 27 Mitsubishi G4M1 Type 1 ('Betty') bombers of the 4th Air Group was scheduled three days later. Escorting the bombers from Rabaul would be A6M2

A6M Naval Type 0 carrier-borne Fighter. Known to Japanese airmen as the Reisen (Rei Sentoki) or Zero Fighter, this aircraft opened the eyes of the world to the capabilities of the Japanese aircraft industry with a shock. When the A6M2 was used against the Americans and British in December 1941 at Pearl Harbor and over Malaya, its speed and manoeuvrability took them by surprise. The Allies adopted the official code name 'Zeke' but commonly referred to the aircraft as a Zero. Its armament consisted of two 20 mm cannons in the wings and two cowl-mounted 7.7 mm machine-guns. During the first six months of the Pacific war, A6M2s of Japan's Striking Force and 11th Air Fleet proved more than a match for the heavier and less manoeuvrable fighters used against them. It was not until the Allied pilots learned not to try to engage the Zero in a dogfight that the A6M began to lose its ascendancy. Nevertheless, it remained a formidable weapon and was produced in larger numbers than any other Japanese aircraft. Another amazing aspect of the A6M2's performance was its range of 1010 nautical miles, which could be increased to 1675 nautical miles with the use of drop fuel tanks. (AWM)

Zero fighters from the crack Tainan Kokutai. Included among the fighter pilots was Petty Officer SecondClass Enji Kakimoto. From Oita-Ken, 22-year-old Kakimoto had been a farmer before joining the Japanese Navy at Sasebo in July 1937. He had served aboard the cruiser Myoko before entering flight training and had graduated in the forty-seventh term flight class in October 1939. This day, he and Petty Officer Third Class Kazushi Uto would fly in the 2nd Shotai (section or flight) of the 3rd Chutai (Squadron) as wingmen to the ace pilot Petty Officer First Class Saburo Sakai.

As Kakimoto and his comrades checked each other's equipment in preparation for take-off, a runner came into the operations room with a radio message for Captain Masahisa Saito. Shortly afterwards, the CO announced that American marines had invaded Guadalcanal and Tulagi in the Solomons.

The Milne Bay mission was scrubbed immediately and, instead, an attack was made against American transports anchored off Guadalcanal. The Japanese pilots encountered opposition in the form of US Navy Grumman F4F Wildcats and Douglas SBD Dauntless dive-bombers. In the ensuing air battle, Kakimoto claimed a Grumman near Guadalcanal and an SBD over Tulagi. Meanwhile, as Sakai attacked a flight of SBDs from behind, he was caught in crossfire from the tail gunners and severely wounded. After an agonising five-hour flight, he managed to reach Rabaul and land out of fuel.

Japanese resources at Rabaul and Lae were suddenly stretched to their limits, the air groups having to cover an area which extended south-east to Guadalcanal and south to Port Moresby and Milne Bay. Air fighting, particularly over Guadalcanal, was growing in intensity, and during the period from August to October 1942 the Tainan Kokutai would claim 201 enemy aircraft shot down (including 37 uncertain) for the loss of 32 pilots.

August 11 saw an air battle over Milne Bay in which twelve Zeros were intercepted by 22 RAAF Kittyhawks.

During a fierce encounter, although they were outnumbered almost two to one, the Japanese gave as good as they got and shot down four P-40s. [*In this, Milne Bay's second air raid, KIA were F/s M. Sheldon and Sgt F. Shelley of 75 Squadron and P/O A. McLeod and Sgt G. Inkster of 76 Squadron for a claim of 4 probables: P/O F. Coker (1), F/O J. Olivier and P/O W. Withers (1) for 75 Squadron; Sgt J. Dempster (1), Sgt R. Carroll (1) for 76 Squadron. AA gunners claimed three more.*]

Meanwhile, because of heavy losses suffered on Guadalcanal, Major-General Kawaguchi's 124th Infantry Regiment,which had been reserved for the attack on Port Moresby, was ordered to move against the Americans. However, the use of Kawaguchi's force, and its subsequent defeat on Guadalcanal, did not mean that plans to attack Milne Bay had been abandoned. The task fell to Admiral Gunichi Mikawa, Commander of the Outer Pacific Fleet, a gifted tactician who had won a brilliant naval victory on 9 August when, off Savo Island shortly after midnight, his cruisers surprised Allied ships guarding the approaches to Guadalcanal and were responsible for the sinking of three American cruisers and HMAS Canberra without loss.

Knowing he could not count on help from the Army, and estimating that Milne Bay was held by not more than three infantry companies and 30 aircraft, Mikawa allocated 1500 men for the invasion, code named RAT. Most of them were to come from Kavieng and they included 612 marines of the 5th Kure, Special Naval Landing Force (SNLF), under Commander Shojiro Hayashi; 362 of the 10th Construction Unit under Engineer Tsutsui; and some detached 5th Sasebo marines

(228 under Lt Fujikawa). The Kavieng convoys were to sail up Milne Bay and land at Rabi, about five kilometres east of the Gili Gili jetty.

At the same time, 353 marines of the 5th Sasebo SNLF from Buna, under Cdr Tsukioka, would be carried in seven big, wooden, motor- driven barges, landed at Taupota on the Solomon Sea side and marched over the mountains to Gili Gili from the north.

[*In fact, Mikawa's intelligence was hopelessly inaccurate. The Allies at Milne Bay now consisted of some 4500 Australian infantry, supported by 3000 Australians and 1300 Americans in engineer, artillery and service units. Air defence consisted of the Kittyhawks of 75 and 76 Squadrons and a combined flight of 6/32 Squadron Lockheed Hudsons.*]

Preliminary orders for the RAT assault were sent out on 21 August. Signals to advance were sent to 5th Sasebo at Buna two days later. After some delay due to a transmission error, Tsukioka immediately completed preparations and led his 347 marines onto seven barges which left at midnight. His intention was to land at Taupota early on 26 August.

Sixteen Zeros of the 5th Air Raid Unit transferred from Lae to Buna, ready to start raiding Milne Bay in support of RAT Force. These were sent into the area on the 23rd but they failed to locate the target because of cloud. A single P-40 was bounced and damaged before it disappeared back into the haze. [*F/Lt Frank Coker of 75 Squadron was jumped and his aircraft suffered superficial damage to the fuselage from cannon fire. Australian anti-aircraft gunners sighted four Zeros through the clouds.*]

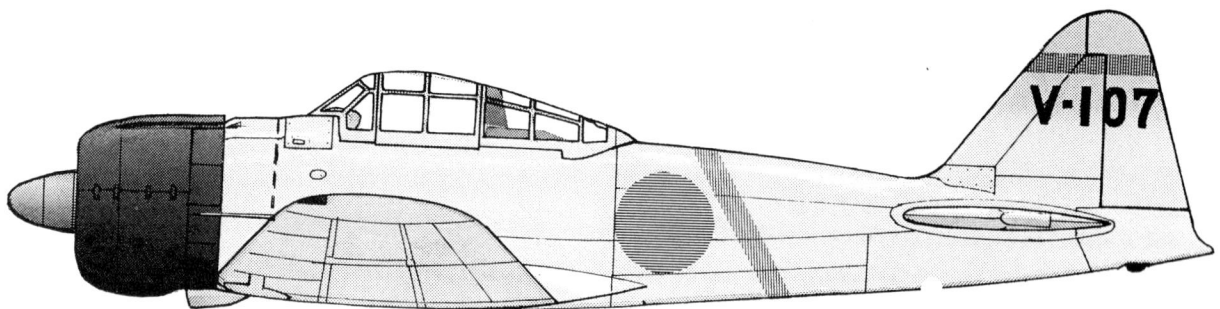

Mitsubishi A6M2 Type 21, V-107, of the Tainan Kokutai. V-107 was one of many Zeros flown by the highly successful Japanese ace Petty Officer Saburo Sakai. On 7 August the Tainan Kokutai was briefed to escort an air strike against Milne Bay by 27 Mitsubishi G4M1 Type 1 'Betty' bombers of the 4th Air Group but the American invasion of Guadalcanal and Tulagi in the Solomons caused the mission to be scrubbed. Instead an attack was made against American transports anchored off Guadalcanal. The Japanese pilots encountered US Navy Grumman F4F Wildcats and Douglas SBD Dauntless dive-bombers. In the ensuing air battle, Sakai, flying Zero V128, claimed a Grumman and two SBDs but as he attacked a flight of SBDs from behind, he was caught in crossfire from the tail gunners and severely wounded. After an agonising five-hour flight, he managed to return to Rabaul and land out of fuel. It was a testimony to his courage and the Zero's long-range capabilities. (Dennis Newton)

Next day, the Buna Zeros were luckier. They found the target and made a strafing attack along the full length of the airstrip. In 30 minutes of air fighting they claimed nine P-39s and one P-40 shot down without loss. [*Twelve Zeros strafed the airstrip at Milne Bay. F/Lt V. Sullivan together with P/O Giffin and Sgts B. Carroll and R. Glassop of 76 Squadron were jointly credited with one Zero destroyed while two more were claimed as probables by F/Lt C. Wawn. AA gunners claimed two more.*]

At 7 a.m. that day the main body of RAT Force set out from Rabaul, escorted by vessels of the 18 Cruiser Squadron. Altogether, it comprised of two transports, two cruisers, three destroyers and three sub-chasers. The General Orders read: 'At the dead of night quickly complete the landing and strike the white soldiers without reserve. Unitedly smash to pieces the enemy lines and take the aerodrome by storm.'

Meanwhile, misfortune was about to overtake the overland force. As Tsukioka's seven barges chugged down the coast under cloud cover they were sighted by a coastwatcher and reported moving past Porlock Harbour in the direction of Milne Bay. The following day, the marines beached their craft on the western coast of Goodenough Island and went ashore for their midday meal. At that very moment, nine Australian P-40s swooped in on low-level strafing runs. [*They were two flights from 75 Squadron led by F/O John Piper and F/O Geoff Atherton.*] All the barges were destroyed, together with large quantities of weapons, radio equipment and medical and food supplies. Actual casualties were light, five dead and six wounded, but the Buna marines were now stranded and there would be no threat to Milne Bay coming from Taupota.

The main assault force had been sighted too. It came under almost continuous contact with Allied aircraft and was attacked by Lockheed Hudsons and bomb-carrying P-40s. Resulting from these actions, Hayashi's 5th Kure suffered ten killed and six wounded and Fujikawa's unit lost two killed and one wounded. There was some damage to barges loaded on the transport Nankai Maru, but repairs were made before reaching anchorage.

By 7.45 p.m., RAT Force was entering Milne Bay. The moon was two nights before full, but the weather was cloudy with poor visibility and no clear landmarks. During a downpour of rain shortly before midnight, Hayashi began the landings at a point he believed to be Rabi, but without a reliable map, and in the darkness and rain, he in fact landed eleven kilometres to the east on a swampy coastal shelf where the mountains came down almost to the water. His only means of advance westward toward Gili Gili was a muddy three-metre-wide track.

Immediately on landing, part of Lieutenant Fujikawa's unit discovered two patrol boats approaching. These were attacked by two barges. One escaped to the west but the other ran aground and prisoners were taken. These were questioned about the position of the airfield but they replied that they did not know. The rest of Fujikawa's men, with the cooperation of Tsutsui's construction unit, hurriedly built a jetty for unloading. Amongst the material to eventually reach shore were two Type 95 light tanks, the first to be landed on the New Guinea coast. Although the road was sufficiently wide, it was muddy and difficult for vehicles.

It was vital to ensure the assault was made before the following dawn in the expectation of cooperation and cover by friendly aircraft on 26 August. CPO Yasumura was ordered to reconnoitre. Because of the required speed of the operation and the impossibility of moving at night through dense jungle on both sides, he made a rapid advance along the road at the head of his platoon. At 3 a.m., they were suddenly fired on at close range by at least ten enemy with automatic weapons. Yasumura was killed. The troops dispersed and attacked. After 30 minutes the Australians withdrew. Apart from Yasumura's death, there were fifteen wounded.

After advancing another 2 kilometres, fierce fire was met and the Japanese immediately deployed. The warships gave a covering bombardment but without clear results. At 2.10 a.m., still stubbornly resisting, the defenders withdrew about 100 metres. After three charges, the Japanese had advanced about a kilometre, reaching the line of a river but dawn was near and it was obviously no longer possible to penetrate to the airfield.

Lt Fujikawa's men continued to land supplies until 5 a.m. when the transports had to leave the bay to avoid air attack. They then concentrated on sorting the landed goods, grouping weapons and ammunition at dispersed points and concealing the barges. This was still incomplete just after dawn when Australian P-40s and Hudsons were seen approaching to attack the ships. Fifteen minutes later the landing point was located and attacked.

Two barges loaded with bombs exploded in a huge detonation near the jetty causing fuel drums which were either stacked or floating just offshore (they had been thrown into the sea from the hastily unloading transport Nankai Maru) to catch fire. The whole area was engulfed in flames and the remaining ten barges either caught fire in succession or were damaged and sank.

Return fire with 13 mm machine-guns mounted near the camouflaged food and ammunition dump was ineffective and drew more intense strafing. Ammunition and food stores were destroyed by fire. Fujikawa had six men killed and five wounded. The remainder withdrew into the nearby jungle.

Wrecked Japanese barges along the dense jungle foreshore of Milne Bay, the victims of strafing and bombing by RAAF Kittyhawks and Hudsons. (AWM)

Forward troops also came under heavy attack from the P-40s and they too were forced to withdraw into the jungle.

The Australian P-40s remained extremely active throughout the day, working in relays bombing and strafing in sections and flights. Company commander Lt Fujimura was killed and platoon commander Ensign Hiramoto assumed command. Half of the other platoon commanders were killed or wounded. Communications were disrupted between Hayashi's main force and Fujikawa at the rear and the situation became obscure. The only information received was that most of the landed stores had been lost by fire. To advance during daylight was impossible.

Hayashi's promised air support was busy elsewhere. Lt Junichi Sasai, who claimed 54 aerial victories and was planning to break the famous Red Baron's record set in World War I, led the Tainan Kokutai from Rabaul to escort Betty bombers attacking Henderson Field on Guadalcanal. In a combat with Wildcats over the target, the Japanese lost three bombers and three escorts, one of the casualties being Sasai himself. At Buna, just as a flight of Zeros was about to take off to support RAT, they were attacked by Allied aircraft carrying out the first of what would be a series of attacks against the airfield. Another force of fifteen fighters and bombers did take off from Rabaul but it was turned back by bad weather.

During breaks from the persistent air attacks, Hayashi sent out patrols but these were unable to locate the position of the airfield. According to information from natives, there were two airfields, one north of Gili Gili and one north-west of Rabi, which was unfinished. The airfield was apparently thirteen kilometres from his present position and he resolved to penetrate to the objective by night attack on 26/27 August.

Hayashi's first objective was a plantation astride the track at KB Mission, lightly held by Australian militia. Advancing along the road and preceded by a flame-thrower, his troops tried to outflank the defenders by wading into the bay on one side and the swamp on the other. His men met greater than expected opposition and the terrain was worse than anything they could have imagined. Amid heavy fighting, the main force advanced through the jungle for six hours, the furthest point of the advance being about a kilometre west along the road. At first light, still unable to reach the airfield, he ordered retirement into the jungle to avoid the new day's inevitable air attacks.

Shortly after 8 a.m., Milne Bay had another air attack in the form of an eight-aircraft strike by Val dive-bombers of the 2nd Air Corps from Rabaul. One of its members was Warrant Officer Ota Genga, a veteran navy flier who had been recalled from retirement and who was familiar with the area. They were escorted by twelve fighters from the Tainan Kokutai. Men below leapt into muddy slit trenches as the first shotai of dive-bombers commenced to bomb and Zeros began strafing along the airstrip. Enemy AA guns put up a terrific barrage and within seconds every rifle and machine-gun in the area seemed to be shooting into the air. One man was seen firing a revolver at an attacking Zero until he collapsed to the ground. [*John Olivier, an-off duty 75 Squadron pilot, had ignored the danger and started taking pot shots at an attacking Zero with his revolver. He was severely wounded.*]

Five Zeros led by Lt. Joji Yamashita sweeping through on a strafing run, were met by a hail of light anti-aircraft fire. On Yamashita's wing, Enji Kakimoto noticed fuel spurting from a hit in his leader's fuel tank. His own aircraft was struck too but it continued to respond to the controls. On the airfield, a huge B-24 bomber was in flames. Two bombs from the Vals exploded at the side of the runway and the remainder burst wide some distance away. [*The Liberator had force-landed back on the 20th. Engineer officer Bill Matson and his maintenance crew had dragged it to the side of the runway, jacked it up and were repairing it.*]

Climbing to 450 metres and heading west, the Zero pilots suddenly encountered twelve USAAF B-26 Marauders. Joji Yamashita, knowing his damaged Zero was losing fuel and that he could not reach home, led his flight after the fast-flying Americans and commenced a series of rear and beam attacks. He closed in on one Marauder and to Enji Kakimoto it seemed that Yamashita shot it down before his Zero crash-dived into the sea. [*There were several USAAF aircraft operating in the general vicinity. The Marauders were from the 22nd Bombardment Group. One bomber was damaged and the American gunners claimed two of the attacking fighters destroyed. As well, a B-17 Flying Fortress of the 435th Squadron, 19th Bomb Group, undertaking a reconnaissance of the Buna, Normanby Island and Milne Bay area, was attacked and damaged by three Zeros.*]

Alone and with the oil pressure of his own engine falling, Kakimoto at first tried to join up with another pair of Zeros flown by First Class Sergeant Sadao Yamashita and First Class Airman Kihachi Ninomiya, but it was no good. As his power failed, he lost height and managed to successfully ditch on the water. Kakimoto abandoned the plane and swam to shore. Scrambling onto land, he could see the other two Zeros attacking his almost intact plane which was still floating on the surface.

Sadao Yamashita and Kihachi Ninomiya, intent on their task of destroying Kakimoto's Zero to prevent it falling into Allied hands, did not notice until too late the three Australian P-40s which appeared overhead. They were taken by surprise. During a head-on attack, one Zero pulled up into a stall and ran into a hail of bullets. It half

rolled and dived into the sea. The other Zero was attacked from the beam at a range of 25 metres and hit the water seconds later. [*Patrolling 75 Squadron aircraft had been recalled and these intercepting Kittyhawks were flown by S/Ldr Les Jackson, Sgt Roy Riddel and P/O N. Todd. The Zeros fell to Jackson and Riddel.*]

Kakimoto disappeared into the jungle.

More P-40s arrived to defend the airfield. One was chased off and shot down. [*Sgt 'Stu' Munro in Kittyhawk A29-110 was last seen being pursued in a north-westerly direction. The wreckage of his P-40 was not discovered until October 1943 in the hills 600 metres above Hagita Mission.*]

At 150 metres, four incoming dive-bombers were attacked by two of the Australians fighters. One Val, suddenly aware of the hazard, zoom climbed away quickly into cloud cover, leaving the others stranded in close formation in the centre of the bay. The P-40s attacked together and then followed up with numerous individual assaults from above, beam and below. The Vals jettisoned

Petty Officer Enji Kakimoto of the Tainan Kokutai and Saburo Sakai's wingman on 7 August. Drawing based on a captured group photograph taken at Rabaul on 4 August 1942. During the raid on Milne bay on 27 August, his Zero was damaged by ground fire and he was obliged to ditch.
(Dennis Newton)

their bombs but stayed together for mutual support. By the time the P-40s were finished, there were only two battered dive-bombers remaining, one trailing smoke as they flew low over the water half-way down the bay. [*F/ Os B. Watson and P. Jones were credited with destroying one Val, probably a second and damaging a third.*]

Altogether, the mission cost the Japanese five fighters and two dive-bombers. According to the records of the Tainan Kokutai for the 27 August raid on Rabi/Milne Bay, besides Enji Kakimoto, Joji Yamashita, Sadao Yamashita and Kihachi Ninomiya, Petty Officer Third Class Takeo Matsuda also failed to return.

On the ground, Commander Hayashi, considering the failure of the past two nights, was acutely aware of the need to pinpoint the enemy positions. But his men were given no respite by the strafing planes. By the approach of nightfall, his patrols sent to find and reconnoitre the airfield had not reported back. Nevertheless, the second echelon from Kavieng had arrived during the night and he determined to attack in greater force.

A good omen for the success of the attack occurred just on dusk. Two patrolling P-40s sweeping over KB Mission towards Sanderson Bay discovered a large body of Hayashi's troops with a tank emerging from a gorge and onto the main track. Flying low over Cameron Plateau, they tried to obtain a clear line of fire into the ravine, but one plane clipped the top of a tall tree and crashed into the jungle. [*S/Ldr Peter Turnbull and F/Lt Ron Kerville of 76 Squadron had been up hunting for the tanks. Turnbull's Kittyhawk, A29-108, flipped onto its back and dived, apparently with its guns firing, straight into the gorge. It crashed into the jungle about kilometre east of Australian troops assigned to defend KB Mission. A patrol was ordered to try and locate the wreckage, but the task was impossible because visibility from the track was less than two metres, so thick was the jungle, and darkness was falling. A veteran of 3 Squadron in North Africa and the fighting over Port Moresby, S/Ldr Peter Turnbull, DFC, had twelve enemy aircraft (nine in the Middle East, three in the Pacific) to his credit.*]

Abandoned Type 96 light Japanese tanks. During the vicious night battles of 27/28 August, the driver of the leading tank was killed. He was replaced immediately by another driver but the tank left the road and went over into the mud. The second tank, trying to avoid it, also went over and both had to be abandoned.   (AWM)

His body was not able to be recovered for some days but his place as CO of 76 Squadron was taken by S/Ldr 'Bluey' Truscott, DFC, who was already serving with the unit as a flight commander.]

In the dark, the tanks were brought into action. Each had a strong headlight which, shining through the rain, enabled them to illuminate the Australian positions while the attackers remained in darkness. These lights were set deeply in heavy steel reflectors directly beneath a machine-gun. Wherever the lights moved, the ground ahead was illuminated giving the gunners a good field of fire along the beam. The obvious tactic would have been to shoot out the bulbs but these were so small, and so deeply set inside their steel reflectors, that only a carefully-aimed shot at very close range fired from the front, aimed at the very centre of the beam, had any hope of success. To attempt to do this would have meant almost suicidal exposure to the machine gun.

With the tanks' help, Hayashi's men cleared KB Mission and reached the Gama river. There they encountered about 20 of the enemy in defence positions on the opposite bank. While assaulting these, the driver of the leading tank was killed as a result of mortar fire or by a sniper. He was immediately replaced by another driver but the tank left the road and went over into the mud. The other tank, trying to avoid it, also went over and both had to be abandoned.

In spite of this setback, the Japanese successfully crossed the river and advanced to where the jungle opened out on both sides; leaving thin forest with grassy spaces. The airfield? [*It was actually Airstrip No. 3*] At this stage coordinated concentrated fire was received from the front and on both flanks. It was now 3 a.m. The action continued for over an hour but the front line was stalemated and could not move. Expecting air support they held on, but after dawn Australian aircraft attacked again and the force withdrew into the jungle on both sides of the road.

During this day, air strafing and bombing was particularly severe but Hayashi was resolute, wanting to complete his attack that night. That evening, he concentrated his remaining forces at a point one and a half kilometres in front of the enemy positions. On inspection he found that, in the higher ranks, his killed and wounded were unexpectedly high, while among NCOs and men the figure was about 33 per cent. Even among the uninjured, mobility was impaired by foot disabilities because of the constant wet. Loss of automatic weapons had also been severe also and there were some dispersed elements which he could not find. Lt Fujikawa's unit had suffered severe bombing (three killed and five wounded) and was unable to make contact with the forward troops. There was little choice but to abandon the attack and withdraw.

Hayashi had already asked Admiral Mikawa to send reinforcements. The situation looked bleak. His overland force has disappeared and he had lost much of his food and ammunition when the barges ferrying it ashore had been destroyed. Morale of his men was suffering after three days of combat because of lack of success in battle, constant air attack, the shortage of rations, marching through endless mud; and extreme exhaustion and distress caused by dampness, cold, wounds and foot disabilities. The officers were unable to exercise restraint or control and the result was a breakdown in discipline. Some men halted and rested without order, others entered huts and searched for food, and yet others entered the palm plantations to get coconuts.

Reinforcements were landed on the night of 29 August under cover of heavy mist. They were 568 marines of the Kure 3rd SNLF and 200 of the Yokosuka 5th SNLF, all under Commander Minoro Yano. Aboard the cruiser Tenryu, Yano took reports of the situation from Lts Fujikawa and Sakurai.

Yano met Hayashi immediately he landed, at Fujikawa's HQ. Being senior to Hayashi, he took command of RAT operations. He strongly criticised 5th Kure's withdrawal and stated that the aim of the reinforcements was to capture the airfield that night.

There were no attacks by enemy aircraft during the morning. [*The P-40 squadrons had withdrawn to Port Moresby overnight because of the anticipated attack on the airfield.*] In the afternoon there was some gunfire and scattered mortar attacks, but activity was light.

Before 1 o'clock on the night of 30/31 August the combined Japanese forces launched a furious assault on the airstrip. Defending Australian infantry and American engineers fired flares and exposed the attackers, who were revealed grouped around the eastern side of the airfield.. They offered easy targets to the defenders firing across the open ground of the field. Artillery and mortar fire crashed down. Three times the Japanese formed up and attacked and three times they fell before the hail of fire which caught them.

Lt Nagata, Adjutant of Yano's 3rd Kure, was with Hayashi prior to the deployment of 5th Kure, aiming to maintain close contact between both units, but contact was almost completely lost between the two HQs when fighting broke out.

With no prospect of a successful frontal attack, Hayashi issued repeated orders to outflank the enemy. When he was hit in the face and leg by mortar fragments, he refused to withdraw but, advised by the adjutant and others, he went to an abandoned trench about 20 metres back. Unfortunately, this did not offer any protection from enemy fire and Lt Sakurai, the adjutant, was hit in the abdomen by mortar fragments and died at once. Soon

Kittyhawk A29-147 being taxied by Australian ace S/Ldr 'Bluey' Truscott, DFC along a steel mesh runway to dispersal at Milne Bay. (AWM)

after that, Sapper Chadanai who had accompanied the CO as a runner, was hit in the face and left shoulder. One by one the officers around Hayashi were killed but he firmly refused to leave the forward area. In the end nobody survived.

During this time the 5th Kure front-line medical unit (five men led by Lt Chisaka) were extremely active treating and evacuating the wounded. Chisaka himself carried men on his shoulders as he directed their evacuation.

The night attack had clearly failed, and those surviving were exhausted physically and mentally. Meanwhile, Commander Yano and 3rd Kure HQ moved through the jungle on the left of the road and attempted to cope with the battle as it had developed, but the position was extremely obscure. Reports were received that Hayashi was dead and subsequently there were signs that the front units were withdrawing, mixed with the wounded. The withdrawal was not explicitly ordered but it was happening and there were no specific arrangements for covering fire. Dawn was now close, so Yano decided there was no course other than to retreat for the moment to regroup. Before daybreak three Japanese bugle calls rang out, the signal for retreat.

The Australians pursued, allowing no respite. For the Japanese there was no chance to coordinate for uniformity of action. Contact between units could not be established, and there had to be frequent shifting of positions in the jungle to avoid strafing aircraft [*from 75 and 76 Squadron, whichs had returned from Port Moresby*], and mortar attacks. As well as this, the force became increasingly dispersed through exhaustion, poor visibility and foot disabilities. Consequently, all trace was lost of more and more members. Yano estimated that Japanese personnel fit for combat by evening on 31 August totalled about 400.

Next day, Lt Fujikawa's unit at the rear was relieved of the duty of attending to evacuation of dead and wounded. It moved forward to the front line and came under Yano's command. All of its members found movement difficult, again because of foot disabilities and exhaustion. Australian air attack was so intense that it was difficult to even secure the HQ. In the afternoon, the Australians brought mortars forward and casualties steadily increased.

By nightfall on 1 September, the Australians had retaken KB Mission.

On 2 September, a light cruiser and a transport vessel

were spotted entering Milne Bay. [*They were, in fact, the Allied freighter Tasman escorted by the new Australian destroyer HMAS Arunta.*] Dive-bombers from Rabaul were ordered against them. A three-aircraft strike led by W/O Ota Genga took off escorted by six Zeros. Three hours after leaving the Zeros had to break off as their fuel was running low, but the Vals continued heading south on their own. They disappeared and never arrived over Milne Bay.

Setting up defences on the track to block pursuit, Commander Yano cabled Admiral Mikawa on 3 September requesting permission to withdraw from Milne Bay. He himself had been wounded, he had lost 600 men and there were now more than 300 wounded on his hands. The rest of the men, most of them suffering from trench foot, jungle rot and tropical fevers, could not hold out. Mikawa sanctioned evacuation.

In view of the Yano's severe wound, the steady increase in front- line casualties and signs of disorganisation of command, Lt Fujikawa, after getting approval from Yano, organised all available personnel capable of combat into four mixed platoons. Swearing to serve the Imperial Cause to the end, they took up the second line of defence. At this stage, Lt Nagata, Adjutant 3rd Kure, arrived and protested, asserting that he was the senior surviving combatant officer. Fujikawa yielded command to Nagata and returned to his usual duty.

On the night of September 3, Japanese ships Arashi and Hamakaze again entered Milne Bay and contacted the landing force. Commander Yano went aboard Arashi to make a detailed report and in the hope of obtaining urgent treatment for his wound. After landing supplies, Hamakaze bombarded the Rabi area heavily before

leaving. Yano remained on the Arashi and returned to Rabaul.

With daylight, the enemy, who had remained quiet under fire from Hamakaze, swung again to the offensive. Strafing and bombing became particularly intense. 5th Kure's signal unit which was operating from commandeered native huts, had up to now escaped detection but just after 8.20 a.m. the houses were attacked. Unit commander, CPO Tsutsumi, with others near the houses, died in action and all arms were destroyed. Fujikawa's unit also suffered three killed and two wounded.

On the night of 4 September, the cruiser Yayoi arrived. In a scene of considerable disorder, men rushed to be first aboard the boats and some tried to push ahead of those more seriously wounded. Calm was finally restored by the efforts of the medical officers, the chief medical orderly and Lt Fujikawa. After landing rations and evacuating 224 wounded with Lt Nagata, Yayoi left for Rabaul at 1 a.m.

All remaining units were combined under Fujikawa. Wounded and construction personnel were concentrated and withdrawn. The remainder mounted a strong guard on all sides and prepared for Australian attacks. The bombardment and strafing remained intense throughout the day and during the morning about 50 enemy attacked forward positions on the west. Ensign Hiramoto, in charge of defending this front, led his troops in a charge but they were caught by flanking fire from machine-gun positions set up in the jungle. All died in action.

The enemy continued with fierce attacks through the afternoon, forcing successive withdrawals. From 4.30 p.m. there was a final strafing and bombing, followed by an enemy attack from the east which was repulsed.

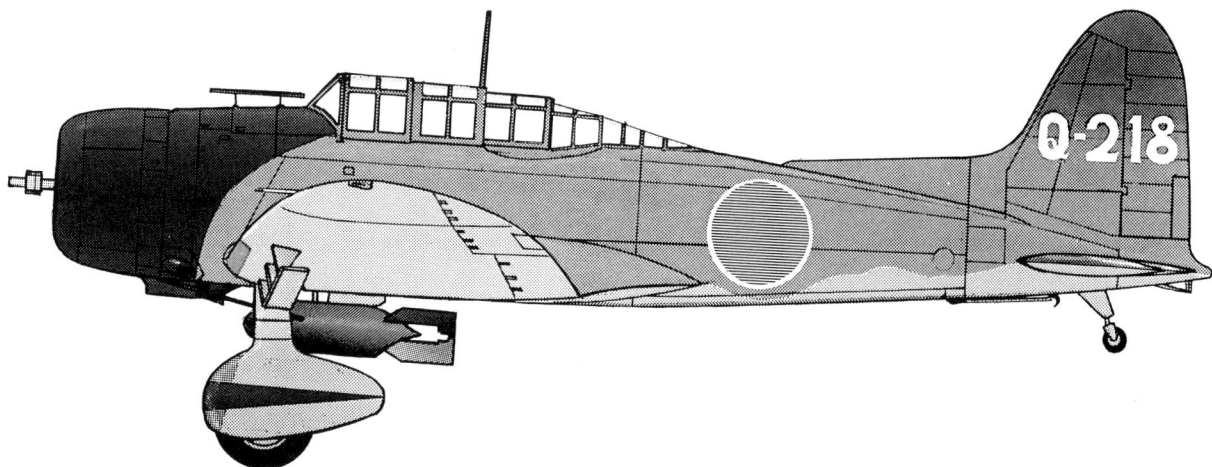

Aichi D3A1 Naval Type 99 Carrier-Bomber Model 11 (Code named 'Val') Q-218 of the 2nd Air Corps at Rabaul. On 2 September, a three-aircraft strike by Val dive-bombers, including Q-218, took off escorted by six Zeros to attack the Allied freighter Tasman *escorted by the new Australian destroyer HMAS* Arunta *at Milne Bay. Three hours after leaving the escort had to return but the Vals continued heading south but became lost.* (Dennis Newton)

That night, only snipers replied when flares were used to signal the warships. Evacuation was started in the order: wounded, construction unit and marines. It was completed by 2 a.m.. By dawn of 6 September, the remaining members of the 1900-man invasion force were on their way back to Rabaul.

There were still stragglers to try and recover, and on 6 September Arashi and Tatsuta were brought into the bay. A large enemy hospital ship and a transport vessel of 4-5000 tons were found anchored in the neighbourhood of Lau Lau Island. The transport was bombarded and severely damaged, while a patrol boat was shelled and sunk on the coast near Rabi. An ammunition dump ashore was shelled and set on fire. Signals were made to the coast but no survivors were discovered. [*The hospital ship Manunda was anchored in the bay. She was illuminated by Japanese searchlights but the Red Cross was respected, and she was not attacked. The motor vessel Anshun, the first supply ship to berth at Milne Bay since the battle began, was being unloaded at Gili Gili wharf when she was struck by a salvo of shells and afterwards capsized.*]

The following night Arashi and Tatsuta were again brought into action at night but, apart from the hospital ship, no transports or other ships were found. In these conditions enemy losses were not clearly known, about 400 reported by 3 Kure but they were considerable with obvious signs of efforts to reinforce and to evacuate wounded. Nor were there any stragglers to be found.

But stragglers and survivors there were and Australian troops spent the next weeks mopping up. There were several violent clashes.

One survivor was Enji Kakimoto. After ditching his Zero and escaping into the jungle, he eventually made contact with natives who handed him over to the Australians. To be a prisoner was to be in disgrace. During interrogation, he submitted to questioning but gave misleading responses. Eventually, he was interned at Cowra POW Camp in NSW where he joined the militant group of dissidents who organised the mass breakout of 5 August 1944. Afterwards, Kakimoto was found hanging from the rafter of his hut, having taken his own life. He was buried in the Japanese War Cemetery at Cowra.

What happened to the three-aircraft strike force led by Warrant Officer Ota Genga? Apparently unable to find the target and almost out of fuel, the Vals landed on the beach at Table Bay, between Abau and Milne Bay, on the southern coast of Papua. Genga and the others removed what they could, set fire to their machines and tried to reach their own lines over the mountains. Native trackers eventually led Allied soldiers to the six airmen who were killed in a couple of brief skirmishes. The three beached Vals were spotted from the air and an Australian party which reached the scene found that each plane had been badly burned around the cockpit area but was otherwise in good condition. The least damaged aircraft was later recovered for examination.

For the first time, a Japanese invading force had been thrown back into the sea and, because of this, the two-pronged thrust to capture Port Moresby had been frustrated. The Japanese landings had been undertaken by 2043 marines who suffered around 1150 casualties, of which some 750 were killed or went missing. Total Australian battle casualties were 377, of which 167 were killed. Also killed were 14 Americans. The bitter campaign back along the Kokoda trail would come next.

8

BOOMERANG

On 19 February 1942, just over ten weeks after the attack on Pearl Harbor, Japanese bombers appeared in the skies over Darwin for the first time. The defences were not ready. No RAAF aircraft was capable of defending the town or even of intercepting the bombers, so the raiders escaped unscathed Thus began a period of unprecedented danger for Australia — one which has never been equalled before or since. As well as the raid on Darwin, attacks followed on Broome, Port Hedland, Wyndham, Katherine, and Townsville, and these served to accelerate the development of Australia's first indigenous fighter plane, the Commonwealth Aircraft Corporation' Boomerang

The bombing of Pearl Harbor planted the seeds from which sprang the design concept for the first Australian-designed fighter. At the time, Mr T. W. R. Air was the Chief Engineer of the Commonwealth Aircraft Corporation (CAC), who noted in a later interview:

> From January 1937 I was Chief Engineer of the Commonwealth Corporation [now Hawker de Havilland Victoria] responsible directly to the manager, L. J. Wackett, for all technical aspects of our aircraft programs throughout the war years and on to 1952. This included the Boomerang fighter projects CA12 and CA14.
>
> The Japanese assault on Pearl Harbur was announced on the early radio news on Monday 8th December 1941 (Sunday 7th Hawaiian time), and as soon as I reached my office that morning I called a meeting with my senior design engineers, a team headed by Fred David during the war years. It was during discussions at that meeting that the concept of a new fighter aircraft was born.

The third production Boomerang A46-3. (CAC)

Head on view of a Boomerang. (Bill Air)

We had by then built up a most competent design and development team, starting with the development of the Wirraway Advanced Trainer based on the North American NA33 Basic Trainer. In all, 811 Wirraways were delivered to the Royal Australian Air Force, commencing early in 1939. Then followed the Wackett Trainer, and then the CA11 twin-engined Torpedo Bomber using the P&W R1830 engine which wasbe coming available from the CAC engine factory at Lidcombe, NSW...

During that second week in December, following Pearl Harbur, sketch plans were made and the concept of a single-engine fighter emerged, and by 24th December a Design Proposal was documented. By that time the seriousness of the Japanese threat in the Pacific area became clearer and on 20th January 1942 formal approval of the design was received from the RAAF and production design was able to proceed.

The man who created the preliminary 'sketch plans' — in fact a three-view engineering layout for the new aircraft — was a young graduate aeronautical engineer, Alan Bolton. He recalled:

The man who deserves almost all credit for the Boomerang and its concept was Fred David, the then Chief Design Engineer at CAC. This man was a brilliant engineer and aircraft designer, a gentleman and fine teacher and leader. The following are the circumstances, as I vividly recall them.

By the end of 1941, the Japanese were in full glorious flight, taking all before them on land, sea and in the air and there seemed nothing would stop them reaching Australia. The RAAF had no fighter except the Wirraway Trainer and these had been shot out of the sky at Rabaul. There was only one Hurricane Fighter on loan from the R.A.F. in our Air Force, the UK had its hands more than full and could not help and the U.S.A. was not yet in the war.

Fred David had been a very senior design engineer for Heinkel, had escaped Nazi persecution and gone to Japan, where he had again designed military aircraft, escaping once more to Australia, when Japan joined the Axis Powers. Things looked indeed black for Australia and no-one was more aware of this than Fred David.

Early in December 1941, (in fact, prior to Bill Air's meeting) I recall vividly going into the Design Office at CAC early one morning, to find myself alone with Mr David. He was sitting at his desk, next to mine, in a very emotional state. I sat down next to him and waited. After a short time, he said in his heavily accented German English —
'What can we do Mr Bolton — what can we do?'
I hadn't the foggiest idea, but waited. Then he said —
'Design a fighter, to fight the Zero and use the biggest engine we make and as much as possible of the Wirraway jigs and tools.'

Here was one man, a German, classified as an enemy alien and being forced (at that time) to report weekly to the police, calling for the immediate start on the design of a fighter for the belated defence of Australia, a responsibility, surely, of the Air Force and the government of the day, and I was being given the job, at age 23.

The original design proposal of 24 December 1941 emerged as follows:

- The objective was the production of a highly manoeuvrable aircraft which would be put into production with the least possible delay and flown within three months.
- Performance would be limited by the adoption of the R1830 engine, the installation design for which could be taken largely from that already available for the CA11 twin-engine bomber.
- There would be no time to examine options, and the design had to be fixed from the start for the whole first contract run. Wind-tunnel testing was to be limited to a single model, to confirm aerodynamic balance, and the best drag reduction obtainable by adjustment of external fairings.
- To advance quickly to production, materials should be selected from the large stocks already on hand for the Wirraway contracts, thus avoiding long delivery lead times. Any other requirements would be limited to those obtainable quickly from suppliers.
- To save tooling time the wing centre section should be patterned basically on the geometry of the Wirraway, and a duplicate jig would be built for this substantial

assembly. The Wirraway landing gear, already strengthened for this aircraft two years earlier, could be used unchanged. This item set the limit for all-up landing weight.

- The Wirraway tail units could be used. The fuselage would be of welded steel tube frame with a plywood fairing to avoid the time involved in development and structural testing of a metal monocoque design.
- Armament would be four .303 Browning guns, and two 20 mm Hispano cannon, mounted in the wings. It was realised that there were no supplies of the Hispano guns available and CAC would plan to manufacture the requirements for the Boomerang in a separate factory made available by the government.
- Protection for the pilot would be provided by a zirconium steel bulkhead, and bullet-proof fuel tank fitted in the fuselage.
- Though the program proposed was a hasty one, there would be a properly controlled -making process. All essential steps were subject to schedule check on a critical path analysis aimed at test flying the first aircraft in 100 days from the time production was commenced. In the event, the test program commenced after 98 days from issue of the first production order.

DESIGN AND DEVELOPMENT

All the foregoing preliminary concepts were set down, to accompany Alan Bolton's drawings for obtaining formal approval. However, Bolton recalled that their design implications required:

(1) Strengthened landing gear supports.
(2) Strengthened wing centre-section within the Wirraway contours and profile, permitting the use of the Wirraway wing centre-section assembly jigs.

(3) A for-shortened fuselage, with other structural changes, particularly to house the large fuselage fuel tank.
(4) A new engine mount.
(5) The design of a completely new outer wing, (with 'lamina flow' section for low drag, required wing loading and aspect ratio — all for highest possible performance and manoeuvrability) and to house the two Brownings and the 20 mm cannon and their magazines — also for strength to withstand an acceleration of 10g, including safety factor. The stressed skin outer wing and its stiffness requirements and the stiffness of the control systems were most important to achieve the strength and flying characteristics we wanted. A full-scale wing was built with all cutouts in skin and spars necessitated by the armaments and tested to destruction at the Aeronautical Laboratory at Fisherman's Bend under simulated aerodynamic load of 10g. I remember my wing showed signs of failure under test at about 9.0g, which was about ideal. It only required a small local strengthening placed at the weak point (at a cut-out), to easily exceed 10g in strength. I also completed extensive wing and controls static stiffness testing, to ensure compliance with these requirements.
(6) The tail units of the Wirraway could NOT be used without modification, though their profiles were originally made identical, allowing the use of the Wirraway jigs.

The selected powerplant, a Pratt & Whitney R-1830-S3C4-G Twin Wasp 14-cylinder radial, was the most powerful engine available in the country and necessitated the re-stressing of the forward fuselage for its installation. To cater for its correspondingly heavy fuel consumption, the aircraft's 45 Imperial gallon (204.6

CAC Wirraway. Speed was essential to develop and get the Boomerang into production quickly. To save tooling time the wing centre section of the Boomerang was patterned basically on the geometry of the Wirraway, the Wirraway landing gear was used unchanged and so was the tail unit. Materials were selected from the large stocks already on hand for Wirraway contracts, thus avoiding long delivery lead times. (Dennis Newton)

A flight of 2 OTU's CA-12 Boomerangs over Mildura aerodrome, just visible below. (Bill Air)

L) self-sealing wing-root fuel tanks were supplemented by a 70 Imperial gallon (318 L) self-sealing tank just behind the pilot's cockpit, and provision was made for the attachment of a flush-fitting plywood ventral drop tank of the same capacity if required.

Some interesting problems were encountered in providing the Boomerang with its two 20 mm Hispano cannons. Because Australia might soon be isolated, it was obvious that this weapon had to be manufactured locally, but there was no sample of the gun immediately available, and only a few handbooks which described it. Fortunately, through an extraordinary piece of luck, probably the only example in the country at the time was located. An RAAF sergeant, who'd had the cannon mounted on the back of his truck in the Western Desert, had brought it back to Australia from North Africa. Using this, and the handbooks, the CAC team was able to draught production drawings so that a local sub-contractor, Harland Engineering, could manufacture the weapon. At the same time, the team designed for it a spring-fed magazine and recoil-driven belt-feed booster.

According to Alan Bolton:
All resources were harnessed very quickly — Drawing Office, Engineering Department, Production Department., etc. It was decided to run the great risk of putting the fighter straight into production on an assembly line, before the prototype was anywhere near completion, so that when it flew under test, production models were already coming down the line.

The first CA12 Boomerang (A46-1) began flight trials on 29 May 1942, only sixteen weeks and three days after the approval for detail design to commence had been given. With CAC test pilot Ken Frewin at the controls, the machine completed taxi trials and flew for the first time. Frewin was delighted by the handling characteristics displayed by the aircraft and ,although its level speed was not particularly fast, its manoeuvrability and climb rate exceeded all expectations. Tests showed that the machine had a maximum speed of 296 mph (476 km/h) at 7600 feet (2,300 m), a range of 930 miles (1500 km) and a service ceiling of 29 000 feet (8850 m). It had no serious vices and therefore required no major modifications. During tests with a loaded weight of 7368 pounds (3.342 kg) it displayed an initial climb rate of 2940 ft/min (14.93 m/sec) which was better than the Curtiss P-40E, the Hurricane I or the Spitfire I. An altitude of 10 000 feet (3,048 m) could be reached in four minutes and 20 000 feet (6096 m) in 9.2 minutes.

An initial production order for 105 aircraft was given to the CAC factory at Fishermen's Bend, Victoria. A maximum effort was made to complete the first five Boomerangs as quickly as possible for RAAF evaluation. The first two featured an external oil cooler duct underneath the engine cowling, but this was incorporated into the cowling itself on later aircraft. An airscrew spinner was introduced to improve engine cooling during a sustained climb. The first Boomerangs arrived at Mildura for No. 2 OTU during the late summer of 1942.

COMPARISON TRIALS.

A series of mock combats between the first Boomerang, a P-40E and a P-39 Airacobra was arranged by the

Department of Air. The resulting report stated that the Australian fighter was more manoeuvrable than the P-40 at 10 000 feet, could turn inside it and that the speed advantage of the American fighter was not enough to allow its pilot to dictate the type of combat. Although the P-40 was capable of out-diving the Boomerang, the latter's better pull-out and superior climb resulted in the two aircraft being level at the apex of their ensuing zoom. Once combat was joined, the P-40 proved unable to evade the Boomerang and could not break off the action except by a sustained dive.

The P-39 enjoyed a greater speed advantage over the Boomerang and its much better climb-and-dive capability initially allowed the Airacobra pilot to dictate the terms of combat. However, the Boomerang proved it could always outmanoeuvre its opponent at the same height in concentric attack.

TEETHING TROUBLES

At Mildura, No. 2 OTU began to encounter teething problems which stemmed from the speed with which the fighter had been evolved. In some aircraft the backplate of the airscrew spinner revealed cracks, so the spinners were removed. This had a detrimental effect on performance because cylinder head temperatures could only be kept within the specified limits by flying with the cooling gills partly open. The problem was eventually corrected by the provision of a heavier gauge backplate.

The guns showed a tendency to freeze at altitude. This was eventually overcome by diverting hot air from the exhaust system to the wing gun bays.

It was necessary to reposition the reflector sight because its original location obliged the pilot to sit bolt upright, in a posture which increased the possibility of him blacking out while sighting and shooting. It was also a hazard in the event of a forced landing.

When they were hot, the brakes tended to lose their effectiveness and so needed modification.

The locating pins of the ventral drop tank had to be strengthened to retain the tank in the correct position. Prior to this the tanks on some aircraft had shifted 90 degrees in mid-flight.

Besides these teething problems, inexperienced pilots at Mildura were encountering difficulties while landing the fighter and several aircraft were damaged as a result of ground loops. An investigation revealed that the majority of the landing accidents were occurring on cambered runways during crosswinds. The Boomerang, with its short wheelbase and substantial side area, had a tendency to swing if handled clumsily and this, coupled with the other factors, accounted for the high accident rate. Experienced pilots found that the swing could be counterbalanced by a combination of brakes and rudder accompanied by a short burst of power to increase rudder control. Once this procedure was adopted, the landing accident rate was reduced to a normal level.

COMBAT

The first unit to operate Boomerangs was 84 Squadron. Early in 1943, after a short period of working up, this unit, under the command of S/Ldr. N. Ford, was despatched to Horn Island, off the Cape York Peninsula,

CA-12 Boomerangs from the first production batch. (Bill Air)

from where it flew across the Torres Strait to provide standing patrols over the Allied base under construction at Merauke, New Guinea, some 200 miles away.

Boomerangs made their first interception of enemy aircraft on 16 May 1943, when two planes of 84 Squadron flown by F/O R. W. Johnstone and Sgt. F. J. Stammer, on patrol over Merauke, met three Mitsubishi G4M 'Betty' bombers and attacked. The guns of one Boomerang refused to fire because of an electrical fault but the other managed to deliver a short burst from about 250 yards (230 m) without any obvious effect before the Bettys melted into cloud cover and escaped. Return fire from the bombers was ineffective.

The squadron kept up its standing patrols during June, July and August, especially during the middle of the day when the airfield was most vulnerable. It was a long trip from Horn Island and the Boomerangs could only stay for about an hour because of their limited range. In July, a squadron of RAAF P-40 Kittyhawks arrived at Merauke to provide permanent fighter defence.

On 9 September a newly installed radar station at Cape Kombies detected an enemy force of sixteen bombers escorted by as many fighters heading for Merauke at 20 000 feet (6100 m). Fourteen Kittyhawks of. 86 Squadron and four Boomerangs of 84 Squadron took off to intercept. The Kittyhawks shot down three enemy aircraft without loss, although only four were able to fire their guns, but the Boomerangs did not manage to reach the battle on time. Meanwhile, the Bettys bombed the airfield, causing only minor damage to installations but destroying a Boomerang on the ground.

Two other squadrons also received Boomerangs at this stage. These were 83 Squadron, which had been initially formed with a few Bell P-39 Airacobras supplied by the USAAF, and 85 Squadron which had initially operated the Brewster Buffalo. These two units were despatched to Gove, near Millingimbi in the Northern Territory, and Pearce, WA. However, because they were retained for local defence duties on the mainland, these squadrons had no real chance to meet the Japanese in the air.

The leading Australian fighter ace, Group Captain Clive 'Killer' Caldwell, who was in charge of Darwin's Spitfire wing, was asked to test the Boomerang. He was not impressed with its performance as an interceptor. In his trials, he found that it could not sustain a battle climb because of overheating by the time it reached 11 000 ft (3350 m) where he had to open the gills and ease off the throttle to cool it down. Upon resuming the battle climb, the same thing occurred after another 4000 or 5000 ft and the cooling procedure had to be carried out again, and so it went on...

Combat exercises with six B-25 Mitchells of the Dutch No. 18 Squadron, RAAF, at 12 000 feet over Canberra revealed that the speedy Mitchells were too fast for Caldwell's three intercepting Boomerangs.

Although its all-round performance was such that it was inferior to that of the standard Japanese fighters such as the Mitsubishi A6M Zero or Nakajima Ki-43 Oscar, as a stop-gap measure it could have been effective as a last line of defence (the role for which it was envisaged) against the less well armoured Japanese bombers had the necessity arisen. The speed at which the Boomerang was

Boomerang A46-163 was from the second batch ordered by the RAAF. Because of minor modifications, this new order was given the designation CA-13. (Bill Air)

The experimental CA-14 Boomerang A46-1001, port side showing the huge air-intake blister. (Bill Air)

Experimental CA-14 Boomerang A46-1001 again, starboard side. (Bill Air)

designed and built, with such limited resources available, was a considerable achievement in itself and the aircraft became a symbol of Australian defiance. Fortunately for Australia, the flow of American equipment was never interrupted and, instead of being thrown into the fray against superior-performance enemy aircraft, the tough, tubby little Boomerang found its role changed to one for which it was superbly suited — army cooperation.

PROGRESSIVE IMPROVEMENT

By June 1943, CAC had completed the initial order for 105 CA12 Boomerangs (A46-1 to -105), and commenced production of a second batch of 95 aircraft (A46-106 to -200) which incorporated the various minor modifications made in the light of initial service experience.

This new order received the designation CA13 and modifications included:

- replacement of the light alloy seat by one made from laminated timber;
- replacement of fabric by light alloy for the skinning of the ailerons;
- introduction of wooden wingtips;
- fitting of Beaufort-type flame-damper exhaust tubes;
- replacement of the hydraulic cocking system for the guns by a system in which the guns were cocked mechanically before take-off; and
- introduction of an external rear view mirror.

While production of the CA13 was proceeding, CAC initiated a development program aimed at improving high-altitude performance. An experimental aircraft was built as the CA14 (A46-1001), utilising modified production components. The S3C4-G Twin Wasp offered its best performance with high-speed blower at 12 500 feet (3800 m), so a General Electric turbo-supercharger was installed in the rear fuselage. The location of the turbo- supercharger intake on the port side of the rear fuselage resulted in trim problems and some tailplane buffeting, but a gain in speed in the order of 20 per cent was obtained at altitude. This

arrangement was intended as a quick way to get the turbo-supercharger into the air, for proving the complex system and to allow flight performance testing and aerodynamic refinement while the CA14A engine and higher tech fan and air intake cowl were designed and built.

The CA14 and CA14A were the same aeroplane. The latter modification merely required the removal of the port-side intake blister assembly and the fitting of the new modified engine and cowl and new ducting. Also replaced were the fin and rudder with a new larger area. The production model would also have had a retracting tailwheel. Bill Air described the work:

The experimental aircraft CA14A, detached from the Boomerang production line was the subject of a series of design changes aimed at improving the altitude performance. With the active encouragement of General George, then commanding the 5th US Army Air Force, a General Electric Model B-12 turbo-supercharger was installed. This was taken from an unserviceable Liberator Bomber and flown especially to Melbourne for us.

The experimental development of the CA14A aircraft proceeded in two stages. The turbo-supercharger was inset on the right-hand side behind the cockpit and fuselage tank area and the exhaust pipe extended back to this position. The intercooler was installed and fed with cooling air from a large external scoop on the left side of the aircraft. To improve engine cooling the normal intercylinder baffles were replaced with a closer fitting system, and the cooling flaps improved considerably.

We decided to test the aircraft with this installation to get some idea of the performance with the engine boosted by the turbo Supercharger. This proved greater than anticipated, but at altitude was limited by cooling for the P&W radial engine.

The next step was to mount a cooling fan driven by a 3:1 ratio gear box attached to the main engine reduction gear housing with a redesigned propeller shaft. This system was later used on the German Fw 190 fighter very successfully and appeared before the end of the war in Europe. To improve directional stability the fin and rudder were enlarged with a flat top which distinguished this aircraft from the standard Boomerang.

It would have been essential to redesign the aircraft to incorporate a pressurised cockpit if this were to be taken further. Performance tests were done and the aircraft flown to 45 000 feet [13 700 m] on the limited oxygen system then available to us.

With hundreds of high-altitude American aircraft arriving, there seemed little to be gained in further development effort and the aircraft, then numbered A46/1000, was delivered to the RAAF for experimental flying.

Alan Bolton recalled:
The CA14 prototype flew for many years for the Meteorological Bureau, taking high altitude weather observations, up to about 50 000 feet [15 200 m], which was high in those days. The aircraft's most unusual feature was a fan, rotating at three times propeller speed in the nose of the more streamlined cowl. This and other ducting design features, provided maximum 'head' for engine aspiration, engine and turbo-supercharger cooling and cooling for the inter-cooling air. Maximum speed was at the critical altitude of 35 000 feet [1 ,000 m] and the production model would have had a performance higher than all contemporaries until the advent of the Mosquito.

One other Boomerang model left the Fishermen's Bend factory before the last example of this aircraft was completed in January 1945. This was the CA19 of which 49 (A46-201 to-249) were built. Changes to the first few were relatively minor, being largely confined to standardisation of Dunlop eight-ply tyres and the omission of previously provided jacking joints, but an F24 vertical camera for tactical reconnaissance was installed into the rear fuselage of the eleventh CA19 (A46-211) on the assembly line and this became standard equipment for all subsequent aircraft.

ARMY COOPERATION

Over the kunai and jungle of New Guinea, the Boomerangs began to set new standards for this type of work. Flying in pairs, they led bomber formations to specific pinpoint targets and guided artillery fire by dropping smoke bombs as markers and strafing with tracer bullets. Among the mountains and valleys of the Finisterre Range, pilots flew by the seat of their pants, using the amazing nimbleness of their planes to duck in and out of valleys, swoop down on Japanese artillery positions and troop concentrations and finally zoom up and away to evade anti-aircraft fire and call up a formation of Kittyhawks which they would then lead to the target.

Besides enemy anti-aircraft fire, low flying over rugged mountainous terrain and possible enemy aircraft, another problem faced by Boomerang pilots was the fact that, under combat conditions, their aircraft could be mistaken for Zeros. At least two Boomerangs of. 4 Squadron, , were shot down by American fighters and two others were lost because of ground fire. One was chased from Lae to Salamaua by an aggressive P-38 Lightning. It made a forced landing on the airstrip at Salamaua but crashed into a ditch and had to be written off. The pilot escaped.

On another occasion, a Boomerang belonging to 4 Squadron was shot down by American gunners expecting a Japanese raid while it was flying a reconnaissance sortie over Salamaua. This time the pilot was killed.

In the middle of 1944, with the redeployment of Allied forces, II Australian Corps took the place of the XIV American Corps on Bougainville. In the air, the Australians were assigned support in the form of the New Zealand Air Task force under the command of G/Capt

A line up of Boomerangs on Bougainville in 1945. (George Hunt)

CA-14A Boomerang featuring a modified tail. (Bill Air)

CA-12 Boomerang A46-30 once played the role of the Lady Southern Cross *in the film* Smithy, *on display in the Australian War Memorial, Canberra.* (Dennis Newton)

G. N. Roberts. Since the New Zealanders had no army cooperation organisation, the RAAF supplied an army co-op wing included in which was No. 5 Squadron equipped with eighteen Boomerangs and four Wirraways.

The problem of aircraft recognition persisted and when a Boomerang met RNZAF Corsairs during the campaign, the pre-arranged signal was for the Boomerang to lower its undercarriage so the New Zealanders would not mistake it for a Zero. Nevertheless, the familiar pattern of operations was repeated and an excellent working relationship soon developed, born out of mutual respect for each other's ability. Having located a target, the Boomerang pilot would lead his flight of Corsair fighter-bombers to the spot and, after marking it, he would then circle nearby, observing the bombing and calling corrections over the radio. According to G/Capt. Roberts: The excellent pinpointing by the Boomerangs has made the job a great deal easier and much more effective, while the accuracy of our bombing has improved immeasurably.

END OF THE LINE

When production of the Boomerang ceased a total of 250 had been delivered to the RAAF from CAC's Fishermen's Bend factory and this stop-gap fighter had earned for itself an honourable place in the history of Australian aviation. Bill Air summed up:

It was always realised that the Boomerang would have inevitable performance limitations with the 1200 hp P&W engine, the only one available at the time. The most serious lack was high-altitude climb. Some improvement was later obtained when the Lidcombe factory was able to offer a higher ratio supercharger on the R1830 engine... Contrary to the story put around at a later date, this was no 'Panic' program. There was an understandable delay of a few weeks before the original authorisation was given to us which enabled work to proceed, but this worked to our advantage giving time for the design team to think over our attack. (During this time, Alan Bolton continued the development of the design, working unofficially and on his own.) We realised time was of the utmost importance, and once the decks were cleared, the whole project went ahead in a most organized fashion.

After the war, in accordance with the Australian government's policy, the Boomerangs were sold for salvage and ended up as scrap or were melted down. Only one aircraft survived intact. This was Boomerang A46-30, a CA12 which had been used on patrol duties by. 85 Squadron in Western Australia. It was saved from the melting pot because, towards the end of 1945, it was selected to feature in the film Smithy, suitably painted as the Lady Southern Cross, Kingsford Smith's Lockheed Altair, VH-USB. Afterwards it was turned over to the Australian Air League and left at Blacktown, where it deteriorated into a state of disrepair and decay over almost 20 years. The Australian Restoration Group found it and in 1966 arrangements were made through a group member, W/Cdr Keith Isaacs, AFC, to have it returned to the RAAF and transported to Williamstown for restoration. This was duly carried out and for several years it was mounted as a gate guardian at the RAAF base. The effects of weather began to take hold but fortunately it was realised that, because of its rarity, the plane should be protected. Itwas moved under cover to Point Cook.and was llateracquired by the Australian War Memorial. At the time of writing it was on display in the AWM's Aircraft Hall.

A number of enthusiasts have managed to recover various parts of the indigenous fighter from several areas in New Guinea and northern Australia and are in the process of using these to restore and rebuild some examples for display.

CAC PROJECT TEAM INVOLVED IN DESIGNING THE BOOMERANG

This team covered the CA12 and CA14 projects.

Lawrence Wackett — General Manager

Bill Air — Chief Engineer responsible directly to General Manager

Fred David — Chief Design Engineer, head of the project team.

Alan Bolton — Boomerang design engineer, overall design responsibilityand stressing and detail of outer wings, tail surfaces, tailwheel, engine mount, turbo-supercharger installation and mountings, inter-cooler installation and all ducting; structural strength and stiffness testing, etc.

Ian Fleming — Flight Testing and aerodynamics

Joe Solvey — Detail wing aerodynamics

Doug Humphries — Wing Centre-section and under-carriage stressing

Colin Bellwood — CA14A engine modification, fan, spinner and cowl

Lionel Stern — Design copy and production of 20 mm Hispano cannon

Ernie Jones — Chief Draftsman

Morrie Lodge — Project Engineer

CA12 BOOMERANG SPECIFICATIONS

POWER PLANT: One Pratt & Whitney R-1830-S3C4-G Twin Wasp 14-cylinder two-row radial air-cooled engine rated at 1200 hp at 2700 rpm for take-off, military ratings of 1200 hp at 4900 ft (1494 m) and 1050 hp at 13 100 ft (3993 m) for five minutes, and normal rated output of 1100 hp at 2550 rpm at 6200 ft (1890 m) and 1,000 hp at 12 500 ft (3800 m). Hamilton Standard Series 3E 50 three-bladed constant-speed airscrew of 11 ft 0 in (3.35 m) diameter.

ARMAMENT: Four 0.303 in (7.7 mm) Browning machin- guns with 1000 rpg and two 20 mm Hispano cannon with 60 rpg.

WEIGHTS: Manufacturer's empty, 5373 lb (2437 kg); normal loaded, 7699 lb (3492 kg); maximum overload, 8249 lb (3,742 kg).

PERFORMANCE:
Max. speed (at 7368 lb/3342 kg): 302 mph (486 km/h) at 7400 ft (2250 m),
305 mph (491 km/h) at 15 500 ft (4700 m);
Max. permissible dive speed: 410 mph (660 km/h);
Recommended climb speed: 140 mph (225 km/h) between sea level and 7000 ft (2134 m);
Stalling speed (engine off): 92 mph (148 km/h) with undercarriage and flaps up, 76 mph (122 km/h) with undercarriage and flaps down (engine at 2000 rpm), 79 mph (127 km/h) with undercarriage and flaps up, 69 mph (111 km/h) with undercarriage and flaps down;
Initial climb rate (at 7368 lb/3342 kg): 2940 ft/min (14.93 m/sec), (at 7699 lb/3492 kg), 2150 ft/min (10.92 m/sec);
Service ceiling, 34 000 ft (10 363 m);
Normal range: 930 mls (1 500 km) at 190 mph (306 km/h) at 15 000 ft (4570 m);
Max. range with 70 Imp gal (318 L) drop tank: 1600 mls (2575 km) at 175 mph (282 km/h) at 10 000 ft (3050 m).
Max. endurance: 4.9 hours.

DIMENSIONS:
Span: 36 ft 0 in (10.97 m);
Length: 25 ft 6 in (7.77 m);
Height (tail down): 9 ft 7 in (2.92 m);
Wing area: 225 sq ft (20.90 m).

For illustration of Boomerang, Commonwealth CA-13 , see page 8.

9

LOW-LEVEL SPECIALIST

In September 1939, three weeks after the outbreak of war with Germany, the UK had put forward a plan for a scheme in which Canada, Australia and New Zealand would be jointly involved in the training of pilots and aircrew. After a conference in Canada the following month, the four countries adopted the proposal which became the Empire Air Training Scheme (EATS), later the British Commonwealth Training Scheme. Southern Rhodesia (now Zimbabwe) also entered the scheme. On 25 December 1940, a group of twelve officers and 23 sergeant pilots, all Australians, arrived in England. These men had left Australia the previous July and completed their flying training at the Royal Canadian Air Force's No. 2 Service Flying Training School at Uplands near Ottawa, Canada. They were the first of a multitude who were trained under the EATS. It was hoped that 15 946 aircrew of all categories could be trained by 1 March 1943. This figure was later increased to 48 948 but it was never reached; when the scheme ended on 31 March 1945 a total of 41 248 men had completed their training.

During 1941 the Australian presence in the air war over Europe and the Middle East increased dramatically. Under the EATS between April and December around 3000 aircrew and 1500 ground staff reached England. Three fighter squadrons (452, 456 and 457) and three bomber squadrons (455, 458 and 460) were formed in the UK; two fighter squadrons (450 and 451) were formed in the Middle East, where 3 Squadron RAAF was already operational; one squadron (453) was created in Malaya. By the beginning of 1943 there were two RAAF squadrons and fourteen Australian EATS squadrons in the Middle East and UK. This had increased in November to two RAAF squadrons and fifteen Australian EATS squadrons in the Mediterranean and UK, plus two Australian EATS squadrons in the Pacific operating with normal RAAF units. At the same time, many Australians were scattered throughout RAF squadrons, mainly in Bomber Command and also in Coastal Command.

This is the story of one EATS volunteer. In the words of French air ace Pierre Clostermann, DSO, DFC, he
was '...an incredible Australian...' who '...feared neither God nor the Devil...'

Between October 1968 and October 1969, Group Captain J. I. (Bay) Adams, DFC, AFC, commanded the RAAF Contingent at Vung Tau, South Vietnam. In his end of tour report, he warned of the vulnerability of helicopters in low-level operations: 'even with a limited amount of light anti-aircraft fire in any area these helicopters would not survive without a great deal of tactical fighter escort... I personally believe that in any future wars helicopter operations will be largely restricted to secure areas.'

The dangers of anti-aircraft fire were something Bay Adams knew about from first-hand experience...

Bay Adams in flying gear. (Bay Adams)

John Irwin Adams was born on 6 December 1922, at Cheltenham, Victoria. He was the second youngest of the family and had three brothers and two sisters. While he was still an infant, when they and their friends wanted to go swimming they would tell him that they were 'going to the bay' and he would keep repeating 'bay... bay...' until they took him. Eventually they just called him 'Bay'. The nickname is even entered on some official school rolls and has stayed with him ever since. After primary school he received his secondary education at Malvern Grammar School and then commenced work as a clerk for a real estate agent.

Meanwhile, World War IIhad erupted and on 7 November 1941, a month before his nineteenth birthday, Bay Adams joined the RAAF. For initial training he was sent to Victor Harbour and afterwards to Parafield, South Australia, for elementary flying. Late in June 1942 he found himself being shipped out to Canada. Two months later he was flying Harvards at a SFTS. Apparently he flew them too well because, instead of being posted to England for operational flying after training, he was made an instructor, much against his own wishes. This was to remain his occupation for almost two years but finally, after numerous requests, he was finally sent to fly Hawker Hurricanes at an OTU near Quebec and then on to England where he arrived on April Fool's Day, 1944.

After a refresher course on Spitfires, W/O Bay Adams was posted to No.3 Squadron, RAF, stationed at Newchurch. The squadron's commanding officer at that stage was S/Ldr A. S. Dredge, AFC, who had flown as a sergeant pilot in the Battle of Britain. Bay found that the unit contained a number of Australians, including W/O Roy Torpy of Marrickville, NSW; P/O Ron 'Scratch' Adcock of Mosman, NSW; F/Lt Bruce McKenzie of Launceston, Tasmania; and P/O Bert Bailey of Booborowie, SA.

No.3 Squadron had a long history and was one of the original squadrons in the Royal Flying Corps having been formed at Larkhill on 13 May 1912. More recently, during February-March 1944, together with 486 (New Zealand) Squadron, it had received the first Hawker Tempest Vs. The third member of the Newchurch Wing (150 Wing) was 56 Squadron, which had traded its Spitfire IXs for Tempests in June. In overall command was W/Cdr. Roland Beamont, DSO, DFC and Bar.

In the Hawker Tempest V, the RAF had the fastest, low to medium altitude fighter available. Powered by a 2200 hp Napier Sabre IIB, 24 cylinder, liquid-cooled engine, this machine had a maximum speed of 392 mph (630 km/h) at sea level, 416 mph (670 km/h) at 4600 feet (1400 m) and 430 mph (690 km/h) at 17 000 feet (5180 m). It could climb to 10 000 feet (3,050 m) in 2.7 minutes, to 20 000 feet in 6.1 minutes and had a service ceiling of 36, feet. In essence, it was an aerodynamically refined version of the earlier Hawker Typhoon powered by a similar engine. During fast dives, the Typhoon used to experience sudden and sharp increases in drag accompanied by changes in aerodynamic characteristics which caused serious nose heaviness and pitching. As early as 1940, Sydney Camm, Hawker's chief designer, commenced preliminary work on the development of a thinner, high-speed aerofoil to delay the onset of compressibility. Because of its thinness, this new wing was not able to house a comparable amount of fuel and, in order to maintain a suitable range, it was found necessary to install a large fuel tank within the lengthened fuselage. Six prototypes were built with different engines. As it turned out only the Tempest II and Tempest V reached quantity production. Because of more detailed modifications required for fitting the 2520 hp Bristol Centaurus radial, air-cooled engine to the Tempest's fuselage, the Mk II version did not see service until after the war, so the Tempest V preceded it into RAF squadrons. It was the only variant to be employed on wartime operations.

Tempests met enemy aircraft in combat for the first time two days after D-Day in an engagement during which three Messerschmitt Bf 109Gs were shot down without loss but it was as a countermeasure against V-1 flying bombs that Tempests made their greatest early impact. When these 'malignant robots' began coming across the Channel in June, 3 Squadron was diverted from its roll of an intruder fighter squadron to deal with them. The first was shot down on 16 June and by the end of that same day eleven had been destroyed. July proved to be a very busy month, with 146 destroyed.

Powered by a pulse jet, these 'doodlebugs' flew between 3000 and 5100 feet (900-1550 m) at speeds varying between 320 and 400 mph (515-640 km/h) and were controlled by servo-gyroscopes which became locked in one desired position as soon as the missile was launched on its predetermined course. It could not be directed against pinpoint targets and was only really suitable for deployment against larger, sprawling urban areas. The British quickly established belts of anti-aircraft guns (later equipped with radar proximity fuses), zones patrolled by fighter aircraft and, as a final barrier, zones of anti-aircraft barrage balloons. Of the aircraft employed, except for a few Spitfire XIIs, Spitfire XIVs and P-51 Mustangs with uprated engines, the Tempests were the only ones with enough speed to be able to overhaul the bombs in level flight.

Although the V-1s were pilotless and flew straight and level, attacking them could be quite a dangerous affair. Coming up from behind the RAF pilots found that they had a target only three feet (90 cm) in diameter across the fuselage with wings only eight inches (20 cm) thick. In spite of their successes they often missed the target.

Firing from 400 yards was useless because of the spread harmonisation pattern of their cannons according to standard Fighter Command practice. If a pilot closed in to 200 yards the resulting explosion from the detonation of the warhead would more than likely blow the attacker out of the air or inflict crippling damage to his plane. Cockpit air vents had to be closed during an attack because more than one airman had his arms scorched by flames from disintegrating V-1s searing back through the openings. The best procedure was to point harmonise the cannon to a distance of 300 yards and trust to the accuracy of the pilot's shooting. With this sort of practical application and practice, squadron marksmanship improved dramatically and more bombs were destroyed. Although the Germans launched flying bombs against England for the rest of 1944, and a few in 1945, the real threat posed by these weapons was virtually over by the middle of August 1944, as far as the Tempests were concerned because of the high degree of accuracy of the radar- controlled AA guns. Towards the end of this month, Tempest pilots on anti-diver patrols, as they were called, often intercepted V-1s only to see them shot down by ground fire before they could attack.

During August, Bay Adams was engaged in numerous anti-diver patrols. At 1.30 p.m. on 24 August, while flying as No. 2 to F/O D. J. Butcher, four miles north of Rye, he intercepted and shot down his first flying bomb. Four days later, over the same area, he closed in and destroyed his second, but this time he came too close. His plane was engulfed by the explosion and struck by debris. After flying through it into clear sky, he discovered that he had lost part of his wingtip but the Tempest was still under control and he was able to land without difficulty back at Newchurch. On the 30th, in the squadron's Operations Record Book it was noted, 'Usual diver patrols today but little diver activity'. The doodlebugs were becoming exceedingly rare but at 1.45 p.m. on the 31st, Bay shared in the destruction of a third.

With the -.1 menace well under control it was time for the Tempest squadrons to return to their original role, that of air support over ground troops with the 2nd Tactical Air Force (TAF). Late in September 3 Squadron together with 56 Squadron, moved to Mutlask for five days and from there proceeded to the Continent to B-60 Grimbergen airfield, six miles north-east of Brussels. By doing so they became part of 122 Wing.

Operations began immediately flying over the Arnhem and Nijmegen areas where Allied units of the British 2nd Army were involved in heavy fighting to hold the recently captured Nijmegen bridge. It was here that Bay Adams encountered, and learned of the accuracy of, German anti-aircraft fire for the first time. Before the first day was over 3 Squadron had lost one aircraft to flak. By now the Luftwaffe had been dominated by Allied air supremacy so that opportunities for air-to-air combat did not come all that often. Two days later, on 1 October, the three squadrons (3, 56 and 468) of 122 Wing — 468 Squadron had arrived at Grimbergen on 30 September — moved to airfield B-80 at Volkel in Holland. One aircraft was shot down by flak en route over the Nijmegen pocket north-west of Eindhoven. The wing's new home was found to be in a very battered condition owing to American bombing and to demolition work carried out by the retreating Germans. Nevertheless, operations were carried out immediately. The Tempests were employed on patrols over the forward positions, on armed reconnaissance sorties and sometimes on patrols to catch the highly elusive Messerschmitt Me 262 jet fighters. Especially for this last task, a pair of Tempests was kept at constant readiness, the pilots strapped in and ready to take off as soon as an Me 262 was reported crossing the lines. On 7 October two more Tempest units (80 and 274)

V1 Flying Bomb. These were also known as 'doodle bugs' and more sinisterly as 'malignant robots. (IWM)

joined 122 Wing at Volkel, bringing its strength up to five squadrons.

Soon there was an additional assignment — that of paralysing Germany's railway system from the Rhine to Berlin through a systematic, constant air attack on trains. The procedure for attacking trains, and indeed for any ground strike, was to dive in for a single surprise attack, sweep through and disengage behind trees wherever possible. Unless the target was especially vital there was to be no second run,as the anti-aircraft defences would obviously be better prepared and there was no sense in giving them a second chance.

On 12 October, W/Cdr Beamont led No. 3 Squadron down to strafe an exceptionally long troop train travelling between Nijmegen and Vocholt. As they came in the locomotive screeched to a halt. Light flak from a gun position immediately behind the engine greeted the Tempests as they raked the target from stem to stern. Soldiers could be seen jumping out of doorways and windows of the slowing carriages and throwing themselves flat onto the grass. The flak position was soon silenced. Seconds later the Tempests had swept out of range. In spite of all the usual procedure, Beamont decided that the target was important enough for a second strafing run. As the Tempests swept back, exhausting their ammunition on the hapless train, they encountered light machine-gun and small-arms fire but none of the planes was hit. Against his own rules, Beaumont decided to turn back and inspect the damage. As he made his third run over the train the gun on the flak truck opened fire at point-blank range. Someone had climbed back on board to man the gun. He did not feel any hits but after reforming, his number two reported that his plane was trailing smoke. Beamont was obliged to crash land in German territory where he was swiftly taken prisoner. He remained in captivity until the end of the war.

Flak was not the only danger. Low-level operations were hazardous at any time with the ever-present possibility of striking objects such as trees, high power wires, buildings and other obstacles. Often the Tempests were struck by exploding debris from their own targets. On one occasion while conducting a rocket attack on a train, Bay Adams saw it explode in a huge fireball showering debris everywhere. One of its wheel and axle assemblies hurtled up into the air, narrowly missing his plane it as it cartwheeled past.

Patrols and ground sweeps continued through November but, as end of the year approached, operations became seriously hampered by deteriorating weather conditions. With the AlliedTAF becoming more and more inactive because of this, the Germans under Field Marshal Gerd von Rundstedt chose 16 December to launch their surprise counter-attack into the Ardennes, the weakest sector of the Allied lines. The assault swept all before it under a secure blanket of low cloud which prevented the Allies flying in any strength, but on the 23rd the weather cleared. Rocket-firing Hawker Typhoons, Spitfires and Tempests, and USAF P-47 Thunderbolts and P-51 Mustangs, were concentrated against the German armour which, in the desperate attempt to break through, had to operate in the open in full daylight. The Germans were completely routed.

Meanwhile the Luftwaffe, which had been carefully conserving its strength, launched a massive assault against Allied airfields in the early hours of New Year's Day, 1945. As luck would have it, B-80 Volkel was one of the few airfields not attacked. In any case, many of 122 Wing's Tempests were already in the air on early-morning patrols and, upon being recalled, intercepted several of the German planes. No. 3 Squadron, which had lost one Tempest to flak while on patrol, was able to claim two Messerschmitt Bf 109s destroyed.

During February the Canadian 1st Army and the British 2nd Army commenced an all-out assault to close up to the Rhine. As the fighting approached the German border the Luftwaffe began to make more frequent appearances in a desperate last-ditch effort. No. 122 Wing also suffered heavy losses to flak, which was becoming increasingly intense and accurate. From its arrival on the Continent in September 1944 to the end of January 1945, 26 Tempests were lost in action, eight of them in aerial combat and the rest to anti-aircraft fire. In February this figure more than doubled, with 28 lost in as many days, eight of which belonged to 3 Squadron, all victims of flak. On 8 February the squadron lost its commanding officer, S/Ldr K.F. Thiele, DSO, DFC and Bar, shot down by ground fire while strafing a train. On the credit side, the wing had accounted for the record total of 484 locomotives, 32 enemy aircraft, 485 vehicles, 118 barges and 650 railway trucks.

On 28 March six Tempests from 274 Squadron on a sweep over Hamm-Munster-Osmabrick strafing locomotives and trucks encountered 40 Focke-Wulf Fw 190s. It was obvious that the regularity of the Tempest's patrols to catch trains had attracted this Luftwaffe ambush. Two Tempests were shot down in the clash, causing the death of S/Ldr D. C. Fairbanks, DFC and two Bars, an American serving in the RAF who had been one of the 2nd TAF's most successful pilots. Immediately after this, 122 Wing was ordered not to penetrate enemy territory in formations less than sixteen strong and under no circumstances was it to engage in further ground attack sorties. This caused an abrupt halt to the wing's personal war against the German railway.

No. 3 Squadron flew back to the United Kingdom on 1 April to attend an armament practice camp at Warmwell.

The formidable long-nose Focke-Wulf Fw 190D-9, the type shot down by Bay Adams on 30 April 1945. (MAP)

It returned to the Continent to B-112 Hopsten on the 17th, and nine days later moved to B-152 Fassberg.

A new arrival in the squadron was the flamboyant Free French ace F/Lt Pierre Clostermann, who had been posted from 56 Squadron. In The Big Show, written after the war, Clostermann graphically captured the nature of the times, describing many of the Tempests' most hair-raising exploits. He gave a vivid account of a costly attack made on the German airfield at Schwerin late in April. When the Flying Order was put up those pilots chosen 'hadn't shown any marked enthusiasm, except Bay Adams, the Australian member of the party, who was quite imperturbable and feared neither God nor the Devil.' According to Bay's recollection, he was far from being 'imperturbable'. He was scared stiff of what lay ahead but chose to cover his nerves by wisecracking and joking to ease the tension. Clostermann went on to relate how eight Tempests dived into an inferno of 20 mm and 37 mm flak and only two emerged. After completing his run the Frenchman looked back to see a single Tempest (Bay's) climbing in zigzags with flak bursting in hot pursuit just behind it. He and Bay were apparently the only survivors.

At 9 a.m. on 30 April, Bay was flying as Red 3 in a formation of Tempests which was vectored onto five enemy aircraft in the Lauremberg area. There were two of the formidable long-nose Fw 190Ds and three Messerschmitt Bf 109s flying on the same level at 3500 feet (1050 m). The three Messerschmitts reacted quickly and zoomed up into the cloud layer at 4000 feet (1200 m). Together with Red 1, Bay closed in on the two

Focke-Wulfs and at a range of 500 yards he fired a two-second burst from his four 20 mm cannon and saw strikes on his selected target. The stricken machine dived into low cloud but Bay, taking full advantage of this rare opportunity for air-to-air combat, followed it down, breaking through the cloud at 1000 feet. The German fighter was still in front. From dead astern at 300 yards he fired again, without any obvious effect. Startled, the German plane shot upwards back into cloud, still with Bay in close pursuit. Seconds later the Focke-Wulf came down again with its pilot apparently struggling with the controls but unable to retain height. Quickly positioning himself dead astern again, Bay sent off a long burst and smoke blossomed out behind his victim. Sensing the kill, he closed in to 200 yards and fired yet again. The FW 190 rolled onto its side and hurtled down into the ground.

During April the losses suffered by the Tempests, the majority of which were caused by flak, were the highest of the war. Since its arrival on the Continent, 122 Wing's losses in action to the end of April totalled 23 for 3 Squadron, 18 for 80 Squadron, 18 for 486 (New Zealand) Squadron, 16 for 56 Squadron, and 16 for 274 Squadron. Of two units which had arrived later and flown with 84 Group, 33 Squadron had lost eight and 222 Squadron five.

Patrols over the Schwerin area continued during the early days of May. With the war in Europe almost over, many members of the Luftwaffe were trying to escape to Norway and the air over northern Germany witnessed increased and sometimes frantic activity involving all types of aircraft. The Tempests made full use of the opportunity to inflict as many casualties as possible.

On 2 May, Bay Adams was leading a formation of Tempests on patrol about 15 miles east of Kiel when he spotted a Junkers Ju 88 parked beside what appeared to be an airstrip near Lutionburg. Diving in from 2000 feet (600 m), he lined up his target, fired a three-second burst from his 20 mm cannons and had the satisfaction of seeing it burst into flames. As he left it was well and truly alight, with ammunition exploding in all directions. He and his flight continued the patrol and then doubled back flying, over his target again ten minutes later. The Ju 88 had been reduced to a burnt-out wreck but ammunition was still exploding around it.

Climbing back to 2000 feet (600 m) once more, he resumed the patrol in a northerly direction. Approximately ten miles east of Kiel his number two called up reporting a Fieseler Storch army cooperation plane below. Bay peeled off anticipating an easy kill but the slow Storch turned out to be a jet-propelled Messerschmitt Me 262 flying at low level in a south-easterly direction. Using the speed built up from his dive, the Australian closed to within 600 yards and pressed the firing button to deliver a short burst from astern. Hits registered on the jet's starboard wing and something fell away from under the fuselage, possibly an auxiliary ventral fuel tank, and dropped into a lake below. Black smoke suddenly streamed from the 262's engines as it dramatically accelerated away. With the German machine now at full throttle the Tempests were unable to close in and it was useless to pursue it further.

On the following day the Tempests of 3 Squadron had a field day amid the fleeing German planes. In The Big Show, Pierre Clostermann described the shooting down of an Fw 190 and a Bf 109, both with the assistance of Bay Adams. Altogether, fourteen German aircraft were

Messerschmitt Me 262. The Tempest squadrons mounted rat catching patrols in an effort to shoot down these jet fighters while they were landing, their most vulnerable moment. (MAP)

claimed destroyed and eleven damaged for the loss of one Tempest.

At 6.20 p.m. on 4 May Field-Marshal Montgomery, Commander of the 21st Army Group, received the unconditional surrender of the German forces in Holland, north-west Germany and Denmark. Three days later at General Eisenhower's headquarters in Rheims, German representatives signed the unconditional surrender of all German armed forces to the Allies, effective from one minute past midnight on 9 May. The war in Europe was over at last.

With the hostilities ended, 3 Squadron joined 135 Wing and became part of the British Air Forces of Occupation (BAFO), the duties of which were policing the peace and maintaining a high degree of readiness because of the increasing tensions which had grown up out of the relationships between East and West. Bay Adams stayed with the occupation forces for about a year before returning to Australia in 1946. He had decided to stay in the RAAF.

After serving with several squadrons in Australia he was transferred to the British Commonwealth Occupation Force (BCOF) in Japan in 1948. The force, which included units from Britain, New Zealand, India and Australia, was subject to the command of General Douglas MacArthur, who had been appointed Supreme Commander Allied Powers. As its share of the occupation force the RAAF had assigned its No. 81 Fighter Wing consisting of. 76, 77 and 82 Squadrons, all of which were equipped with leased North American F-51 Mustangs. The wing's base was at the southern Honshu town of Iwakuni which had previously been a Japanese naval air station and training base for Kamikazi pilots. F/Lt Bay Adams joined 77 Squadron as a flight commander.

In 1949, Nos. 76 and 82 Squadrons were withdrawn back to Australia, leaving only 77 Squadron in Japan. On 17 March, Bay was involved in a mid-air collision while flying Mustang A68-811. Twelve of the unit's Mustangs were manoeuvring in battle formation when the wing of W/O Geoffrey (Bluey) Thornton's machine let down on top of Bay's port wing, bending and breaking it downwards as it went past. Much of the wing was broken off and Bay struggled with the controls to maintain altitude. At approximately 5000 feet (1500 m) he turned the crippled plane onto its back and bailed out over the freezing waters of the Sea of Japan. Even as he was floating down, an air-sea rescue launch was being called but he was coming down into the sea a mile to a mile-and-a-half east of Otake and too long a time in the water could be fatal. He splashed down not far from a Japanese fishing vessel but it made no attempt to pick him up. Speed in the rescue was essential and in its dash to reach his position the rescue launch was guided by a Wirraway

A Mustang of 77 Squadron RAAF landing at Pusan during the days of crisis in Korea. (Cec Sly)

which maintained contact by radio. It took fifteen minutes.

Meanwhile, Bluey Thornton's Mustang A68-765 had only been slightly damaged and he managed to land safely back at Iwakuni. An inspection revealed it had a broken flap and aileron.

It had been a near thing. This was underlined by the news that some 200 miles further north an American pilot had also crashed into the sea that day but the unfortunate man had spent 50 minutes in the water before being picked up. By the time his rescuers arrived he had frozen to death.

Someone from the squadron had quickly informed Bay's fiancée, Bonnie, that he was safe and well. Bonnie, from Cowra, NSW, was employed in Japan as a teacher and tutor of the children of European servicemen. The couple were married on 13 August that year and the wedding was fully reported in the Cowra Guardian of 13 September.

In the Far East Gunnery Contest of 1949, invitations were issued to all fighter wings in the command requesting that they each send three representatives to participate. Held at Yokota, the competition included air-to-air shooting, air-to-ground shooting, dive-bombing and skip-bombing. No. 77 Squadron's three representatives were S/Ldr. Graham Strout, F/Lt. Bay Adams and P/O Terry Fitzsimmons, who put up an impressive and highly professional display. As a team they came in second, but the star of the show proved to be Bay Adams, who achieved the highest personal score and took out the individual trophy. He was later awarded an AFC for his efforts.

At 4 a.m on 25 June 1950, Communist troops of North Korea crossed the 38th Parallel and invaded South Korea. Pyongyang radio just after midday announced a formal declaration of war.

Two days earlier, on 23 June, the Australian squadron had completed its last scheduled flying for its period of occupation. In accordance with Canberra's policy, it was due to be withdrawn from Japan and there had been quite a party on the 24th to celebrate the idea of going home. The pilots were shocked when they heard of the invasion the following day. When Graham Strout contacted him by phone, Bay was still in his dressing gown at home and did not at first believe the news.

Although US authority over 77 Squadron did not cover operations outside Japan, the commanding officer, W/Cdr L. T. Spence, immediately placed his unit on readiness in line with other FEAF squadrons. As the days passed and the Americans became more and more involved in the crisis, the Australian pilots became impatient to know whether or not Canberra would permit them to join operations against the advancing North Koreans. On the 29th word came that General MacArthur made a formal request to the government but it was not until late the following evening that news arrived. Prime Minister Menzies had committed the squadron to the war.

Bad weather prevented operations immediately, but they began on Sunday 2 July,. There were three separate missions. The first involved a flight of four Mustangs led by S/Ldr Graham Strout to escort C-47s bringing back wounded from Korea but the Americans did not rendezvous.

The second mission consisted of eight Mustangs led by W/Cdr Spence and included Bay Adams, ordered to escort B-26s while they bombed railway bridges over the Han Rivers south of Seoul, capital of South Korea. Shortly after take-off one machine had to abort and return to Iwakuni. The remaining Mustangs rendezvoused with the

The UN air forces quickly established air superiority over Korea. An abandoned Illyushin Il-10 of the North Korean Air Force. (Cec Sly)

seventeen B-26s over Tongnae, near Pusan. The American air gunners regarded the seven Australian planes with suspicion at first, particularly as they were expecting a high escort and not a close escort. There was a possibility that North Korean Yak-9s could be in the area but the moment of tension passed when identities were established. With the Mustangs weaving from side to side just above, they set course for the target. Some flak was encountered near Seoul but nobody was hit and the bombing was successful. On the way back to Japan, two F-80 Shooting Stars, suspecting that the RAAF roundels were actually North Korean markings, made a firing pass at one of the Mustangs which saw the threat and avoided being hit by turning inside the faster jet fighters.

The third task was another successful escort mission, this time for Boeing B-29 Superfortresses from Okinawa.

By the end of the day 77 Squadron had flown sixteen sorties with only two aborted for no losses. It had been a successful though unspectacular day and one that gave no indication of the tragedy about to happen.

On 3 July, the first ground attack mission was assigned to the squadron. At 1.59 p.m., eight Mustangs, each armed with six 60-pound rockets, took off from Iwakuni to attack enemy troop movements along the main highway between Suwon and Pyongtack. W/Cdr Lou Spence led Able section while Bay Adams led Baker section. Before leaving Spence had voiced doubts about the assigned target area because it seemed too far south, but after checking with the 5th Air Force Tactical Control Centre at Itazuke and receiving assurances that the North Koreans had advanced that far, he had been instructed to proceed with the mission.

Arriving over the assigned area, a river estuary and a railway junction were clearly pinpointed and, as luck would have it, there was a train just waiting to be attacked.

After double-checking the location, Bay declared that he was going after the train with his four aircraft. Lining up the locomotive and allowing a little for deflection, he was down to 1500 feet (450 m) and about to open fire when he noticed a familiar symbol mark on the train. The red and blue orb divided by a curving line through its centre was the symbol of the Republic of Korea. Without firing he pulled up abruptly, warning his section not to attack because the train displayed South Korean markings. Scanning the map on his knee, Bay checked the area again. He was obviously in the right place and it seemed probable that the North Koreans could have captured the train and were using it for their purposes. By radio he called to an American Forward Air Control plane which was further south and this assured him that the area was under enemy control.   Convinced, he brought Baker aircraft around again and prepared to attack. As he was coming down, before he could open fire, the locomotive he was lining up was suddenly blown off the rails and over onto its side. Looking up, Bay saw Spence's section attacking from the opposite direction. He had been robbed of his train but there were plenty of other targets. He ordered his section to concentrate on a convoy of trucks. For the next 20 minutes the Mustangs spent their time rocketing and strafing every vehicle they could find and when they departed they left behind them an absolute mess.

Back at Iwakuni the fliers were celebrating the success of their strike when news came that there had been a horrible mistake. The trucks had been carrying the advance battalion of the 24th US Division, the first American troops to be rushed to Korea, as well as South Korean reinforcements, while the train had been loaded with ammunition. From a technical point of view the Australians had delivered a devastating blow — but not to the enemy. The story of the Australian planes bombing

American ground forces were reported in the US wire services, United Press and Associated Press, and given a wide distribution in the United States. The 4 July edition of the New York Times carried the reports from both news sources.

Investigations into the incident revealed that lengthy delays had occurred between the initial report of a North Korean truck convoy being on the move, its reception by General Macarthur's headquarters in Tokyo, and the time it was finally passed onto the 5th Air Force Operations. Several more hours then passed before the report was acted upon. The officers concerned noted the delay and estimated the point they thought the trucks might have reached by the time 77 Squadron could arrive. They were not even aware of the fact that American and South Korean troops were in the area. The Australians were completely cleared of blame but, exonerated or not, the shock of bombing and strafing his own men was something which Bay Adams never forgot.

Soon after this episode, taking effect on 7 July, General Macarthur instructed the establishment of a realistic bomb line which was to be updated throughout each day, and also ordered that both South Korean and American vehicles were to have clearly visible white stars painted on their tops and sides to avoid confusion. Later in the month a system of forward air controllers was inaugurated, in which army air observers were carried in North American T-6 'Mosquito' spotter planes so they could report on enemy activity and direct incoming fighter-bombers onto their targets.

As the intensity of operations began to pick up there was not time to dwell upon what had happened. For the remainder of July and August the squadron was heavily occupied in trying to slow down the advance rate of the North Koreans and relieve pressure on the US 8th Army making its stand on the Pusan Perimeter. The effectiveness of the enemy's anti-aircraft fire began to increase, but it was nothing like that experienced by Bay over Europe. Operations were also complicated by the wet season. Korea could receive up to 16 inches of rain in July and, mixed with the mountainous Korean terrain, this created hazardous conditions. The Australians' first casualty occurred on 7 July when S/Ldr Graham Strout's Mustang exploded during a strike on the east-coast railway near Samchok.

Because the Americans had swiftly established air superiority over the numerically smaller North Korean Air Force, enemy aircraft were not in evidence and ground attack sorties intensified. On 9 August, Bay led four Mustangs on a close support mission for a ground controller near Chunggyo-ri and Chogye. A town containing enemy troops and field equipment was attacked and set on fire. Three trucks were damaged and a field piece attacked. Bay's wingman, Stan Williamson, was hit by flak and, unable to lower his flaps, he was obliged to crash land at Pohang. His Mustang, A68-775, was a complete write-off but he was uninjured.

On the 14th, Bay provided close support under the directions of a ground controller near Yongsanni, where he and his section attacked an enemy-held hill. The controller reported good results and at least one tank was destroyed.

In the morning of the 23rd, Bay Adams led an armed reconnaissance of eight Mustangs over the Wonsan and Hamhung areas. The Australians proceeded first to Wonsan but, owing to deteriorating weather conditions they could not go further. They turned instead to a patrol over the roads on the east coast from Wonsan to Chumunjin, when they strafed a convoy of trucks and left several on fire. Next they found a small railway yard at Uman-ni and severely damaged a goods shed and three boxcars. During the afternoon, Bay was up again leading

A Mustang damaged by ground fire during a low-level attack. (Cec Sly)

three Mustangs on a close-support mission to Tosong Dong. Following the directions of a ground controller, the town was attacked, several fires were started and two camouflaged vehicles were strafed.

On the morning of the 25th, Bay Adamsand another Mustang provided close support under the direction of a ground controller and attacked a large building in the town of Kunwi. Afterwards they patrolled the road from Kunwi to Andong but no enemy was sighted.

During another close support mission on the morning of the 27th, Bay and two others attacked and destroyed an observation post complete with radio tower near Waegwan. Enemy troops and equipment were reported located in a nearby orchard and this was thoroughly strafed. At least four large vehicles were destroyed and an adjacent bridge was set on fire. Shortly afterwards the Mustangs strafed another camouflaged vehicle and left it blazing. A nearby large haystack, which was hit during the attack, burned with a thick black cloud of smoke and was believed to have hidden a fuel storage dump.

Next day, during a rocket strike on the North Korean airfield at Taejon, no enemy aircraft were seen on the ground, so Bay and the others delivered their rockets into a radio tower on an adjacent hill.

In the early afternoon of the 29th, Bay led an armed reconnaissance near Seoul and over the area to the north. They rocketed a large factory building at Chinnamop, destroyed three trucks and following railway lines, attacked several railway trucks and strafed personnel working on a railway bridge. Just over an hour after landing at Iwakuni Baywas off again on a close-support mission directed by a ground controller in the Hyopchong area.

And so it went on... These operations were typical of those carried out by Bay Adams and the other pilots. By the end of August the squadron had destroyed 35 tanks, 212 trucks and other vehicles, 4 locomotives, 14 box cars and 15 ammunition or fuel dumps.

On 9 September, while leading a close-support mission to Pusan, W/Cdr. Louis Spence was killed when his aircraft failed to pull out of a dive and crashed into the centre of the town of Angang-ni. After Spence's death, Bay took over leadership of the squadron in the air while Air Cdr. A. Charlesworth, Chief of Staff of BCOF, came from Tokyo to look after administration at the base until the arrival of more officers from Australia. The unit's new commanding officer turned out to be S/Ldr Richard Cresswell, a World War II veteran and one of the most experienced fighter pilots in the RAAF. On 20 September, he flew his first sortie as Bay's number twoand within a week he had flown eleven missions.

The Americans presented a number of decorations to 77 Squadron on 22 September. The flight commanders, Bay Adams and F/Lt. S. 'Brick' Bradford, had by now chalked up 50 sorties and both received US Air Medals. This award was one of Bay's most valued possessions because it was his first. He later received the British DFC for his service in Europe and Korea.

The war situation changed dramatically when the largest amphibious operation since World War II, at Inchon, deep behind the enemy's lines, was a resounding success, relieving pressure and breaking the enemy's will to fight. They fled northwards to avoid being trapped but many were cut off and captured. At the beginning of October, United Nations armies crossed the 38th Parallel in pursuit of the enemy.

With the fighting apparently racing to a conclusion, the Australians found they were having to fly longer missions from their base in Japan to find fewer targets. The squadron transferred to Pohang on the south-east coast of Korea on 12 October. Such was the situation when Bay Adams finished his tour of duty and returned to Australia.

After a course at East Sale during which he flew his first jet, the Australian-built de Havilland Vampire F Mk. 30, he served with No. 21 Squadron at Laverton which

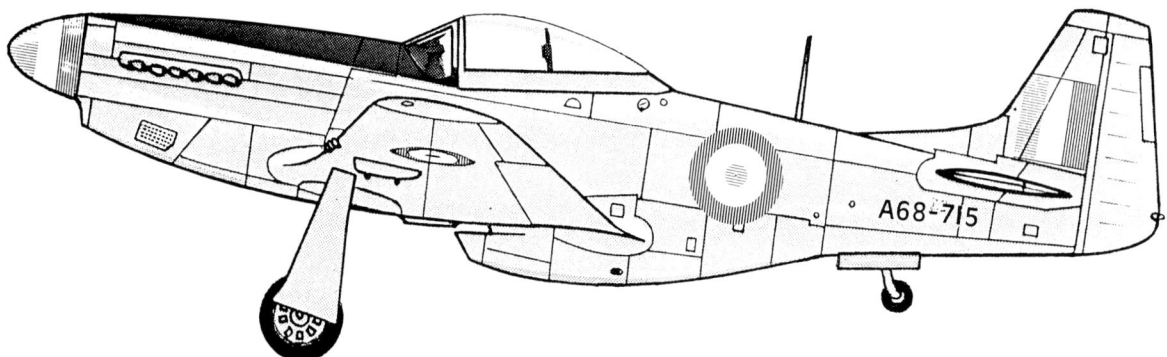

North American F-51D Mustang A68-715 of 77 Squadron RAAF, one of the aircraft flown by bay Adams in Korea.
(Dennis Newton)

at that time was equipped with both Mustangs and Vampires while changing over to the jet.

In 1952 the RAAF had commitments in both Korea and Malaya but in March the government announced that two more squadrons would be sent on a third overseas assignment to Malta. Together,. 75 and 76 Squadrons would form No. 78 Wing and the commanding officer of No. 76 would be S/Ldr. Adams, DFC, AFC. Appointed to command the wing was W/Cdr. Brian Eaton, DSO and Bar, DFC. They would fly leased British-built Vampire FB MK 9s, which Bay found to be delightful machines and superior to the Australian version.

Although the RAAF wing on Malta was not part of the NATO forces, it was there in support of the RAF and participated in many NATO exercises, usually operating as the air defence force of the island. For armament practice the Australians flew to North Africa and Cyprus. During the Middle East Gunnery Contest for the 'Imshi' Mason Cup (named after the British World War II ace) the Australian pilots took out first and second places, Bay being runner up to Bill Horsman.

During 1953, No. 78 Wing represented the RAAF in the Queen's review of the RAF at Odiham, England, not long after her Coronation. In July it was assigned to the 2nd TAF in Germany for 'Coronet', a NATO exercise which simulated an atomic war.

From 1961 to 1964 Bay was in the USA, stationed first at Norfolk, Virginia, with the Armed Forces Staff College and then as Intelligence Officer for the RAAF at the Australian Embassy. He returned to Australia to take up a position as Deputy Director of Intelligence for the next two years. For twelve months, beginning December, 1966, Bay was Officer Commanding the RAAF airbase at Townsville, where he checked out on Lockheed P2V Neptunes and Douglas DC-3 Dakotas. At one stage the base was inspected by Gough Whitlam MP, the future prime minister.

In October 1968, G/Capt J. I. Adams took up his appointment as Officer Commanding, RAAF Contingent Vung Tau, Vietnam, his third posting to a war zone. As if underlining his appointment, on the night of the 18th the base was subjected to a rocket attack which resulted in the deaths of six Vietnamese civilians and the wounding of several others. All lived in the nearby village of Bin Dink, located close to the RAAF's living quarters.

Based at Vung Tau were the Bell UH-1 Iroquois (nicknamed 'Huey' by the Americans) helicopters of 9 Squadron and the de Havilland C-7 Caribou STOL transports of 35 Squadron. At this time the Iroquois helicopters were being used for such roles as transport, leaflet dropping, medical evacuation and troop airlifts. It was not possible to use them as gunships or command and control helicopters. In May 1968, the Australian

W/Cdr J.I. Adams, DFC, AFC, prior to his promotion to group captain and his appointment as Officer Commanding, RAAF Contingent Vung Tau, Vietnam, in October 1968, his third posting to a war zone. (Bay Adams)

Chiefs of Staff Committee had recommended the purchase of gunship kits from the US Army to provide 9 Squadron with this added capability and while awaiting final RAAF approval Bay's predecessor, G/Capt. J. W. Hubble, DSO, AFC, had authorised the borrowing of kits and the carrying out of trials. The squadron was then in the process of being re-equipped with the UH-1H model of the Iroquois, powered by a 1400 shp Lycoming T53-L-13 turboshaft engine which gave a greater lift capacity than the unit's previous UH-1B variant. The new machine could carry two seven-tube rocket pods, two 7.62 mm mini-guns with 9600 rounds of ammunition carried in sixteen storage bins strapped to the floor behind the pilots, plus four side-firing, twin-mounted M60 machine guns with a total ammunition load of 4000 rounds. It was decided to mount the mini-guns on the front pylons to overcome shock wave-effects. This positioning moved the helicopter's centre of gravity forward, which improved stability and made it a better weapons platform. If necessary, this gunship, named a 'Bushranger', could be converted back to a troop carrier in an hour. The first mission carried out by Bushranger helicopters occurred on 11 April 1969 and they soon proved their worth.

No. 35 Squadron, with seven Caribou aircraft on strength, was known affectionately as 'Wallaby Airlines' throughout Vietnam. Its tasks included the airlifting of passengers, mail and cargo, dropping of paratroops including Australian Army SAS troops), medical evacuation of battle casualties, dropping flares for night operations and mercy missions such as the resettling of Vietnamese families quite often with all of their household goods. During a typical day of operations, a crew could visit as many as nine or ten airfields of extreme types from dirt airstrips to strongly defended major air bases. During a typical month in 1968-9 the Caribous clocked 320 hours flying time, 99 of them in support of the Australian forces. One day in July 1969, one crew flew an outstanding 23 sorties and moved 152 drums of fuel, the equivalent of 35 tons of cargo, a record which lasted until the following year.

Operations could suddenly become more hazardous because of unexpected enemy action. On 19 January 1969 one Caribou, while taxiing into a parking bay at Katum, a small Special Forces strip close to the Cambodian border and north-west of Saigon, came under mortar attack. The plane was hit by shrapnel in over 100 places and the aircraft's captain F/Lt. R. J. 'Tommy' Thompson, was wounded in the right leg while his co-pilot, F/O R. McGregor, was showered by flying glass from the shattered windscreen and cut about the face. Fortunately no one was seriously injured and there were no direct hits. Thompson turned the aircraft about ready to take off as soon as possible. Before moving away, the loadmasters, Corporal B. Gracie, who was nearing the end of his second tour of duty in Vietnam, and Corporal B. Barnes, swiftly offloaded the cargo. Then, taking advantage of a brief lull in the attack, Thompson wrenched the Caribou off the ground, but their problems were not yet over because the undercarriage refused to retract and had to be pumped up. Later, when landing at Bien Hoa, the emergency system had to be used. For their swift and decisive action, and other service in Vietnam, Thompson received the DFC and Gracie was awarded the DFM.

While commanding at Vung Tau, Bay Adams logged as many flying hours as he could. On average he flew with the helicopter crews twice a week and with the Caribou crews one day per week. In his own estimation he was not much of a helicopter pilot and he was aware of the younger airmen tossing a coin to determine who would be his co-pilot. Thinking back to his experiences

of flak over Europe in World War II, he was very conscious of the vulnerability of the slower flying helicopters to concentrated anti-aircraft fire. If the enemy in Vietnam had been able to utilise such weapons as the superb 20 mm anti-aircraft batteries used by the Germans instead of sending off the occasional rocket they could have inflicted crippling losses. He stated as much in his end of tour report.

Bay had one frightening experience. Just after taking off in an Iroquois, a piece of cardboard off a ration box was handed to him over his shoulder from behind. On it was a scrawled message: 'You are hijacked - take us to the back beach. For an instant he froze, fearing the worst, and then he slowly turned around to find the grinning face of his co-pilot. The 'back beach' was a well known R and R area — to go there was a much more palatable idea than going on a sortie. Bay's comments are not on record.

Bay Adams' tour of duty ended in October 1969, when he handed over to G/Capt R. J. McKimm, AFC, and for his work he was awarded the CBE on 20 April 1970. In 1970 he was Staff Officer (Operations) at Operations Command Penrith, NSW. During his time there he became responsible for the organisation of the Jubilee Fly Past for the RAAF's fiftieth anniversary. Bay and his team had to organise seven aerial displays and as they went from base to base to make preparations they received from the men their own unofficial title of 'Dad's Army from Fort Fumble'. Nevertheless, the quality of the displays received widespread acclamation.

From November 1971 he was stationed at the Defence Central, Canberra, as the Director of Joint Operations and Plans (DJOP). Next came Singapore at ANZUC as Air Commander and then commander of the Integrated Air Defence System (IADS) for the next few years. He returned from Penang in January 1978 to become Chief of Air Force Operations in Canberra. Bay's last appointment was as AOC Operational Command until his retirement on 5 November 1979, after 38 years of service.

Interviewed in May 1985, AVM, J. I. (Bay) Adams CBE, DFC, AFC, US Air Medal (Ret'd) looked back on his career in the air force and remarked: 'I loved it all, the whole bloody lot.' Then he added this advice for up and coming airmen: 'Be qualified, be available for the job you're after and be ready to serve.'

He always was and he always did.

10

THE LAST DOGFIGHT

By the time of the surrender of Japan in August 1945, the RAAF had become the fourth largest air force in the world. Its total wartime enlistments reached 21,900 men and women of whom 10 562 were killed and another 3192 injured. At its peak, it had 76 flying squadrons operating over 8000 aircraft backed up by a large training and support organisation.

After the war, the RAAF continued with overseas commitments in support of United Nations activities. From early 1946, a fighter wing comprised of three Mustang squadrons and nearly 2000 personnel participated in the occupation of Japan. In 1948/49 the aircrew equivalent of a transport squadron delivered supplies into besieged Berlin during the Berlin Airlift. By June 1950, only one Mustang squadron was still in Japan when the Korean War broke out. No. 77 Squadron become the first UN unit, besides those of the USA, to commence operations over Korea. A transport squadron was also committed while, at the same time, a bomber and transport squadron undertook active operations against Communist terrorists in Malaya.

The arrival of Russian-built MiG-15 jet fighters in Korean skies in November 1950 marked the beginning of a new era in air combat. UN air forces did not possess a plane to match it until the Americans introduced their F-86A Sabre in December. Realising the inferiority of the Mustang, the decision was taken to re-equip 77 Squadron with jets but no Sabres could be made available for RAAF. The Gloster Meteor, at that time the RAF's front-line fighter, was selected instead but to the Australian pilots a comparison between the MiG and the Meteor did not seem encouraging. Nevertheless, the first batch of Meteors arrived on the British aircraft carrier HMS Warrior on 24 February 1951.

One of the tourist attractions of Mildura, on the southern side of the Victoria-New South Wales border is the War Birds Aviation Museum which houses a collection of exhibits and articles, some of them rare, from World War

II and beyond. Located among them is the cockpit section of a Gloster Meteor Mk. 8.

The curator of the museum, Mr Pierce Dunn, whose interest in aircraft restoration led him to discover the Meteor relic in a shed at Woomera some years ago, transported it back to Mildura for cleaning up. While finding the cockpit section was interesting enough in itself, as he was carrying out restorative work, removing layers of paint, Pierce made another discovery — one which raised his interest to out of the ordinary. Coming to light, one painted red and the other green, were the unmistakable symbols of two small aircraft. They looked like Russian MiG-15s! Was it possible that this Meteor had actually shot down a MiG?

The new find set Pierce Dunn on a trail of investigation. He found out that the Meteor had once carried the serial number A77-851 and that it had definitely been flown in the Korean War by 77 Squadron RAAF. Not only that, he discovered that it had been given a name: 'Halestorm'.

Gloster Meteor Mk.8s arriving in Japan on the deck of the aircraft carrier HMS Unicorn. (George Hale)

Meteor WK-683 (British serial number) being offloaded.
(George Hale)

More facts began to emerge. On 1 April 1952 the Defence Preparations Committee of the Australian government approved the purchase of 36 Gloster Meteor Mk 8s from the British Government at a cost of £1.7 million. This was the third purchase of these aircraft made so that 77 Squadron would be able to remain operational in Korea until mid-1953. In August 1952, this third batch of Meteors arrived in Asian waters on the deck of the aircraft carrier HMS Unicorn. One of the planes sported the British serial number WK-683.

The new planes were modified for combat operations at Iwakuni, Japan, which was the home of No. 91 Wing.

Modifications included ADF (ARN-6 radio compass) which was an American requirement for all Allied aircraft operating over Korea, and Zero-length pods for rocket launching which were an Australian adaptation. WK-683 now became A77-851. It finally arrived at Kimpo airfield, Korea, in March 1953, when it was allocated to Sgt. George Hale.

George Hale came from Claremont, Tasmania. After attending Hobart High School he worked as an accountant and then, in February 1951, he joined the RAAF. as a pilot/navigator trainee. Eighteen months later, after completing training at Point Cook, he graduated as a sergeant pilot and was awarded the trophy for topping the course. From there he was posted to No. 4 OTU at Williamtown, NSW, where he remained until November 1952, gaining experience on Mustangs and Vampires until he was posted to Iwakuni for conversion to Meteors. He arrived at 77 Squadron in Korea early in December.

In general, the Australian pilots were allocated the use of a certain aircraft but, depending upon serviceability, they did not necessarily just fly the one machine. The plane George Hale flew regularly was Meteor A77-510 which he named 'Halestorm and Snow', a play on words referring to the name given to his elder brother and the severity of the Korean winter weather. 'Snow' Hale was in the army serving in Korea and on one occasion he took the opportunity to visit Kimpo. There was plenty of hail and snow at the time, the temperature was minus 32°F.

Meteor WK-683, renumbered A77-851 and named 'Halestorm'. (AWM)

* THE LAST DOGFIGHT* 115

Lockheed RF-80 Shooting Star of the USAF's 67th Tactical Reconnaissance Wing. (George Hale)

By the end of February 1953, George Hale was an experienced combat pilot with 64 missions behind him. He was also by now regularly flying in the No. 3 position as a section leader. Meteor A77-510 had long since passed into other hands and he found himself flying various aircraft, depending upon availability. On 9 March he received A77-851, which was the latest type of Meteor Mk 8 with spring-tab. ailerons for a greater rate of roll and enlarged bell-mouth air intakes to give greater thrust for take-off and low level flight. The name he gave it was 'Halestorm' — an abbreviated version of the name he had given to his earlier aircraft.

Clashes in the sky over Korea between MiG-15s and Meteors seldom favoured the Australians. The Meteor Mk 1 had been the RAF's first operational jet fighter, beginning service in July 1944. The MiG-15 did not make its maiden flight until 2 June 1947, almost three years later, and in terms of performance the Meteor's vintage showed. Added to this, the Communists adopted highly effective tactics. Allied pilots were hampered by the political restrictions of the UN Command. They were directed never to fly across the Yalu River into Chinese airspace. Consequently, the enemy could take off safely from their Manchurian bases without fear of attack, form up and then climb until they were well above the Allied formations before crossing into Korea. The MiGs always retained the initiative, attacked from above and maintained a numerical advantage of about four to one.

Early missions over 'MiG Alley' were without result and it was not until 25 August 1951 that the first inconclusive encounter took place. Then, four days later, the MiGs drew first blood when one Meteor was lost (the pilot, W/O Ron Guthrie, bailed out and was captured) and another was heavily damaged.

On 1 December, the Meteors were involved in a huge dogfight over Sunchon when the squadron was bounced by 50 MiGs. The Australians scored their first confirmed kills when two MiGs were claimed but three Meteors failed to return. F/O Bruce Gogerly attacked a MiG which was hammering another Meteor. He fired a five-second burst. The Russian-built machine took heavy punishment and exploded in flames as it fell. The second MiG was credited as a squadron kill. Of the lost pilots, Bruce Thomson and New Zealander Sgt. Vance Drummond bailed out but the third, Sgt. Ernest Armit, was killed.

The last dogfight. News of the encounter spread quickly and George Hale was met by a battery of reporters and photo-graphers clamouring for news of the combat. Someone, using a finger, scribed the words 'MIG KILLER' on the fuselage between the powder-blackened cannon ports. (AWM)

MiG-15 in North Korean markings. (Cec Sly)

Without a plane to match the MiGs' performance, the Australians could only look forward to more losses, so nobody- was very surprised when they were taken off fighter sweep duties the next day.

No. 77 Squadron was given a new task — ground attack — in which role the Meteor proved highly successful. It was a steady platform for gun and rocket, could sustain tremendous damage and still fly, and had the additional advantage of two engines. By the war's end the squadron had been credited with the destruction of 3700 buildings, 1500 vehicles and 16 bridges. Flak became the main enemy and accounted for most Meteor losses during the rest of the war.

MiGs were encountered on odd occasions but now at lower altitudes where the Meteors stood a better chance. One was probably destroyed on 4 May 1952 when P/O John Surman found himself with a sitting duck. He poured

George Hale (left) and Dave Irlam examine what a MiG's 37 mm cannon can do for a Meteor's jet outlet pipe. An in-spection of Irlam's aircraft revealed 112 holes! (George Hale)

cannon shells into it as he closed to 25 yards. The MiG took no evasive action and went down through low cloud. It was only counted as a 'probable' because it was not seen to crash.

Four days later, P/O Bill Simmonds saw red tracer bullets skim over his wing. The attacking MiG overshot and Simmonds slipped onto its tail and fired. It fell in a spiral dive and crashed after the pilot bailed out at 13 000 feet (4000 m).

In October, after another clash with MiGs, F/O Oliver Cruikshank, an RAF officer serving with the Australians, was killed while attempting to bail out of his Meteor.

The last air battle occurred on 27 March 1953. Four Meteors were scheduled to take part in an armed road reconnaissance in the early afternoon. W/Co. John Hubble, 77 Squadron's CO, would lead the flight with F/ Lt. Sainy Rees as No. 2.; George Hale was No. 3 and his wingman was Sgt. David Irlam.

They flew northward until they reached the road junction at Namch'onjom where the formation parted. Hubble and Rees took the northern road while Hale and Irlam turned westward along the road leading to Sariwon. The idea was to follow the roads in a roughly circular route until the two pairs of Meteors rendezvoused and crossed over on the outskirts of Pyongyang and then traced the roads back to Namch'onjom so that each pair completed a full circuit. That was the plan. . .

In an interview with this writer, George Hale told what happened next. We were sitting in the study of his Sydney home unit and spread out on the coffee table in front of us was a large map of North Korea. It was a composite of several detailed military maps which had been taped together to form a panorama of the RAAF's area of operations. On it had been pencilled symbols to represent flak zones, gun positions, times, etc.

Hale: It happened at 1420, I pencilled that in shortly afterwards. We were descending, both Dave Irlam and myself, in loose line astern to carry out a road recce up this road [referring to the road extending westward from Namch'onjom towards Sariwon]. On the right-hand side I saw two American RF-80s in very, very close formation heading south-east... that would be with the sun to the west on the left hand-side.

Shortly afterwards, there was a third aircraft I reported as a bogey following close behind the RF-80s. I wasn't sure what that was until I had a close look at another aircraft which appeared close behind it and saw the swept wings and high tail. At this stage of the game I made an announcement that they were MiGs.

The thing that intrigued me about the two RF-80s was that they were so close in formation. Usually in any enemy area you should fly in battle formation so you can see behind each other's tail, but they were tucked in tight. That's usually what people do when they are scared — when there's somebody after them. They had no armament so they stuck together so they would have a sporting chance.

I met those guys afterwards — I can tell you about that too. In fact we became quite friendly.

I turned in after the last MiG and followed him in a south-westerly direction. I jettisoned the ventral tank in the turn and, incidentally, this was below 10 000 feet — remember we had just descended for the road recce.
Newton: This was rare for MiGs, wasn't it?
Hale: Yes... they were right down low, obviously chasing these guys who were getting lower and faster trying to get away from them. Somewhere around here [referring to the map and indicating an area just south of Sinmak] I realised I had to get rid of my rockets while I was following the second one. I switched the gun's RP. switch across which fired my two rockets and started the camera running — it ran out of film.

Then the MiG I was following turned left and went straight up this way, going home. I turned in after him and just as I was sort of getting on his tail, I heard Dave Irlam call up and say: 'I've been hit... what will I do?'

I think I replied: 'Head for the nearest cloud' There was plenty of scattered cloud around the area. That was the last I saw of him, or anybody, until I got home. What I did see was two MiGs coming out of the sun, one was attacking him and one must have been attacking me. I looked over on my left-hand side and there was a MiG overshooting me on the inside. They were a lot faster than we were and they were coming out of a dive. He had his speed brakes up, obviously trying to brake back behind me. The Meteor's got those finger-type speed brakes — they're so good you almost go through the windscreen. I just pulled out my speed

Crew Chief, Bob Cherry, standing next to the two MiG symbols, the top in red and the other in green, he painted on 'Halestorm'. (George Hale)

brakes and dropped back and he was right there. I just had to kick left rudder and start firing. I was hitting him sort of right beside the cockpit. You could see the metal strips falling off and black smoke. Then he just peeled over and went down like that. [At this stage George had been demonstrating with his hands, holding them up, palm downwards, one behind the other. He turned his leading hand over and downwards to indicate the path of the falling MiG].

As I was about to follow him, I saw another two coming down behind me. I S-turned into them until they went past and then turned in behind them and had a parting shot. The thing you never do is turn your back on the enemy. I was firing at those two when I saw another two coming down on me.

That second lot were going pretty fast and I was 'S' turning so they couldn't hit me and then turning back behind them when I first started to get the feel of the gunsight. Normally you turn it backwards so the graticules get bigger as you close in on the aircraft... I was doing the other thing... I was using my wrist the wrong way and bringing them in to try and hit them as they were going away at high speed. And that's when I hit the second one, the one on the left-hand side. He blew off a stream of dense white smoke [fuel] and he and his mate then just put on full bore and climbed away, the bloke on the left leaving his trail of white.
Newton: Was he losing power?

Hale: Well... I don't know, he was getting away pretty quick and he was going up pretty steeply.

It was at this stage of the game that my guns stopped and I realised that, with all this, I had used up every drop of ammunition so I did a screaming left-hand dive at full bore and headed back towards Kimpo. There was no point me being caught up here. By this stage we'd probably reached up here somewhere. [George pointed to an area on the map just north of Sinmak.]

The standard in Korea was that any aircraft on its own, regardless of what it was, could be shot down by anybody. There always had to be two. You never flew around on your own. My object then was to get home as quickly as I could.

Newton: With the first one, how definite do you reckon it was? You claimed a 'probable'.

Hale: Well ... I said probably ... I reckon if a bloke gets a broadside from four cannons at no more than 50 yards, all around the back end of his engine area, and he starts blowing black smoke, there's something pretty seriously wrong with him.

Newton: One would assume so...

Hale: He sort of rolled over and disappeared. He didn't have too far to go, of course, we were probably at about four or five thousand feet at this stage of the game. In fact, I doubt if he would have got out of the roll and dive.

Now, while this was going on, John Hubble and Sainy Rees must have been up here somewhere. [He indicated a point on the northern road near Suan]. They were going up this other road. After I announced in no uncertain terms that the bogeys were MiGs, they must have cut a corner somewhere across here. They said they met some MiGs head-on and traded some passing shots with them.

Newton: So they were actually cutting them off?

Hale: They were cutting them off this way, and that's obviously why the MiGs broke off and headed home. They probably saw these other two Meteors coming and thought they would be trapped. At any rate, there

had already been some Sabres scrambled from down south ... I passed them on my way back.

And that's it. That's all that happened, as close as I can recall. And that is the last time that an Australian took part in aerial combat. We didn't meet MiGs after that and we didn't use fighters in Vietnam. That was the last time ...

More than four decades have passed since the Royal Australian Air Force has fired its guns in anger in air-to-air combat. I then asked about the RF-80 pilots.

'Oh yes,' came the reply. 'Here's the word from the two guys. They came up to the mess that night.' [George opened up a black-covered book titled the 67th Tactical Reconnaissance Wing. This book had been produced by the wing itself and it contained blank pages at the back for autographs. He pointed out two of them: ' Charles Abby, United States Air Force, and James Schneider.'

Under Charles Abby's signature was the inscription:'Buddy for life!' James (Jim) Schneider had written: 'George, we met in a rather unusual way and I will always thank you for getting one of the MiGs. With luck perhaps I will see you again. I wish you happiness.'

'Yes, they came up that night and gave me a large bottle of bourbon ... terrible stuff,' George said, grinning, 'real rot-gut.' The grin became wider. 'I remember sitting in a slit trench there one night when the Po-2s came across on a nuisance raid. They were all firing away. I sat in my trench and drank my bourbon ... But that's another story.'

After the four Meteors landed safely back at Kimpo that day, an inspection revealed that Dave Irlam's plane had collected 112 holes, but against this George Hale could claim the probable destruction of one MiG-15 and damage to another. News of the encounter spread quickly and George Hale was met by a battery of reporters and photographers. Someone, using their finger, had scribed the words 'MIG KILLER' on the fuselage in between the powder-blackened cannon ports.

That evening, as he was servicing 'Halestorm', Crew Chief Bob Cherry painted two little MiGs, one red and one

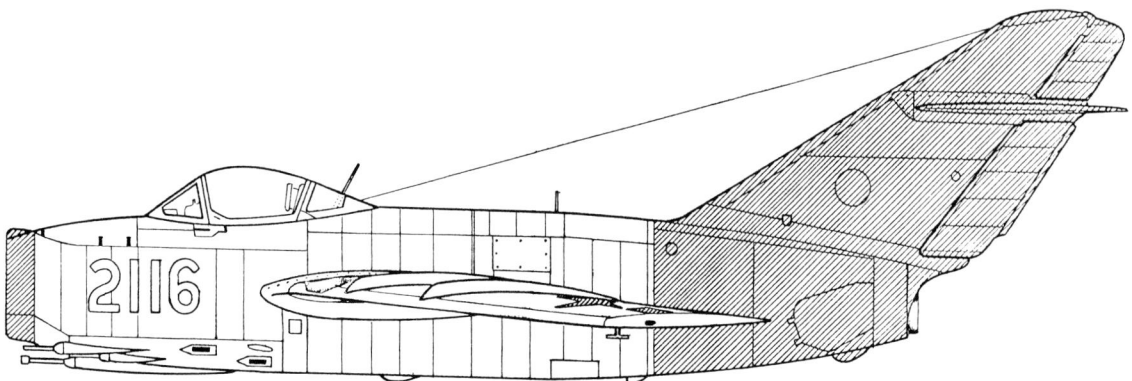

MiG-15 in Chinese markings. (Dennis Newton)

'Halestorm' showing details of markings — caption on drawing. Credit: Dennis Newton

green, on the fuselage just below the emblem. Later, W/Cdr Hubble ordered that they be removed so he painted over them. These were the two MiGs symbols discovered by Pierce Dunn during restoration work in Mildura many years later.

George Hale s tour of duty in Korea finished on 14 June 1953. Altogether he had flown 131 combat missions, 40 of them on A77-851. He considered 'Halestorm'to be a lucky plane, for although he did collect 'one or two holes' in the aircraft, none of them was punched into 'Halestorm'. In fact, the only damage it received he inflicted on it himself. One day while taxiing back to his revetment after a mission, he misjudged his position and bent the pitot.

Back in Australia, George Hale transferred to.11 Squadron and flew anti-submarine Neptunes. Then, in 1954, he completed an instructors course at East Sale which led him into instructing on Wirraways at Point Cook. He finally left the RAAF and joined Qantas in March 1958, where he in due course flew as a Senior Check Captain on Boeing 747s. He has since retired to Queensland's Gold Coast.

How did part of 'Halestorm' end up at Mildura?

After the war, 77 Squadron's remaining 41 Meteors were loaded aboard aircraft carrier HMS Vengeance on 3 December, 1954, and transported to Australia where they formed part of the equipment of No. 78 Wing stationed at Williamtown, NSW. With the introduction of Avon-powered Sabres into the RAAF, the Meteors were relegated to the training role and A77-851 its 'Halestorm' emblem long since removed, was sent to 23 Squadron at Amberley in September 1956. It stayed on the squadron's strength until 1960. On 17 October that year the Department of Air approved of the disposal of A77-851 and it was sold to the Weapons Research Establishment (WRE.) at Woomera, South Australia. Before going there,

it was issued to Fairey Aviation Company of Australia Pty Ltd for modification to U 21 standard and was converted into an unmanned target aircraft.

In September 196, the converted A77-851 was ferried to Salisbury Field, SA, for installation of its control and guidance equipment. From there it went to Edinburgh Field in March 1963, where it crashed while landing during an unmanned flight trial and was considered to be 'uneconomically repairable'. Useful components, including the cockpit section, were removed and the remainder of the plane was scrapped. It was officially written off on 8 January 1964.

At one time it was envisaged that the cockpit section taken from 'Halestorm' would be used for making up a jet simulator for the Royal Australian Navy, but this did not proceed further than the idea stage. So A77-851's remains stayed in the shed at Edinburgh Field for years until they were finally discovered by Pierce Dunn.

In the Line Book, the signatures of Charles Abby and James (Jim) Schneider, the two RF-80 pilots rescued by George Hale on 27 March 1953. (George Hale)

11

BLACK DIAMOND LEADER
THE STORY OF VANCE DRUMMOND

An uneasy peace was reached in Korea in July 1953, but fighting erupted in Indo-China where Viet Minh forces, aided by Communist China, won a decisive victory over the French at Dien Bien Phu in May 1954. The French withdrew from the country altogether. To meet what was seen as the rising threat of Communist China, the Manila Treaty was signed by Britain, the USA, France, Australia, New Zealand, Pakistan, Thailand and the Philippines on 8 September 1954. By this means, these nations set up a regional defence organisation known as the South-East Asia Treaty Organisation (SEATO), with headquarters at Bangkok. It was a collective effort to strengthen the defences of South-East Asian countries against subversion which persisted in Thailand, Malaya and Indonesia.

Australian participation in the SEATO pact was part of its quest for security. The belief was that Australia should meet any challenge as far from Australian shores as possible and that the country could not expect collaboration from friends and allies in its defence unless it was itself prepared to share in the responsibility. By the beginning of the 1960s, the RAAF was firmly committed to a forward defence posture in Asia. At Butterworth, Malaysia, two fighter squadrons, a bomber squadron and a transport support unit were located, but in the face of the worsening strategic situation Australia felt the need for the security of having 'powerful friends' like Britain and the USA.

Australia was travelling along the road which would lead to Vietnam . . .

There had been a fight. They were landing in ones and twos and the sides of their planes around the cannon ports were blackened by powder. They were excited. Someone had shot down a MiG, the squadron's first. Their faces showed the strain of combat but they were happy. The place was Korea.

At debriefing the story of the attack began to unfold. The squadron had run into an estimated 50 MiG-15s over Sunchon. The Reds had come down in pairs and there had been a terrific fight. Bruce Gogerly had shot down one of them for sure and several other pilots had scored good hits on others. Two had been seen burning on the ground, but because of the confusion, noone could be certain who should be credited with the second. A squadron check immediately after the battle had revealed that everyone was scattered but otherwise OK.

F/Lt. Ralph Davidson, 77 Squadron's Intelligence Officer, checked again with F/Lt. Geoff 'Bluey' Thornton who had been leading the mission. Thornton confirmed that he had called a squadron check just after withdrawing from the dogfight. Everyone had checked in. What was worrying Davidson was the fact that not all of the Meteors were back.

Reports were coming in that the MiGs had been out in force and a number of USAF flights had also met opposition. As time went on hope faded. It was obvious that the three Meteors had run into trouble on the way home.

Two of the missing pilots were Australian but the other was a 24-year-old New Zealander serving in the RAAF, Sgt. Vance Drummond. Drummond's Meteor had taken hits until Bruce Gogerly had chased the MiGs off. The plane's electrical equipment had been damaged and it had been last seen in a tight starboard turn trailing fuel from a holed tank.

It was 1 December 1951, and Vance Drummond had disappeared for the second time. . .

Vance Drummond was the youngest son of a large family, four boys and two girls, born to Mr and Mrs L. H. V. Drummond of Hamilton, New Zealand, on 22 February 1927. He grew up in the Waikato district and attended Hamilton East School. Determination, one of the facets of his character, became apparent at a very early age as he always tried to keep up with his older brothers. At eight he demonstrated this by swimming with them across the Waikato River. He began his secondary education at Te Awamutu College but after only six months it was necessary for him to leave to help his father with farm work.

Korea, September 1953. Vance Drummond (left) and Bruce Thompson, still wearing their Chinese POW uniforms, just after their release. (AWM)

He became very interested in horses and by the time he was sixteen he was an accomplished rider, which he proved when he won the Morrinsville Cup. He also won ribbons for riding at the Te Aroha and Paeroa pastoral shows.

But these were the war years and the thoughts of young men were turned towards the armed services. Vance and his brothers were all interested in flying. His eldest brother had been killed in action while flying Spitfires with 111 Squadron RAF in 1941. In Morrinville, Vance joined the Air Training Corps and, as soon as he was able, he joined the RNZAF. He was enrolled in a navigation course which ended in September 1945, the last month of World War II — too late to be posted overseas.

Then the New Zealand Army announced that it was looking for volunteers to go to Japan with the occupational forces. When Vance and his brother, Nelson, found out they were the first in Hamilton to lodge applications. Vance at this time was still under 21 and he had to obtain his mother's consent in order to be allowed to go. He was trained as a cipher clerk and sent overseas with 'J' Force.

Just after his arrival in Japan, he applied for permission to attend a training course for interpreters. The army's reaction was cool. After all, he had already been trained as a cipher clerk, but Vance's determination was undaunted and he finally had his way.

It was while he was acting as an interpreter that he first met the results of aggression. Among his duties, he had to interrogate Koreans who had fled from the

Communist regime in the north. These people had risked their lives in perilous trips in small boats across the sea to Japan. Their stories impressed the young New Zealander and in a letter to friends at home he described their experiences as 'heart rending'. In this, his first experience of Asian Communism, there was nothing he could do to fight back, andhe was obliged to play the role of a helpless observer.

He served in Japan for three months short of three years and returned to New Zealand in 1948. On his arrival Vance found that the air force was now seeking men who had been in the armed forces during the war and offering to train them as fighter pilots. The idea appealed to him and he applied immediately, but the result of his third application to serve in his country's armed forces was a disappointing refusal. He was considered to be too old for the course. He was not yet 22!

Vance was not deterred. Again his characteristic determination came to the fore. He had a goal and he would pursue it. He told his mother that if he was not going to be accepted in New Zealand, he would go to Australia and try there. And that is exactly what he did. He was soon on a plane to Sydney. By chance, the aircraft was conveniently diverted to Williamtown and Vance Drummond had hardly set foot on Australian soil when he enlisted in the RAAF.

In August 1949 he began pilot training as a member of No. 4 FTS Course at Point Cook, Victoria. It was while he was on this course that he disappeared for the first time. He set out, flying a Wirraway, on a low-level navigation exercise and failed to return. It was obvious that he had come down — but where? A search was carried out but as time wore on hope began to fade. Then, some hours later, he was found, wet but safe, clinging to

November 1962. The Black Diamonds aerobatic team with Vance Drummond, Black Diamond Leader in the centre. Others in the team were: left to right, F/O T. Conn, F/O Keith North, Major Joe Turner, USAF, F/Lt Ron Noble. (AWM)

all that remained of his ditched aircraft floating above the waters of Lake Corangamite.

The course finished in February 1951 and Vance not only graduated as a sergeant pilot, he also came first. Graduating with him, also as sergeant pilots, were men who were later to serve with him in Korea.

Sgt. Drummond was posted to 78 Wing at Williamtown where he converted to Mustangs and then to Vampires, the RAAF's first jet fighters.

Meanwhile, the Korean War was now a year old and in August he received a posting to 77 Squadron as a replacement pilot. He arrived at Kimpo on 29 August, the same day that the squadron's Gloster Meteors had their first heavy engagement with MiG-15s. One Meteor had been shot down and the pilot, W/O Ron Guthrie, had apparently bailed out. Another Meteor had been heavily damaged.

The squadron at this time was commanded by W/Cdr. Gordon Steege, DSO, DFC who was fast becoming convinced that the Meteor was outclassed in fighter-vs-fighter combat with the MiG-15.

Vance began operations on 1 September and took part in many of the Meteor/MiG clashes. Flying with him were others from his Point Cook days including Ken Murray, Bruce Thomson, John Myers and Vic Oborn.

At this time, the Australians often acted as escorts for the American B-29s. While on these missions they frequently found themselves involved in running battles between F-86 Sabres, F-84 Thunderjets and Korean MiGs. Several hits were made on enemy planes but there were no definite kills. The Meteors sustained damage on numerous occasions.

The United Nations pilots were always outnumbered, often three or four to one, and they soon found that the only plane which could match the Russian built-jet was the F-86. In fact, the performance and success of the Sabre so impressed the Australian government that the decision was taken, in October 1951, to acquire a licence to manufacture a modified version of the aircraft in Australia. Plans were made for production to be carried out by the Commonwealth Aircraft Corporation.

During the air battles of October, the pilots of 77 Squadron were always worried about hitting the American planes by mistake. In a hectic dogfight, sometimes only a fleeting glimpse was seen of the swept-wing fighter that happened to hurtle by in front. But the Australians did their job well. At the end of one very heavy engagement, the commanding officer of one of the B-29 squadrons, Colonel Wolfe, landed his damaged plane at Kimpo and had a few beers with the 'Aussies' who had given his boys 'such good protection'.

Vance Drummond was in the thick of this air fighting and by the end of October the US authorities had recommended him for an American Air Medal for ' his courage, aggressiveness and tactical skill'. However, it was to be some time before the medal would be officially awarded.

November, 77 Squadron's main task was to cover the return of fighter-bombers and there were numerous clashes with the enemy. Several Meteors sustained damage but the only losses, two aircraft, happened as the result of a mid-air collision on Armistice Day.

Then came 1 December and the air battle over Sunchon. Vance, who had been on combat operations now for three months, was one of three pilots to be listed as missing in action. He had disappeared for the second time. One of the Meteor pilots perished that day, but the other two, Vance and Bruce Thomson, managed to bail out and were taken prisoner by the North Koreans. By the end of December they had been delivered to the Chinese prisoner-of-war camp at Pinchon-Ne. There they met two other Australians, both former pilots of 77 Squadron.

The first was F/Lt. Gordon Harvey who had been captured on 19 January 1951 when his Mustang crash landed during an attack on the North Korean capital of Pyongyang. It had been his 84th mission. Harvey had received some very rough treatment at the beginning of his captivity while he was in the hands of the North

Black Diamonds formation take off. (Margaret Drummond)

Black Diamonds on display. (Margaret Drummond)

Koreans. In July, he had been finally transferred to Pinchon-Ne. The other was W/O Ron , who had been shot down on the day Vance had arrived at Kimpo.

Living conditions were somewhat primitive at Pinchon-Ne. The prison compound had been built around what was once the village school. This was a long building of timber and mud construction which had been built during the Japanese occupation. Some of the classrooms were used for indoctrination lectures and the others were used as sleeping quarters. Each room had a central alley on either side of which the floor was covered with straw mats on which the prisoners slept at night, covering themselves with a padded quilt, a blanket and a greatcoat to keep off the cold in winter. Outside each room, in the passage, stood a stove. A small ration of wood was provided so water could be heated for personal hygiene and washing clothes.

The daily routine was irritating and simple. At dawn the compound was wakened and the men assembled in the former playground, for physical training exercises. Sometimes, on rare occasions, they had a short escorted walk along the road. Afterwards there was a two and a half hour wait until breakfast. After this, the school bell sounded for the commencement of the morning session of political study. At lunchtime there was a break but no lunch. The afternoon study session began at two and ended at four. The second and last meal was at 4.30 p.m. and this was followed by further study sessions. By 9 p.m., lights were extinguished. This was the normal weekday routine.

The meals were hardly of motel quality. On Mondays, Wednesdays and Fridays both meals consisted of an issue of rice and diacon soup. On Tuesdays there was rice and beans for the evening meal, with two and a half buns of bread. On Saturday evenings there was no bread but there were beans. On Sundays and Thursdays there was rice and pork soup in the morning and pork stew and bread in the evening.

On the surface, this tedious and irksome routine was tolerable. However,there was a little more to it — especially the pressure created by the disappearing prisoners. Every so often someone would vanish, wanted by Headquarters for 'further questioning', or perhaps there would be no explanation at all. Those who went were quite often not heard of again.

POW conditions in general had improved considerably since the beginning of the war, probably because of two factors. The first was the publication of the Handley Report on the treatment of POWs by the Communist Command. The second was the continuation of the peace talks. The Chinese spent much time attempting to create good publicity.

There were, naturally enough, not infrequent attempts to escape, and Vance Drummond did not divorce himself from them. One such attempt took place on Good Friday, 1952. While the attention of the camp was focused upon the religious service and the somewhat limited festivities permitted by the Chinese, he and Bruce Thomson, accompanied by three Americans, escaped from the compound. Unfortunately, as was typical of the majority

Vietnam 1966: Vance Drummond and his Cessna O-1 Bird Dog FAC aircraft named 'Snoopy'. (Margaret Drummond)

of these attempts, the escapees were recaptured within a few days.

They were held in the village's old fire station in a form of solitary confinement. After a month they were given a mock trial staged by their captors, accused of having a 'hostile attitude' to the Chinese People's Volunteers, had their 'confessions' (obtained through a combination of intense interrogation, solitary confinement and beating) presented to the court and were all naturally found guilty. Most of them were sentenced to another month of solitary confinement in accordance with the Geneva Convention. This measure was political at the time because the Geneva Convention was being constantly quoted in the leading Chinese newspapers as the minimum standard by which all POWs might expect to be treated. One of the Americans was singled out for a heavier sentence because the Chinese considered him to be the ring-leader of the escape.

Vance Drummond was to be a POW for eighteen months until his release in September 1953.

Meanwhile, in Australia, at the same time as preparations were being made to release the POWs, the prototype CA-27 Sabre was carrying out flight trials. It first flew on 3 August and it was more than just a locally built version of the F-86F. The RAAF had noted the American jet's shortcomings in combat over Korea and sought to remedy them.

The first was in the area of armament The six .5 inch machine gun-armament, which was standard on the US model, was replaced by two 30 mm Aden cannon. The Americans themselves had recognised the inadequacy of the armament and during the closing stages of the war they were testing, in combat conditions, F-86Fs modified with four 20 mm M39 cannon.

The RAAF also considered that the American machine was underpowered and the decision was made to use the

7500-pound thrust Rolls-Royce Avon RA 7 turbojet. Since this engine was lighter, shorter and fatter than the J47-GE-27 in the standard F-86F, it was necessary to reposition it further back in the fuselage in order to preserve the original centre of gravity. Because of this the engine was no longer supported by the forward fuselage. To compensate, the rear fuselage was shortened by 26 inches (65 cm) and the forward section lengthened by the same amount to retain the standard fuselage length.

It was also necessary to increase the size of the air intake because of the greater power of the Avon engine. To do this the front fuselage was split horizontally and lowered 3½ inches (8.8 cm). The intake was thus enlarged without having to completely change the complex cockpit arrangements. As well, in order to support the jet pipe of the Avon engine so that neither the tail unit flight loads nor the tailplane inertia loads were transferred to the engine, the rear fuselage, as well as being shortened, had to be completely redesigned. As a result of these changes, only about 40% per cent of the original fuselage structure was retained. While the CA-27 looked like the F-86F on the outside, internally it was almost a completely new aeroplane.

As the test program continued, no aerodynamic problems were encountered and few modifications were required. The only trouble which manifested itself was a minor centre of gravity problem which was solved by weighting the nose with an 80-pound (36.3 kg) load of lead.

As the test program continued, F/O Vance Drummond returned to Australia. Not long afterwards, he visited his family in New Zealand. He said little about his experiences as a prisoner. To mention Korea in his presence would cause him to 'clam up' for reasons which were both professional and personal.

However, these experiences did not dampen his enthusiasm for flying and, back in Australia, he enrolled in and completed the Advanced Navigation Course. He was posted back to Williamtown with No. 2 (F) OTU as a staff pilot and during this time he completed No. 3 Fighter Combat Instructors Course. He was to remain at Williamtown for five years.

At this time, everyone in the RAAF was watching and waiting for the arrival of the new Sabres. For the pilots at Williamtown the interest was much more than academic because some of them were to be members of the Sabre Trials Flight. Vance Drummond was one of the chosen few. Among the others were Dick Cresswell, two times commanding officer of 77 Squadron in World War II and Korea, and a familiar face from POW days, Gordon Harvey.

The first production Sabre, A94-901, had made its 35-minute maiden flight on 13 July 1954, less than twelve months after the prototype took to the air. The centre-of-gravity problem which had resulted in the weighting of the nose had been solved in the production model by moving forward a pump which supplied emergency power to the controls. Production aircraft also incorporated a new integral starter motor and improved ammunition feed for the 30 mm Aden cannon. The following month the first of these machines was handed over to the Sabre Trials Flight for evaluation and conversion.

Vance and the other pilots soon realised that they had in their hands an aircraft which was one of the most formidable of the Sabre family. It was much faster, had a higher service ceiling than the existing models and had a climb rate almost twice that of the F-86A which had matched the MiG-15 successfully over Korea. If only the Australians had been flying Avon Sabres instead of Meteors in those days!

The initial order for 72 aircraft was progressively increased, and as production continued various modifications were carried out. The first 22 Sabres, designated Mk 30, were powered by imported Avon RA 7 turbojets but sbsequent aircraft used the 7500-pound thrust CAC built Avon Mk 20 and also featured the '6-3' wing leading-edge to aid high altitude manoeuvrability. These were designated Mk 31. Both versions had provision for two external drop-tanks but the later Mk 32 had attachment points for four drop-tanks.

They were heady and exciting days for Vance, flying one of the best fighter planes in the world, and they were made headier and more exciting by the arrival on the scene of a Newcastle girl called Margaret — the future Mrs Drummond. But things were going too well and there had to be a let-down. The bad news came in June 1955.

Bruce Thomson was dead. He had been killed in an aircraft accident on the 9th while formation flying over Werribee, Victoria.

The news affected Vance deeply. It had been Bruce who had befriended him in the Point Cook days and the Thomson family had welcomed the young New Zealander into their home like a newly arrived son. The experiences they shared together in 77 Squadron and as POWs had served to draw them even closer. To have survived Korea only to die in an aircraft accident seemed so futile. . .

On 16 May 1956, a special parade was held at Williamtown. The occasion was the presentation of American decorations by the US Air Attache, Colonel John Hussey, to three RAAF pilots who had served with distinction in the Korean War. Vance at last received the US Air Medal for which he had been recommended back in 1951.One of the other pilots to receive awards on that day was F/Lt. Bruce Gogerly, DFC, who had come to Vance's assistance in that air battle on 1 December 1951.

Vance left Williamtown in February 1959 when he was posted to Headquarters Operational Command. By now he had a clear aim in his mind — to obtain command of his own squadron. The less time he spent away from flying the better, but for the time being he had to be patient. After his stint at Headquarters he attended No. 15 Course, RAAF Staff College, and was then posted to No. 81 Wing.

In December 1961 he returned to an operational squadron for the first time since 1951 when he was posted back to Williamtown as a flight commander of 75 Squadron. This was more to his liking and he was even more delighted when, in October 1962, he was given leadership of the Black Diamonds aerobatic team.

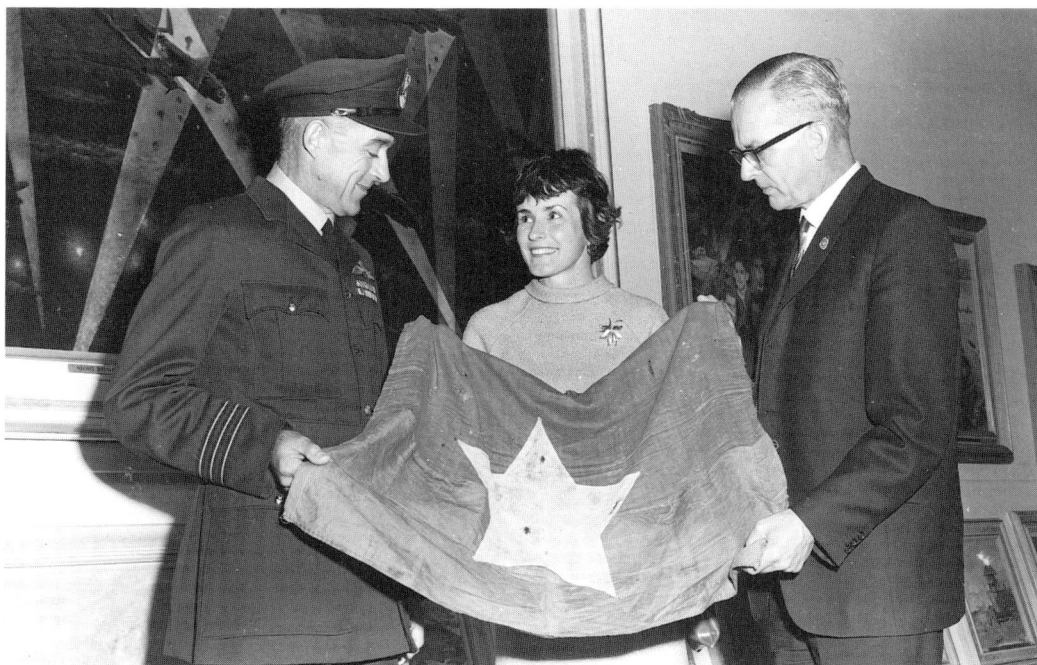

Presentation of the captured Viet Cong flag to the Australian War Memorial, Canberra. Left to right, W/Cdr B. Rachinger, Margaret Drummond, Mr Lancaster, Director of the AWM. (AWM)

The Black Diamonds had been first formed within 75 Squadron in 1961 but they had not been given full recognition by Operational Command. Just after Vance took over they were given notice to prepare for a display within two weeks. Their aerobatic practices were carried out in addition to their normal routine within the fighter squadron. On schedule, they gave their first official demonstration when they entertained visiting cadets from the US Air Academy at Richmond, NSW. The display was a resounding success and from then on the Black Diamonds were acknowledged as the official RAAF aerobatic squad.

Over the next two years the Sabre Mk 32s of the Black Diamonds became a familiar sight over many special functions all over Australia and also in New Guinea. The name Black Diamonds was derived from the shape of the formation in which they flew. This was in a four-aircraft 'box' or 'diamond'. The colour came from the squadron's colours of black and white.

During a typical display, approximately eighteen minutes were taken up with precision aerobatic formation flying led by Vance. Strict discipline and split-second timing were required because at all times during the manoeuvres the planes would only be about eight feet (2.4 m) apart. They flew at speeds ranging from 350 to 510 mph (560-820 km/h). To finish off the formation display, they would hurtle upwards in a vertical climb at 400 knots, increasing power as they went. Black Diamond Leader would then call 'Vertical black delta, bomb blast. . . GO' and the formation would erupt in different directions.

Following that, the fifth member of the Black Diamonds team, Major Joe Turner, USAF, would give a five-minute display of solo aerobatics to finish off the performance. Joe Turner was from Arizona and had joined 75 Squadron in October 1961 on exchange duty. Prior to coming to Australia he had flown F-100 Super Sabres.

They participated in the flypast saluting the opening and closing of the VIIth Commonwealth Games in November 1962, at Perth. They also gave aerobatic demonstrations at that time at Pearce Air Force Base.In February 1963, they headed for Hobart, where they demonstrated their skills over the Royal Hobart Regatta which was presided over by HRH Queen Elizabeth and Prince Phillip. Vance led the Coral Sea flypast over Sydney in May and the Black Diamonds performed over Darwin in July. In September, during Air Force Week, they gave displays at Pearce, Amberley and Richmond. Vance then led the Sabres from Williamtown in the formation of a cross over St Mary's Church, Newcastle, as the Requiem Mass for President Kennedy ended. In June 1964, the Black Diamonds turned up in Port Moresby where they participated in the flypast to celebrate the opening of New Guinea's House of Assembly. Afterwards they gave a 'stunning' aerobatic display before a crowd of 8000 people.

Unfortunately, however, the era of the Black Diamonds was drawing to a close. Not long after Port Moresby, Joe Turner returned to the United States. Also, 75 Squadron was scheduled to be re-equipped with the new Mirage fighter. It would be the first squadron to lose its Sabres and, with the parting, the role of official aerobatic squad would be handed on to another squadron.

Then, in December 1964, Squadron Leader Vance Drummond was posted to the Department of Air in Canberra. It was a sad leave-taking and Vance had to resign himself to the prospect of staff work again for the next three years. But there was compensation. In January 1965 it was announced in the New Years Honours List that he had been awarded the Air Force Cross 'in recognition of his valuable service'.

After twelve months in Canberra, Vance had settled in to the routine of 'flying a desk' when suddenly, out of the blue, he received three weeks notice to go to Vietnam and be attached to the US Air Force for duties with a Tactical Air Control Party. At the same time he was given the rank of acting wing commander.The move was completely unexpected. John Myers, a friend and classmate from Point Cook days and Korea, had been scheduled to take up the appointment but he had been injured in a traffic accident and was unable to go. Vance arrived in Vietnam for what he considered would be his third brush with Asian Communism and he was determined that this third time would be different. Instead of being helpless or on the receiving end, he would dish it out!

At the beginning he was assigned to the 7th Air Force to study tactical air control techniques at the centre at Tun Son Nhut. On 8 July, 1966, on his own initiative, he was posted to the 19th Tactical Air Support Squadron as a forward air controller (FAC) for experience of a more practical nature.

Close air support, controlled by the FAC, was one of the most effective measures employed against the Viet Cong. The VC were elusive and highly mobile. They could set up an ambush, strike hard and fast and be gone. The old method used in the Korean War of having an air liaison officer with a ground unit who called for air support proved to be ineffective because reaction time was too slow. It was necessary for the air liaison officer of Korean times to be airborne and mobile. Hence, the forward air controller.

The first FACs of the Vietnam War were all senior American air force officers with several thousand flying hours up. Vance, the first FAC from the RAAF, fitted in easily among them because of his long hours on Sabres.

The plane used for the job at this stage of the war was the Cessna O-1 Bird Dog. It was a high-wing, two-seat observation plane which had been serving in the US armed forces since 1950. Its slow cruising speed of just over 100 miles per hour (160 km/h) made it ideal for spotting enemy ambush sites and concealed troops. It had several shortcomings, however, such as its lack of armour, no self-sealing fuel tanks and short range. The low number of marker rockets it could carry was also a limitation on the duration of its operations. The later Cessna O-2 was an improvement but it was really only a stopgap replacement until the North American OV-10A Bronco became available.

Vance and his American pilot operated an O-1 Bird Dog they called 'Snoopy'.

The FAC had to know his assigned area better than he knew the palm of his own hand. He had to know the habits of the local people, what sort of traffic could be expected on rivers and roads, and be acquainted with the various tracks in use. If there were any suspicious circumstances he could request an air strike by calling Direct Air Support Centre.

The Direct Air Support Centre could not authorise an air strike without the approval of the local Vietnamese province chiefs, some of whom were extremely reluctant to do so. If permission was given and the attack was to go ahead, the FAC had to circle the area waiting for the incoming fighter-bombers.

When they arrived and contact was established, the FAC would mark the target with smoke rockets or smoke grenades. Then he had to control the action of the attack. This was the most dangerous part of the operation. Generally, before the target had been attacked, the VC chose not to fire on the FAC, hoping that they had avoided detection. Once the strike was under way there was no such restriction and as the FAC swooped down to assess results, the VC, if there were any still alive, would often give the plane a hot reception. The whole affair could be extremely frustrating and dangerous, as Vance's mission on 2 August demonstrated.

On this day there was to be a strike against suspected VC concentrations along the river south of Saigon. Vance was to work with a flight of four F-100 Super Sabres from the 612th Tactical Fighter Squadron based at Phan Rang. When they rendezvoused over the target, Vance's pilot pushed the tiny Cessna into a dive and fired marker rockets. The target area was a grove of trees bordering the river opposite a Vietnamese village.

With the target marked, Snoopy climbed to a vantage point so that Vance could direct the strike. He instructed the first American pilots to attack with their CBUs to catch any VC who may have been in the open under the trees. The CBU-2A was a cluster bomb unit made up of several small anti-personnel bombs designed to separate when dropped to give maximum coverage of the target area. It was very effective against troop concentrations

February 1967: W/Cdr Vance Drummond, CO No. 3 Squadron RAAF. (Margaret Drummond)

in the open away from fortified positions. The following F-100s were to attack with 750-pound napalm bombs.

But as the attack started, both Vance and the F-100 leader noticed enemy fire coming from the village on the opposite side of the river. Apparently the VC had shifted into the village and they were firing from a large stone building situated in the centre. As the F-100s circled above, Vance identified it as a church. There was no doubt about it being the VC position because gun barrels could be clearly seen protruding from the windows.

He immediately asked the Direct Air Support Centre for permission to strike the village. A few minutes later the reply came back and it was negative, the province chief had refused. The Direct Air Support Centre insisted that the F-100s should continue to attack the original target, the trees on the other side of the river.

The Super Sabres screamed in again but it was obviously a waste of fuel and effort because the area was deserted. With each pass the VC, realising that they were safe in the church, increased the volume of their anti-aircraft fire. They even began firing on the Cessna.

Vance kept on pleading for permission to strike the church. Bombs and ammunition were being wasted and it was only a matter of time before someone would be shot down. Finally, the province chief partially relented and gave permission to attack the village but not the church. By this time the F-100s had used all of their ordnance except for their 20 mm cannon. Nevertheless, they came down on strafing runs and with the first attack the anti-aircraft fire decreased, but when it became obvious that the church was not the target the VC redoubled their firing.

The situation was ridiculous. The only VC in the village were undoubtedly in the church but the opportunity to hit them was being denied! The Cessna was also being peppered by a hail of bullets. There was only one thing to do, as painful as it was obvious, and only Vance Drummond, as FAC, could take the responsibility. He, ordered the Super Sabres to attack the church. They swooped down and used up their remaining ammunition on the building. The enemy guns fell silent.

Vance never found out how many VC casualties there were that day. The enemy had already gone, taking their dead and wounded with them, by the time ground forces arrived. Villagers were reluctant to give information because of the possibility of VC reprisals.

More positive results had been obtained on the night of 24 July. There had been a heavy battle in Vance's area in which friendly troops were trapped in forest country and surrounded by the enemy. Vance and his American pilot continually flew in low dropping flares illuminating VC positions and calling up air support in the shape of fighter-bombers and helicopter gunships. They remained over the battle directing the strikes for three hours and only considered leaving when the fighter-bombers had gone, the flares had gone and fuel was running low.

But the enemy was still applying pressure on the encircled troops so, at the risk of running completely out of fuel, they decided to stay until they were relieved by another aircraft with flares. The mere sound of an O-1 circling overhead was enough to inhibit VC movements. After being relieved, they returned to base with the gauge showing empty and landed shortly before midnight. There the plane was refuelled and rearmed. It was 12.15 a.m. when they took off again.

Back over the battle, they found that the enemy had mounted another attack. Again they swooped low marking

Lord Casey presenting Vance Drummond's Distinguished Flying Cross to his son, David. (Margaret Drummond)

targets, directing ground fire and calling up further air strikes. They were in constant contact with the unit on the ground which had suffered heavy casualties. Vance's voice coming over the radio was the only link they had with safety. He and his pilot only left when their fuel was dangerously low again.

Landing back at base was a perilous affair. Base consisted of 1000 feet of dirt airstrip shrouded in darkness and falling rain.

But the trapped ground unit was still under constant attack. After snatching only two hours' sleep, the two men volunteered to again fly back to the area. When they arrived they found the VC had launched yet another assault. Again they fired flares and marker rockets in a bid to keep off the enemy. Again they summoned air strikes and until the fighter-bombers arrived they went in low, firing for all they were worth with the automatic weapons they carried in the cockpit. The O-1 met heavy anti-aircraft fire but emerged unscathed.

When the fighter-bombers arrived they went in again, still in the face of heavy ground fire, to mark the friendly and enemy troop positions. When daylight came they could see that not only had the trapped unit been saved, there were over 150 enemy corpses littering the battlefield.

But the job was not yet over and Snoopy remained in the area to mark the landing zone for helicopter reinforcements. Vance and his companion refused to leave until the area was secured. They had flown four sorties altogether and a total of eleven flying hours, plus five hours they had flown the previous day. The ground unit had received effective cover for at least ten and a half of those hours. For his part in this action Vance Drummond was recommended for the DFC.

Some time later a captured Viet Cong flag was presented to him by American ground forces. He sent the flag to the Department of Defence in Canberra and in October it was presented to the Australian War Memorial.

Meanwhile, Vance kept flying missions without respite and his skills as an FAC won him an enviable reputation. Captain Gene A. Teany, USAF, later wrote 'we all considered him to be one of the best Forward Air Controllers we'd ever seen and at different times he helped all of us out of a tight spot'. Teany had only met Vance personally on one occasion but spoke to him almost daily on the radio 'and felt as though he was a close friend.'

Danger was ever present. Once a bullet from the ground missed Vance's head by millimetres. When they landed they found the bullet on the floor. Vance tossed a coin with his pilot to see who would keep it as a souvenir. Lady Luck went with the American.

While Vance Drummond and his plane Snoopy became well known among the Americans, he only saw fellow members of the RAAF once a month when he landed at Vung Tau to pick up his pay and any mail.

For an action which occurred on 27 October, in which he accurately and effectively located enemy positions for fighter-bombers, Vance received the Cross of Gallantry with Silver Star from the Republic of Vietnam.

By the time he had finished his tour of duty he had flown 381 combat missions, most of them of around three hours' duration. As the RAAF's first Forward Air Controller he had set a high standard for those following to emulate.

Back in Australia, Vance at last achieved his long sought after goal — command of his own squadron. It was not to be just any squadron. It was to be. 3 Squadron, one of the RAAF's most prestigious fighter units. No. 3 Squadron had its origins in the days of the Australian Flying Corps and it won many honours in the Middle East and Europe in World War II. It was in the process of being re-equipped with new Mirage fighters.

The old Sabres were being retired. A total of 22 Mk 30s had been built, 20 Mk 31s and the remaining 69 were Mk.32s. Of those that remained, 16 were given to Malaysia and another 16 went to Indonesia. No. 75 Squadron had been the first to re-equip with the Mirage, and in May 1967 they took their new jets to Butterworth. Meanwhile, No. 3 Squadron, which had been stationed at Butterworth, returned to Williamtown earlier for its change over.

Wing Commander Vance Drummond took over his new command on 2 February 1967.

A little over three months later, at 4.20 p.m. on 17 May, Vance led three other members of his squadron in simulated fighter attack exercises at 35 000 feet (10 668 m) off the coast of Newcastle. They were well above a thick layer of cloud which was at 22 000 feet (6707 m). Vance's Mirage, A3-77, went into a dive and disappeared into the cloud. The other three pilots waited, but the Mirage did not reappear. At last, they decided to descend into the cloud but when they broke out below there was still no sign of their leader.

After reporting their fears, they conducted a search and thought they noticed an oil slick on the surface of the water. There was nothing else, no sign of a parachute, life preserver or rubber raft. It was just on dusk and there was nothing anyone could do but return to Williamtown. An air-sea rescue helicopter dispatched to the area also had to give up because of darkness.

That night and all through next day, radar-equipped, anti-submarine Neptunes from Richmond searched and re-searched the area, but in vain. The RAAF crash boat and air-sea rescue helicopters were also on the job but the result was the same. They were obliged to officially end the search at dusk on the next day. All hope was gone.

Vance Drummond had disappeared for the third time and this time it was different. This time he would not return.

During his years of service with the RAAF those around him had seen Vance mature from a highly skilled, determined and uncompromising junior officer into an outstanding leader. With the command of a fighter squadron he had achieved his aim but there is little doubt that, in terms of his career, much more awaited him. To have survived Vietnam only to die in an aircraft accident...

On 5 April 1968, a small figure walked across the floor of Government House and was presented with a medal by the Queen's representative, Lord Casey. The medal was the Distinguished Flying Cross. Its presentation had been delayed while the citation awaited the Queen's signature. It rightfully belonged to Wing Commander Vance Drummond. The boy who received it was his representative. . .his nine-year-old son, David.

The RAAF's restored Sabre A94-983 in Black Diamond markings. (Dennis Newton)

12

BUSHRANGERS AND EMUS
AUSTRALIAN GUNSHIP OPERATIONS
OVER VIETNAM

At a SEATO conference held in April 1964, the Council expressed serious concern over the critical situation in Vietnam, warning of grave consequences if the South should be overrun by the Viet Cong, who were poised to take advantage of a deteriorating military and political climate. US President Lyndon B. Johnson requested those nations already assisting there to increase their aid. At that stage, Australia had already committed a small group of army instructors who were expert in jungle warfare. On 8 June 1964 Australia announced that additional military assistance would be given, this time including an RAAF transport flight of six Caribou aircraft to assist with airlift support for the Vietnamese armed forces in the field.

By the end of that year the United States was moving towards the commitment of American combat forces in South Vietnam, and during December Australia was asked directly for further military contributions. On 2 March 1965 the USAF began Operation Rolling Thunder, its sustained air assault on North Vietnam. A few days later US Marines came ashore to provide a static defence for Da Nang airfield, from where US aircraft operated. Earlier, the US had suggested that as air pressure on North Vietnam increased it could be very helpful to have Australian aircraft either participating or standing by to protect Thailand, Laos, or South Vietnam. No. 79 (Sabre) Squadron RAAF was already based at Ubon as part of the air defence of Thailand. It would remain there until August 1968.

By the end of March 1965 the Americans had decided to commit their ground forces to offensive ground operations and, on 1 April, President Johnson approved 'The urgent exploration with the Korean, Australian and New Zealand governments of the possibility of rapid deployment of significant combat elements from their armed forces in parallel with the additional Marine deployments'. Australia committed the 1st Battalion,

Royal Australian Regiment (RAR) to operations with the US 173rd Airborne Brigade at Bien Hoa, near Saigon.

Fighting in South Vietnam continued to escalate in 1966 following great increases in the build-up of forces on both sides. US forces alone rose from approximately 185 000 men in December 1965 to some 385 000 in December 1966. The Australian commitment trebled with the arrival in Phuoc Tuy Province, in mid-1966, of a combined Army/RAAF Task Force. This included No. 9 Squadron RAAF, equipped with eight Iroquois helicopters. W/Cdr Ray Scott was CO of No. 9 Squadron. At the same time the Caribou Transport Flight was upgraded and renamed 35 Transport Squadron. A Base Support Flight was added to provide facilities and services for the RAAF contingent.

The main party of No. 9 Squadron RAAF arrived at Vung Tau from Richmond, NSW, on a Qantas charter flight on 12 June and the very next day the squadron was needed to ferry 9000 pounds of ammunition to the 5th Battalion RAR at the new Task Force Headquarters at Nui Dat. The squadron was not yet fully operational, only two of the Iroquois having been fitted with armoured seats for protection from ground fire. W/Cdr Ray Scott ordered these two aircraft to carry out the task and flew one of them himself.

No. 9 Squadron was quickly committed to operations. These involved, along with other responsibilities, the insertion and extraction of Australian Special Air Service (SAS) patrols. On 10 July 1966, when they landed to pick up a six-man patrol, two Iroquois, one captained by F/Lt Cliff Dohle and the other by F/Lt Bruce Lane, came under fire. The helicopter crews responded with their own machine guns. The SAS patrol reported that there had been 20 Viet Cong in the immediate vicinity within 20 yards of the helicopters. Two covering US army gunships (more heavily armed helicopters) were late, saw the exchange of fire but did not join in because they were uncertain of the position of friendly forces in the area.

Dust-off missions involved the airlifting of casualties from the battlefield. A typical dust-off occurred on 25 July when the Task Force suffered three killed and nineteen wounded during Operation Hobart. With one helicopter flying top cover, four others landed in turn to pick up the wounded and fly them directly to the helicopter pad at the US Army's 36th Evacuation Hospital at Vung Tau.

The Australian Task Force had not been in Phuoc Tuy Province long when it fought one of its most successful actions in Vietnam — the Battle of Long Tan. This began on 18 August 1966 when D Company, 6th Battalion RAR, ran into an ambush set up by two regular Viet Cong formations at Long Tan, a derelict village some 4400 yards from Task Force Headquarters at Nui Dat. In a furious engagement, the Australians were raked by heavy fire from the front and both sides. Ammunition became critically low, obliging the company commander to call urgently for more. Two RAAF helicopters were immediately loaded with 1150 pounds of ammunition. Ignoring safety, they flew in at treetop level through torrential rain which reduced visibility below acceptable standards of safety. Despite this, they found the company in the dark and dropped the ammunition on target. Over the radio an excited voice was heard shouting, 'You bloody beaut, that was smack on!'

When it was all over, seven RAAF helicopters on standby flew in to hastily prepared landing pads for evacuation of the wounded. Task force losses stood at 18 killed and 21 wounded but the ambush had cost the enemy 245 killed, several hundred more wounded and the loss of a large quantity of arms, ammunition and equipment.

No. 9 Squadron lost its first UH-1B helicopter (A2-1018) on 18 October 1966 while supporting the army in the mountains of Phuoc Tuy Province. The helicopter was heavily loaded with explosives when it crashed and caught fire. After checking himself for injury, Sgt Gordon Buttriss of Sefton, NSW, a crewman, noticed assistant crewman LAC Thomas Farr lying outside. He was still wearing his safety belt. Buttriss warned Farr to get clear and at the same time he dragged one of the two army engineer passengers through the starboard cargo door onto the ground several yards off. He then returned to the burning helicopter and after removing the second soldier's pack, which was snagging on an obstacle, dragged him clear through the left- hand door. At the same time, he saw that aircraft captain, F/Lt Cliff Dohle, had managed to leave safely. Returning a second time, Buttriss tried to lift out second pilot, F/Lt Peter Middleton but noticed his right foot was jammed against a large tree that had pierced the front of the aircraft. Buttriss ran around to the front and began pulling away parts of the machine to free

April 1968, EMU Slicks in formation over Phuoc Tuy Province. (AWM)

Middleton's leg. Back inside again, flame from the bulkhead singed Buttriss' hair and he sprayed the fire with an extinguisher, but in vain. At last, two soldiers arrived and together they managed to move the co-pilot clear to safety behind some rocks. Not content, Buttriss then returned for the other army passenger still lying beside the aircraft. Ammunition began to explode and the fire became intense just as everyone was safely behind rocks.

F/Lt Dohle had suffered a compression fracture to his back and collapsed as he tried to walk from the scene. Middleton had serious jaw, facial and leg injuries. Both Buttriss and Farr were bruised. For his courageous actions during this incident Gordon Buttriss won the George Cross.

On 16 December, W/Cdr Scott finished his tour in Vietnam and handed 9 Squadron over to W/Cdr Roy Royston. The new CO was soon in action and on 11 January 1967 led four helicopters in an airborne assault landing of 37 Vietnamese Army soldiers into a rice paddy in the Long Hai hills area.

The first RAAF serviceman to be wounded in the Vietnam War was hit on 29 July 1967. He was crewman

LAC John Henson of Cairns, Queensland. During a resupply mission, a burst of enemy gunfire blasted several empty jerry cans out of the helicopter. A soldier sitting on one can had it shot away from under him. Fortunately, he was unhurt after being thrown back onto Henson, who was wounded in the leg. At the 8th Field Ambulance, the fragment was removed from his upper left leg.

A week later on 6 August, S/Ldr Jim Cox became the first RAAF pilot to be wounded in action. Two days earlier, 7 RAR had gone on the offensive south-west of Nui Dat with Operation Ballarat. The battalion entered its area of operations on foot, carrying rations for five days. The stealth of the Australians caught the enemy by surprise and there were several contacts. One turned into the savage battle of Suoi Chau Pha, with two Viet Cong platoons and two Australian platoons locked in a vicious fight at close range. Six RAAF helicopters arrived in the rear and began the slow, dangerous task of winching out the wounded who had to be tied to stretchers. Despite volleys fired at the aircraft, which hit several, the RAAF pilots persisted and evacuated the casualties. Jim Cox's helicopter was hovering over the area to begin winching up casualties from the jungle floor when a bullet tore part of his right boot away and wounded his leg. The winch gear put out of action, P/O Peter Davidson, the co-pilot, took over the controls. Because battle damage had made it incapable of completing the mission, it was flown back to base. Cox's damaged boot was later donated to the Australian War Memorial as a souvenir. Six Australian soldiers had been killed and nineteen wounded. Ten Viet Cong bodies were recovered and it was estimated that many more casualties had been caused to the enemy Cong battalion under the weight of supporting artillery, mortar rounds and air strikes.

That August was a hectic month for the Australian helicopter crews. P/O Michael Haxell landed near Xuyen Moc on the 13th for an emergency extraction of an SAS patrol pinned down by enemy fire. With the patrol scrambling aboard, gunfire severely damaged the Iroquois but Haxell succeeded in making a difficult downwind take-off and nursing it back to a safe landing at Xuyen Moc. The aircraft could not be flown again until repairs were carried out at Vung Tau to where it was airlifted by a US Chinook helicopter. P/O Haxell was later awarded the DFC.

On the 20th, crewmen of two Iroquois fought a battle with Viet Cong at less than 25 yards distance during the emergency winching extraction of another SAS patrol from thick jungle. LAC P. Covington immediately engaged the enemy with his machine-gun and covering US gunships moved into attack with rockets and machine-gun fire close to the RAAF helicopter. Covington was apparently hit by shrapnel from an American rocket exploding close by.

Another RAAF crewman, Corporal John (Snow) Coughlan, earned the Conspicuous Gallantry Medal, the highest flying award then available to RAAF non-commissioned airmen of the RAAF other than the Victoria Cross. Coughlan risked his life, despite being faced with the hazard of exploding ammunition and rockets, to help rescue injured and burned crew members of an American helicopter gunship which had crashed into the jungle on 3 October, five miles north-west of Nui Dat.

Also in October, Canberra announced increasing Australian forces in Vietnam to 8000 including additional navy, army and air force components. This would be the peak of Australian strength in the war and it included boosting the size of 9 Squadron by eight additional helicopter crews and servicing personnel. Incoming crews would include reinforcements from the navy. The RAN detachment would comprise of eight Fleet Air Arm pilots sent to 9 Squadron at intervals from February to May 1968. Lt A. A. Hill, first of the RAN pilots, joined 9 Squadron in February. He was followed a month later by

Unable to land because of thick undergrowth, an RAAF Iroquois winches up a casualty. Called 'hot extractions', this method of evacuation often also had to be used to extract troops under fire. (AWM)

Sub-Lieuts G. E. S. Vidal and M. J. Ward. The remaining pilots joined in May, with Lt/Cdr R. A. Waddell-Wood becoming officer-in-charge of the detachment. In addition to the RAN detachment, thirteen pilots were supplied by the Royal New Zealand Air Force.

Australian Fleet Air Arm crews were already operational in Vietnam — with the Americans. On 2 November 1967, the 135th Assault Helicopter Company of the 12th Combat Aviation Group, US Army, began its combat operations over South Vietnam. Sprinkled among the US personnel were the men of the First Contingent, Royal Australian Navy Helicopter Flight Vietnam (RANHFV). This integration of two nationalities into one company was an experiment. The company was designated as an 'Experimental Military Unit'. Because of this the 135th became known as the EMUs.

The 135th Aviation Company had been formed on 1 July 1965, at Fort Benning, Georgia. At the time it was equipped with Caribou transport aircraft, but in February 1967 it converted to helicopters. Then, early in October, the 135th, now renamed an 'assault helicopter company', was deployed in Vietnam flying Bell UH-1B Iroquois helicopters, known as the 'Huey' by the US Army. Meanwhile, on 14 July 1967, the Australian government announced that eight RAN pilots with supporting personnel would join an American Army helicopter unit in South Vietnam. The Australians arrived on 15 October and from then on carried out training flights to familiarise themselves with local conditions before commencing operations. For a major part of the RAN involvement, the EMUs were controlled by the 164th Combat Aviation Group based at Bien Hoa, north of Saigon, and then later at Can Tho in Phong Dinh province. The motto chosen by the EMUs was both simple and graphic: 'Get the Bloody Job Done'.

The 1st Contingent RANHFV was commanded by Lt/Cdr N. Ralph. When the Australians were integrated with the US personnel, he became second-in-command of the unit. The second senior RAN officer was Lt/Cdr P. J. Vickers who also commanded the 1st Platoon.

The EMUs' first major operation was carried out in conjunction with more than 80 other helicopters in Operation Santa Fe — one of the largest scale efforts of the Vietnam War up to that stage. No. 9 Squadron RAAF was also involved. The task of the helicopters was to airlift troops in a sweep against the 5th Viet Cong Division. Allied forces consisted of the 1st Australian Task Force, the 9th US Infantry Division and the 18th ARVN (Army of the Republic of Vietnam) Division. The EMUs worked with the Americans.

Later in November the first EMU helicopter was shot down. Two gunships were on standby when they were called out to aid a merchant ship which was under fire in the Rung Sat special zone. The helicopters located the enemy positions and began strafing attacks. On the second run in, the gunship flown by Sub/Lt Anthony Casadio, RAN, and W/O Esterhazy, US Army, was struck by ground fire from automatic weapons. The port mini-gun and the fuel tanks were damaged and a fuel booster pump was destroyed. With fuel streaming from the punctured tanks, Casadio searched for a place to land. The VC kept firing as he brought the helicopter down in a cleared area nearby.

Casadio and his men quickly detached the machine-guns and took cover. As the VC attempted to close they were met by a withering hail of bullets. They were also kept at bay by the presence of the other gunship, which continued to circle overhead and give cover until it was short of fuel. Finally it had to return to base but other EMU helicopters soon arrived. By the time the area was secured and Casadio and his crew picked up, they had accounted for two known Viet Cong dead and driven away an unknown number of others. Casadio's gunship was later recovered by a Chinook and carried back to Vung Tau.

The most common EMU flights were troop insertions in whichabout ten troop-carrying helicopters (slicks) transported soldiers from their base and landed them near suspected or known enemy strong points to carry out search-and-destroy missions. The ten slicks were usually escorted by four gunships flying in pairs, known as 'light fire teams'. While the operation progressed a command and control helicopter flew overhead. In this was the air mission commander who coordinated the air and ground operations with the troop commander. After dropping their troops, the slicks would fly to a safe staging point where they awaited their next missions, such as evacuation of the wounded. With the operation over or at the end of the day, the slicks were again called in to airlift the troops back to their base or to take them to a night-ambush position. The EMUs carried out their first successful night combat operation on 16 December when they evacuated the US 199th Light Infantry Brigade which had attacked a well-defended VC bunker system. Lt/Cdr Ralph acted as air mission commander.

Later in December, the EMUs moved from Vung Tau, which was a secure base, to Camp Blackhorse, some 35 miles away. The move committed them to the support of more units over a wider area. The 18th ARVN Division which was responsible for the northern area of Saigon, and the US 101st Airborne Division to the west of Saigon, could also call on them now.

On 12 January 1968, two Australians, Naval Airman K. Wardle and Leading Mechanic K. French, were among those who were injured when their gunship helicopter was forced down into the jungle. The wreck burst into flames and they had to clamber out quickly and dive for cover to avoid being struck by exploding ammunition. Smoke from

A 'heavy duty' American Chinook helicopter shows its capabilities by airlifting a 105 mm howitzer. In the same manner, disabled Iroquois could be transported back out of battle zones to their bases for repair. No. 9 Squadron RAAF had to make use of this service when, on 13 August 1967, P/O Michael Haxell landed near Xuyen Moc to extract an SAS patrol pinned down by enemy fire. As the patrol scrambled aboard, gunfire severely damaged the Iroquois but Haxell succeeded in making a difficult down wind take-off and nursing it back to a safe landing at Xuyen Moc. From there, the aircraft was airlifted by a Chinook to Vung Tau for repairs. (AWM)

the fire attracted the rescue helicopters of 9 Squadron RAAF onto the scene and they were winched to safety.

For the people of Vietnam the celebration of the Chinese lunar new year or Tet was, and is, an important event similar to our own Christmas and New Year festive season. In 1968 it fell at the end of January and both sides called for a temporary cease-fire. The Viet Cong announced that they would observe a seven day truce from 27 January to 3 February. However, intelligence reports suggested otherwise. Massive and widespread arms build-ups were known to be occurring throughout the northern provinces of South Vietnam. General F. Weyland, US Deputy Commander, placed the Allies on full alert 36 hours after the beginning of the declared cease-fire.

On 30 January the Viet Cong and the North Vietnamese launched their Tet Offensive. Bitter fighting seemed to break out everywhere. Attacks were made simultaneously on the government in Saigon, on provincial and district capitals and on key Allied military installations. Viet Cong guerillas raided the US Embassy in Saigon but were wiped out after a six-hour battle. The huge US air base at Da Nang was attacked with mortars and rockets and six planes, four F-4 Phantoms and two A-26 Invaders, were destroyed. There was heavy fighting in 26 of the country's 44 provincial capitals.

Meanwhile, on 29 January, because of the temporary absence of Lt/Col Cory, Lt/Cdr Ralph found himself in command of the EMUs when the fighting began — thus becoming the first RAN officer to command a unit of the US Army. Two days later, when acting as air mission commander, he and his crew emerged unscathed from three separate mortar attacks on the ground while working with the US 25th Infantry Division west of Saigon.

On 8 February, the US 9th Infantry Division found itself heavily engaged against a strong force of VC near My Tho. The EMUs airlifted the troops in and Lt/Cdr Vickers led the slicks. On the third run-in automatic fire hit one of the American helicopters flown by Captain R. D. Freer, US Army. The aircraft crashed into the jungle and there were no survivors. These were the first EMU airmen to be killed in action. In this same battle eight helicopters were struck by ground fire, two of them being damaged beyond repair. Two Australians were forced to land their machines because of battle damage and they spent the night with the American troops before being lifted out and back to Blackhorse.

Lt/Cdr Vickers was again piloting the lead slick two weeks later on 22 February. The mission was to airlift troops of the 18th ARVN Division from an area near Xuan Loc. As he brought the helicopter down the enemy opened fire and Vickers was hit. He passed out. Acting quickly, his co-pilot immediately took over, rushed back to Blackhorse and landed back on the hospital pad within five minutes. Unfortunately, in spite of this gallant effort, the Australian died without regaining consciousness. Vickers was granted the posthumous award of Mention in Dispatches for 'repeated acts of heroism and meritorious service as a pilot'.

The EMUs had their revenge next day by killing 20 Viet Cong while providing continuous air fire support for the 25th ARVN Division south of Saigon.

The Tet Offensive had been the enemy's bid to win the war in one bold stroke but, thanks to accurate intelligence information and Allied preparedness, by the end of February — although sporadic fighting continued — it was obvious that the bid had failed. The Communists suffered heavy casualties.

Camp Blackhorse was not directly attacked during Tet, but there were skirmishes on the boundaries and the supply roads were frequently mined. However, it was subjected to a mortar attack on 9 March. Only eight people were injured and there was some minor damage to some of the buildings.

Meanwhile, at the height of Tet, 9 Squadron RAAF was in the process of replacing its eight UH-1B Iroquois with the more powerful and larger UH-1H model and increasing its strength from eight to sixteen aircraft. Also, since late 1967, the commander of the RAAF contingent at Vung Tau, G/Capt John Hubble, had been proposing that 9 Squadron should be equipped with its own gunships. While awaiting an official response to these proposals, experimentation began to find an arrangement suitable for the RAAF helicopters. Components obtained on loan from local American sources were mounted on Iroquois A2-1025. Included in the system were two rocket-launchers (one each side of the fuselage), each pod carrying seven 2.75-inch Folding Fin Aircraft Rockets (FFAR). These missiles were fitted with either 10- or 17-pound (4.5 or 7.7 kg) high-explosive heads, or flechettes, and had an effective range of about 2200 yards. Also part of the system were four M60C machine-guns fixed to fire forward plus twin-mounted M60s at the side doors, making a total of eight machine-guns on board.

The prototype Australian gunship, dubbed 'Ned Kelly', was completed on 21 January 1968 and tests planned. These had not proceeded beyond the ground firing stage when they were delayed. The weight of operations required A2-1025's urgent conversion back to slick configuration. When the pace of operational activity reverted to normal levels, the system was refitted. Successful ground firings were carried out on 17 February, followed by equally successful flight-handling and air-firing trials which began on 19 February.

Further trials were made later with a UH-1H model and the greater lift capacity of this type allowed for the carriage of two seven-tube rocket pods, two 7.62 mm mini-guns with an ammunition load of 9600 rounds in sixteen ammunition bins strapped to the floor behind the pilots in addition to two sets of twin-mounted side firing M60 machine-guns with a total ammunition load of 4000 rounds. In the meantime, a number of pilots experienced gunship operations with the EMUs at Blackhorse. They found Blackhorse hot and dusty and a very busy base which never seemed to stop. This taught the RAAF pilots much about the techniques of mass formation and large-scale troop airlifts. While initial experience of gunship operations was learned this way, RAAF gunship crews would mainly learn their skills on the job.

Early in May, a convoy of the 18th ARVN Division was ambushed on Highway 1. A quick counter-attack by the EMU gunships, combined with tactical air support, helped to break the ambush and kill 200 Viet Cong. Not long afterwards, during an insertion mission on 18 May, an enemy force ambushed a flight of EMU slicks and gunships. The VC opened up as the soldiers were leaving the slicks. Of the ten aircraft hit, seven were disabled and two had to be written off. Lt B. C. Crawford RAN had a narrow escape when a bullet smashed through the windscreen of his helicopter not more than three inches from his head.

It was obvious that the slicks were most vulnerable when they were either disembarking or embarking troops in the landing zone. New tactics were needed to protect them. It was decided to employ one heavily armed helicopter as a 'smokeship' to cover and lay a smokescreen in front of the slicks. A Huey was modified by placing a spray ring on the exhaust. This sprayed oil into the hot exhaust air and created a dense white vapour. There was one drawback. While this provided excellent cover for the others, it made the smokeship an obvious target. The risk had to be taken and the new technique proved successful.

August 1968 saw increased enemy activity and Blackhorse was the target of a mortar attack during the early hours of 15 August. Lt Anthony Casadio and Petty Officer O. C. Phillips led an EMU light fire team in support of ARVN units defending the area on the 21st. A low cloud base kept the helicopters at treetop height. Suddenly, Casadio's aircraft was struck by a rocket grenade. Flame belched from the jet pipe. The helicopter crashed down through the trees into a ditch and exploded. There were no survivors. Casadio was awarded a posthumous Mention in Dispatches.

The Second Contingent RANHFV arrived at Camp Blackhorse on 9 September, under the command of Lt/Cdr G. R. Rohrsheim, who took over from Lt/Cdr Ralph as executive officer. For a while the two contingents operated together until the First left on 16 October. VC activity was light until 23 October, when the US 9th Infantry Division met heavy resistance south-east of Ben Tre. The EMUs, led by Lt/Cdr Rohrsheim, made seven landings and during the operations two aircraft were shot down and seven were damaged. One of the downed helicopters was piloted by an Australian, Sub/Lt T. F. Supple. He and his crew were rescued by another Australian, Sub/Lt A. J. Huelin.

In mid-November, the EMUs were moved to Camp Bearcat, 20 miles north-east of Saigon in Bien Hoa province. The enemy was more active in this area and, early in the new year, Bearcat was subjected to a number of mortar attacks. On 3 January 1969, Sub/Lt Huelin was detailed to fly from Bearcat to the Seven Mountains area, some 140 miles (225 km) away. Low cloud and fog prevailed at take-off but, because of the importance of the mission, Huelin decided not to abort. He took off early in the morning and a short time later, hampered by thick clouds, he collided with powerlines near Saigon. The helicopter crashed and exploded. There were no survivors.

At this time the EMUs were under the control of the 214th Aviation Battalion and they conducted numerous successful operations against the Viet Cong in support of the 7th and 9th ARVN Divisions in the campaign to the northern IV Corps provinces. These actions continued through January and February 1969.

In what is described as a 'vigorous action' on 2 February in Vinh Long province, Sub/Lt Supple and Sub/Lt W. E. Symons were forced down in their gunship. They dismantled their M60 machine-guns from the helicopter and carried on a running gunfight with the VC until they were rescued by a slick which had been recalled from Ben Tre. Symons was wounded later on a night action on 22 February. During February the EMUs flew a total 2979 hours, had 48 hits on their aircraft and killed at least 52 Viet Cong. They accounted for 80 VC killed in March and added another 56 in April.

Enemy tactics constantly changed and now their units became smaller in numbers and more mobile. EMU tactics changed also and single gunships or small flights carried on with the hunt. On 18 April, an EMU gunship in which Sub/Lt J. M. Hart was co-pilot, engaged a VC company, killed ten and prevented the remainder from escaping while ARVN troops closed in and took 25 prisoners.

Having adopted the familiar Australian word 'Bushranger' for their own gunships, 9 Squadron RAAF was now ready for gunship operations and flew its first Bushranger mission on 11 April 1969. Three Bushrangers were in action, but there was little to report that first day. Eight Viet Cong were attacked by two Bushrangers on 4 May with unknown results. Confirmed success came on 11 May when a North Vietnamese company hiding in a rubber plantation was engaged. Bushrangers shared equally the body count of 14 with a US Army Cobra also operated in the area.

In the middle of May, the VC increased their mortar attacks on Bearcat and the EMU helicopters had to be evacuated back to Blackhorse on several occasions.

On 15 May, three Bushrangers were briefed to attack Viet Cong who had occupied the town of Dat Do, east of Nui Dat. Engaging South Vietnamese Regional Forces had American and Australian army advisers with them. Each time they moved forward they were fired on by heavy automatic weapons from VC entrenched in houses in the town centre. Radio directed the Bushrangers as they swept down firing their rockets and mini-guns. On their second pass, a heavy twin-barrelled machine-gun mounted on a tripod opened fire on them. Because it was too close to friendly forces, the Bushrangers had to fire on the VC from another direction. Ground fire scored only one hit on the helicopters. The Regional Forces then moved forward again and by next day the Viet Cong had pulled out. Bushranger fire had severely damaged the occupied houses and the squadron learned later that six enemy had been killed and 13 wounded during the engagement. Unfortunately, a US Army adviser captured by the enemy was found with his throat cut.

On the 16th, three Bushrangers and three other RAAF helicopters took part in a successful "hot" extraction of an Australian SAS patrol which had been surrounded by VC in the jungle. Because of this, the patrol could not move to where the extracting helicopter could land. There was no alternative but to attempt to winch them up through the trees. In the vulnerable minutes while winching took place, three Bushrangers manoeuvred in and opened fire. The patrol marked their position with a smoke grenade and F/O T. Butler's crew then began to lift the patrol out as the gunships maintained their continuous suppressive fire all around them within twelve yards of their position, despite enemy return fire.

In a sharp action on 21 May, three Bushrangers pinned down a 50- man Viet Cong force located in a bunker complex. Led by F/Lt Robertson, who was on his last mission before returning to Australia, the Bushrangers maintained a continuous suppressive fire for two hours, sometimes only 100 yards ahead of Alpha Company, 7 RAR. Bushranger fire enabled the company to reorganise and launch a highly successful assault on the bunker positions. In addition to the contribution by the Bushrangers two other helicopters of 9 Squadron were used to evacuate sitting and walking wounded and a third was used to resupply tanks with ammunition.

The 'bushies', as they came to be known, were sent to Thua Tich to escort Australian armoured personnel carriers (APCs) returning to Xuyen Moc after a successful ambush on 30 May. Anticipating that the VC might mount a counter-ambush against the APCs, they were provided with Bushranger support. When they had almost reached Xuyen Moc, the Bushrangers left with the intention of flying to the former ambush site to check on enemy movements. No sooner had they departed than a Viet Cong fired a rocket-propelled grenade from close range — about ten feet. It penetrated the side of a carrier and landed on the driver's lap, but fortunately did not explode. The gunships were recalled immediately and, with the carriers, opened up on the attackers. Bushrangers' fire was credited with killing three of the enemy and six probables. Afterwards, the Bushrangers returned to base, rearmed and refuelled and then flew to the original ambush site where more VC were found and killed by mini-gun fire.

On 31 May EMU slicks came under heavy fire as they approached a landing zone five miles west of Dong Tam. The covering gunships engaged the enemy force and the VC attempted to escape into a heavily wooded area. Leading Aircrewman N. E. Shipp was a door gunner in the leading gunship. In order to fire more effectively at the enemy he had to lean forward so that he was partially out of the aircraft. While he was doing this the helicopter came under heavy automatic weapons fire. The pilot was hit and the helicopter suddenly plunged down out of control. Shipp stayed at his post and continued firing until the moment of impact. The explosion scattered wreckage everywhere and there were no survivors.

A Bushranger was forced down by enemy fire for the first time on 5 June. F/Lt Hazelwood with two other Bushrangers were supporting 6 RAR when his aircraft was hit by .30 calibre rounds which slightly wounded his crewman, LAC R. G. Ferry. The loss of transmission oil caused by bullet damage forced the aircraft down. While the other two Bushrangers covered them, another Iroquois lifted out the downed crew. The helicopter was recovered by an American Chinook. Hazelwood was later awarded the Distinguished Flying Cross.

Two weeks later, crew members of an RAAF dust-off helicopter braved enemy mines at night to rescue soldiers of an Australian Army patrol wounded by a mine. Seventeen soldiers of the 5th Battalion had been wounded and three died as a result of the explosion which was followed by a second detonation while attempts were being made to evacuate dead and wounded. Disregarding the danger of further mine explosions, LAC Ron Wilson, medical orderly on the dust-off helicopter, tended the wounded and assisted them back to the aircraft. When Wilson reached the scene the second time he saw only two soldiers, one of whom appealed for assistance to bring out the wounded who were hidden by the darkness and thick vegetation some 30 to 40 yards away. The pilot, F/O Ian Harvey, allowed them to go in after the wounded but warned of the danger that more mines might explode. Wilson and A/C Lee, the gunner, nevertheless went in search of the soldiers, leaving crewman LAC Jeff Smith to man the helicopter's machine-guns. On both journeys back to the base hospital the small space in the helicopter was overcrowded with wounded. Wilson, Smith Lee, were all awarded the Mention-in-Despatches.

Deteriorating weather in June caused the cancellation of numerous missions for the EMUs. On June 16, Naval Airman C. C. St.Clair, the gunner of one of three helicopters attempting to evacuate wounded AVRN soldiers, was himself wounded. In a major action in July, Sub/Lts Supple and Symons, in two-light fire teams,

EMU gunship under fire. Australian commanding officers of the RAAF Contingent at Vung Tau, repeatedly expressed their concern about the vulnerability of the relatively slow-moving helicopters to concentrated ground fire. (Dennis Newton)

attacked and killed sixteen VC while ARVN troops captured eight others.

On 15 August, F/O M. Tardent led three Bushrangers in an action in support of 'B' Company of 5 RAR who were in continuous action with enemy forces. Air strikes and artillery as well as the gunship teams were used in support of the heavily engaged troops all day. The performance of the RAAF gunships on this day was highly praised. Apart from the support they gave they were credited with killing five VC.

Six days later, on 21 August, 'A' Company of the same battalion became embroiled in a fierce jungle battle. Gunship helicopters of. 9 Squadron and the US Army were called in for close support. 'A' Company took heavy casualties, one killed and 31 wounded. RAAF and US dust-off helicopters were scrambled. As F/O Tardent's Bushrangers poured heavy fire on the enemy positions, an American helicopter hovered at 25 feet above the troops and winched up three casualties but was then waved off by the ground commander when the VC return fire built up. A few minutes later, an RAAF dust-off helicopter captained F/O Bob Treloar with F/Lt Jim Satrapa as co-pilot moved down to 25 feet, dropped its jungle penetrator and hauled its first casualty up. A second casualty was halfway up when an enemy grenade exploded at three level, killing one of the wounded Australians waiting on the ground. A third casualty was hauled up but shrapnel peppered the aircraft, holing the perspex windscreen, top window and port door, forcing Treloar to move away. His aircraft was hit again as he gained speed over the treetops. One of the injured soldiers was wounded again. Shrapnel pierced the helicopter's fuel tank and another bullet smashed the instrument panel, passing Satrapa's head to finally embed itself in a steel frame. Treloar brought his damaged aircraft safely to Nui Dat. Meanwhile, F/O Tardent and his Bushrangers continued to make accurate rocket and mini-gun attacks to ensure maximum possible protection for the evacuation helicopters. He was awarded the DFC.

The first of the Third Contingent RANHFV arrived on 10 September 1969 under the command of Lt/Cdr D. D. Farthing, who relieved Rohrsheim on 16 September. Lt R. Giffin was the senior pilot. On 23 September, a gunship piloted by LtGiffin and Sub-Lt Symons wounded and captured a Viet Cong in Sa Dec province. Giffin himself was wounded in action on 1 December.

Troop insertion and ground support operations continued. On 18 November, Sub/Lt R. Marum received a shock when a bullet pierced the windscreen of his helicopter and ricocheted off his flying helmet. In a later incident on 22 January 1970, he was wounded in action. Casualties were not only suffered on operational flying. Leading Air Mechanic E. Shelley, RAN, was injured on

23 December when the supply truck he was driving was ambushed and subjected to rifle and mortar fire. Shelley was wounded in the neck.

Lt R. Marum was back in action again on 17 February when his helicopter was again struck by enemy fire. An American crew member was fatally wounded. Later that month the EMUs obtained retribution by killing 27 Viet Cong in the same area.

On 6 March, as Lt D. B. Gibson was bringing his helicopter down into a landing zone, a booby-trap was detonated. The explosion completely destroyed the slick and killed two soldiers. Gibson was seriously injured and was later evacuated back to Australia.

And so the action continued. Despite the acquisition of Bushranger gunships, most of 9 Squadron RAAF's more eventful missions revolved around the 'hot' extraction of troops under fire and dust-offs, where casualties had to be winched out of the jungle while the helicopters were often under fire. On several occasions helicopters were either shot down or badly damaged in these hazardous operations. Such a mission occurred on 13 February 1970 when F/O M Haxell and crew were ordered to extract a patrol which could not break contact with the VC. Arriving over the landing zone, Haxell's helicopter came under such intense fire that the patrol commander advised him to vacate the area and that the troops would try to make a run for it. Scorning this course of action, Haxell put the helicopter down into the landing zone while his gunners suppressed the enemy's fire. The soldiers, still firing their weapons, leapt aboard the Iroquois and, as the helicopter took off, several enemy soldiers were killed in the landing zone.

The year 1970 saw no reduction in the overall operational activities of 9 Squadron in spite of rumours of withdrawals of Allied forces from Vietnam. With the superb efforts of the ground maintenance crews paying off, the squadron continued to mount in the order of 4000 sorties a month. By March the total sorties flown by the squadron in nearly four years of war had climbed to above the 170 000 mark.

Meanwhile, events were happening in neighbouring Cambodia which were to have a serious effect on the joint Australian/American EMU unit. In spite of Cambodian neutrality, the VC had continued to build up for some time supply dumps and communications networks in the provinces adjoining South Vietnam. There was talk of a '30-mile wide VC belt' along the length of the frontier. In the middle of March, Prince Norodom Sihanouk, the Cambodian head of state, visited Russia to ask the Soviets to persuade the VC to withdraw. However, while he was there, he was deposed by the Cambodian National Assembly and General Lon Nol established a government.

There followed a period of confused factional civil war. General Lon Nol and his supporters, who were sympathetic to US policy in the area, opposed the VC presence and appealed to the US, South Vietnam and Thailand for arms. However, since the Tet Offensive of 1968, there had been an overall change in US policy. America was now in the process of gradually reducing its military presence in South-East Asia. The Cambodian Army received limited aid from South Vietnam and Thailand but no materials came from the US. Little by little, over the next two months, the VC and the factional groups supporting them forced back the Cambodian Army and infiltrated much of the country. This also had the effect of reopening the VC supply routes and of consolidating supply bases and troop concentrations in sanctuaries along the border with South Vietnam. Supplies could now freely flow over the border — but only at night.

The Allies were aware that supplies were coming across the border and used their air power to stem the flow. Because of this aerial blanket, the VC were effectively blocked during the day. New tactics needed to be developed by the helicopter units to counter these nocturnal movements. Night hunter-killer operations were introduced. This meant that a command and control helicopter, fitted with a powerful searchlight, flew at low altitude and pinpointed potential targets. These were then illuminated by a higher flying flare-ship, which was backed up by two gunships ready to attack.

Of great use in operations such as these was a device known as the aerial personnel detector (APD), sometimes referred to as the 'people sniffer'. This device could actually sense pockets of people hidden from sight under the cover of dense jungle foliage or of darkness, and therefore invisible to the eye. But in spite of these measures, an increasing volume of supplies filtered through.

Enemy activity increased sharply in the EMUs' area of operations towards the end of March. April saw it at its highest level since February 1969. During a combat assault on 28 April, Sub/Lt Mayo's helicopter was struck by ground fire and his American crew chief wounded in the legs. On the credit side, at least 30 Viet Cong were killed in the same action.

It was becoming increasingly obvious that something had to be done about the enemy base camps and sanctuaries in Cambodia. For this purpose, the United States/South Vietnamese drives across the Cambodian border were initiated. Limited invasions, supported from the air, were mounted into the sanctuaries in the areas known as the Parrot's Beak, the Fish Hook and the Bulge. These actions caused a serious split in the 135th Assault Helicopter Company.

Although the EMU helicopters took part in the initial operations, they did so without the Australian crews. For political reasons, Royal Australian Navy personnel were not permitted to participate. In spite of being fully integrated into the American unit, they were not allowed to be used in any role which compromised the Australian government's policy on the employment of its forces in Vietnam. The absence of the Australians severely hampered the operational efficiency of the EMUs as a fighting unit and eventually the 135th had to be reassigned to support operations in the Mekong Delta. The political differences of the two separate national groups did not disrupt the harmony which existed between the men.

The EMUs were involved in heavy action in Kien Hoa province on 18 May where the regional outpost had been captured by the VC and then heavily fortified. Three battalions of ARVN troops were inserted by the EMUs. Lt/Cdr Farthing acted as air mission commander. The leading slick, piloted by Lieutenant Marum, took numerous hits and had to return to Bearcat. Sub/Lt A. C. Perry volunteered to lead the remaining troop insertions but his aircraft was also struck by ground fire during the first night mission. Unable to lift off, emergency repairs had to be carried out in the landing zone in spite of heavy enemy fire. When he was at last able to take off, he led the flight for two more insertions which also met heavy resistance. It was discovered later that more than 50 of the enemy had been killed in this action. Local villagers had been forced by the VC to carry off the bodies.

During June, VC activity declined, mainly due to the loss of their Cambodian supply bases. However, on 2 July, Lt Marum acted as air mission commander in a dangerous lift-out of an ARVN battalion. The slicks were mortared during all of the six landings to evacuate the dead and wounded.

For his actions in Vietnam, Marum was to receive the DFC and it was he who, on 13 July, saw a number of Viet Cong in the open and called in the gunships led by Sub/Lt G. F. Cooper. Nineteen of the VC were killed. Two days later, Cooper accounted for seven more.

Early in August, the EMUs airlifted a US Navy Special Warfare Unit, called a Sea, Air and Land team (SEAL) into a suspected Viet Cong village in coastal Kien Hoa. The helicopter force consisted of two slicks accompanied by a command and control helicopter and two gunships. The attack achieved total surprise and the VC scattered in confusion. At least twellve were killed by the gunships. Then the SEALS landed, killed several more and took a number of captives. This success led to other SEAL operations.

On 6 September the EMUs moved from Bearcat to Dong Tam, a primitive camp in Dinh Tuong province. This move took place in time for the arrival of the advance

Line drawing of RAAF Iroquois UH-1H (Bushranger) Gunship showing armament. (Dennis Newton)

members of the Fourth Contingent RANHFV on 10 September. The remainder came on 8 October. Lt/Cdr W. P. James relieved Lt/Cdr Farthing on 17 September and Lt J. Buchanan was the senior pilot and second-in-command.

Heavy monsoonal rain in October flooded the Mekong Delta and kept enemy activity at a low level. The rain also interfered with EMU operations. There were several mortar attacks during October and November, most of them aimed at the US Navy compound about a mile to the south. Five EMU personnel were injured during an attack on 3 November.

The Fourth Contingent's first major action occurred on 11 October, when they carried out a troop insertion near Kien Long. ARVN troops were landed against a well-entrenched, battalion-strength enemy force. The EMUs landed four times on a site exposed to heavy mortar fire. Five helicopters were hit and one, with Lt B. G. Abrahams as co-pilot was forced down close by. The enemy withdrew as night fell leaving behind 26 dead.

On 4 December, LtBuchanan was the co-pilot of a helicopter carrying out a MEDEVAC from a disabled patrol boat when the VC opened up with heavy mortars. A sampan 50 yards away exploded as the wounded Vietnamese were being loaded aboard the hovering aircraft. Realising the danger of the situation, Buchanan hooked the skids of the helicopter onto an upper section of the patrol boat and towed it away to a safer area

On Christmas Eve, the EMUs were required to supply a security force to cover President Nguyen Van Thieu as he spent the night with ARVN troops in the Ca Mau Peninsula Six days later the EMUs were involved in a heavy engagement in combination with ARVN troops, gunships and air strikes. Of 50 VC left dead in the field, 20 were credited to the EMUs

Combined offensive operations took place in January 1971 in the Seven Mountains area and the U Minh. On 16 January, one EMU, while attempting to evacuate a wounded US Army adviser, was hit by heavy ground fire and crashed upside down The American pilot had received a fatal wound and the members of the crew, including Naval Airman J. V. Shaw, were trapped. Unable to escape because they were pinned down by enemy fire from well protected positions, they had to spend an uncomfortable night defending themselves on the mountainside.. Meanwhile, ARVN and American troops tried to kill the VC or drive them off, but it was not until morning that they succeeded and the downed helicopter was at last able to be evacuated.

An insertion near Giong Trom ran into a VC ambush. The enemy chose his moment and opened up as ARVN troops were disembarking from the slicks. Out of 40 men, 22 were killed and ten were wounded. Lt Abraham, in the leading helicopter, quickly took off followed by the others. One slick was so badly hit that it had to force land nearby. Its crew came under heavy attack until rescued by the command and control helicopter.

Early in February 1971, ARVN forces, with US air support, crossed the border into Laos with the intention of blocking the Ho Chi Minh Trail. Progress was slow, mainly because of poor weather conditions which hampered movement and grounded aircraft. Although the ARVN managed to establish a number of positions, mainly to the north of Route 9, traffic on the trail was not disrupted because the VC simply used roads and tracks further to the west, which were out of danger. The VC also began to launch counter-attacks on the 17th which, combined with the bad weather, effectively bogged down the ARVN advance fifteen miles into Laos. Heavy fighting between 25 and 28 February saw the ARVN lose several strategic positions. In an effort to regain the offensive, strong ARVN reinforcements were sent in at the beginning of March but VC and North Vietnamese troops, supported by tanks, were again counter-attacking by 12 March.

Under heavy pressure, the positions held by ARVN troops were abandoned one by one, often being hastily evacuated by helicopter. The last soldiers were lifted out on 25 March and on 9 April President Thieu officially declared that the operation was over.

Although the EMUs did not participate, the heavy fighting in Laos caused replacement helicopters, which would have normally gone to the EMUs, to be diverted to o her units located in that area. This placed a heavier burden on the maintenance crews of the 135th and inevitably seriously reduced the number of gunships available for operations.

US helicopter units suffered heavy losses in Laos (the Americans admitted that 105 had been lost) and, in general, it seemed that the enemy began to react more violently to helicopter operations throughout South Vietnam as well. On 20 March, the RAAF Bushranger gunship flight suffered its first fatality, after an LFT captained by F/Lt N. M. Goodall and F/O C. Freedman was called in to assist a platoon from 3 RAR under pressure in an action north of Xuyen Moc. While Goodall fired on the reported enemy location, Freedman began a pass toward the platoon but flew over the enemy concentration at treetop height and low speed. The helicopter (A2-383) was blasted by ground fire and took 20hits. One round entered the cockpit and struck the co-pilot, P/O R.W. Betts, in the head.

A four helicopter EMU flight met very heavy opposition on 21 March but escaped without damage and killed seven VC in the process. On the 24th another EMU team accounted for four more. This situation continued much the same through April, with forest regions in the U Minh becoming very dangerous.

On 31 March 1971, a 9 Squadron dust-off helicopter was tricked into an ambush by a decoy smoke marker thrown by the enemy. Before the mistake was realised, the aircraft was hit and crewman LAC A. C. Bloxsom was fatally wounded. The Iroquois was badly damaged and forced to put down at a nearby fire support base.

Another dust-off mission went horribly wrong on 17 April. On that afternoon, F/O M Castle and his crew in A2-767 were shot down while trying to evacuate a wounded South Vietnamese soldier in the notorious Long Hai hills. An army medical orderly, L/Cpl J. F. Gillespie, part of the helicopter's crew, was killed, as were two soldiers on the ground, one of them Australian Army adviser, Cpl T.D. Blackhurst, hit by flying debris. The downed crew, one of whom was injured, were later evacuated by another Australian helicopter.

The conflict in Vietnam was not a popular war (if there is such a thing) and in the United States it became increasingly unpalatable as the casualty lists grew into the thousands. Although the Tet Offensive of 1968 had

resulted in a military setback for the Communists, in the political and propaganda areas it gave them a victory because it marked the real beginning of widespread public resentment of the war in the Free World. There were numerous moratoriums and demonstrations, and by the early 1970s American public opinion polls showed a majority in favour of US withdrawal. President Nixon's administration searched for a peace formula. The revelations of the secret 'Pentagon Papers', which detailed aggressive American policies in South-East Asia, further increased opposition to the war. Now, while American economic assistance to the South Vietnamese government remained stable, military aid was steadily reduced. US forces, which had peaked at more than half a million men in 1969 were by 1971 being phased out at the rate of approximately 12 000 men per month .

Similar public resistance to the war was reflected in Australia where Vietnam was linked with the emotive issue of conscription. As in the United States, there were numerous demonstrations. In 1971, the government decided to recall the bulk of the Australian Task Force, with reductions to be continued through 1972. On 30 April 1971, the Minister for the Navy announced that the RANHFV would be withdrawn.

Meanwhile, in the war zone, flying conditions became more hazardous in May because of the heavy monsoon weather. Three EMU helicopters were hit by ground fire on 18 May. Two days later, Australian Naval Air Mechanic A. S. Beales, survived the crash of a helicopter which was being test flown after routine maintenance. On 31 May, EMU helicopters flew into Military Region 3 on a troop insertion to block and surround two North Vietnamese Army companies moving in the open about 15 miles north-east of Dong Tam.

The last RAN pilot to have his machine damaged by enemy fire was Sub/Lt K. T. Powell while on a direct combat support mission. Then finally, on 8 June 1971, the RAN pilots stopped operational flying. For them the war was over. They returned home on the 16th.

During their four years of service with the 135th Assault Helicopter Company, the men of the RANHFV accumulated numerous awards and honours. These included three MBEs, eight DSCs, five DFCs, one BEM, 24 Mentioned-in-Dispatches, 34 Naval Board Commendations and various Vietnamese and US decorations. The RANHFV's parent unit, 723 Squadron, was awarded the battle honour 'Vietnam 1967-71' on 22 December 1972.

In general, the members of the RAN contingents showed themselves to be highly skilled and experienced when compared with their American counterparts. This was because the Australians were all volunteers with long backgrounds of service while large numbers of conscripts were often included among the US personnel. The integration of two different national groups into an Experimental Military Unit (EMU) had been a trial. That it proved to be such a success reflected great credit on all involved, Americans and Australians alike.

For the RAAF the withdrawal began in June with 2 Squadron's Canberra bombers departing from Phan Rang on the 4th and returning home. No. 9 Squadron would follow in December and the last to leave — after being the first in — would be 35 Squadron's Caribou.

Meanwhile, 9 Squadron was still committed. While carrying out a resupply mission for Australian troops engaged in Operation Overlord, Iroquois A2-723 crashed and was destroyed by fire on 7 June 1971. Two of the crew escaped with relatively minor injuries but the captain, F/Lt E. M. Lance, and gunner, Cpl D. J. Dubber, were killed. The latter was an airfield defence guard who had only just returned to Vietnam for a second tour of duty, having been Mentioned in Dispatches for his services on his first. 'Lofty' Lance had been in the RAAF less than two years. He was one of eight former RAF pilots recruited in London as part of an Australian drive to overcome shortages. South African born, he had flown with No. 2 'Flying Cheetahs' Squadron SAAF during the Korean War, where he was awarded a DFC and an Air Medal. He had later joined the Royal Canadian Air Force and the RAF.

No. 9 Squadron's last couple of months in Vietnam were relatively quiet, with its flying rate dropping noticeably. By then it was widely known the squadron would be pulling out and preparations were well under way for that to happen. However, the excellent performance of the squadron as a whole was again officially recognised when it was awarded the Gloucester Cup for 1969/70, a unit award for 'efficiency and excellence', for the third successive year.

On 6 October 1971, No.9 Squadron airlifted 500 troops of the 3rd Battalion onto the deck of HMAS Sydney and, with the withdrawal of the last Australian troops of the 4th Battalion from Nui Dat on 7 November, the actual support of Australian troops in the field ended.

The squadron recorded its last Vietnam operational mission on 19 November 1971 when a 'sniffer' reconnaissance sortie was flown by a single helicopter.

This ingenious activity had become a regular 9 Squadron activity from 1969 and the floor-mounted equipment seemed to work as it could scan several hundred square miles of territory in a single mission. The standard procedure was for a sniffer-equipped Iroquois to go out in company with a Bushranger, find some hidden VC and, after positively identifying them as the enemy, leave the gunship to deal with them. On one occasion in February 1970 a 9 Squadron Sniffer had discovered fifteen people but, fortunately, fire was not brought down on them because they proved to be a group of women and children. The unit's final mission was an anticlimax — nothing was registered by the aerial personnel detector.

On 8 December the Australian helicopters were flown onto HMAS Sydney for the voyage home. They arrived at their new base at Amberley, Queensland, two weeks later, in time for Christmas.

Vietnam was the war in which the helicopter came of age. In its five and a half years of service there 9 Squadron logged more than 55 000 flying hours and flew 223 487 operational sorties out of a total 315 189 flown in Vietnam by the RAAF as a whole. It expended millions of rounds of ammunition from the Iroquois' M60 and M134 guns, wrote off seven aircraft and had serious damage inflicted on eighteen more. More important was the loss of seven lives, four of them battle casualties.

AUSTRALIAN HELICOPTER AIRCREW KILLED IN ACTION IN VIETNAM

Betts, P/O R.W.	9 RAAF	20 March 1971
Bloxsom, LAC A.C.	9 RAAF	31 March 1971
Casadio, Lt. A.A.	RAN/EMU	21 August 1968
Dubber, Cpl D.J.	9 RAAF	7 June 1971
Huelin, A/Sub/Lt	RAN/EMU	3 January 1969
Lance, F/Lt E.M.	9 RAAF	7 June 1971
Phillips, Petty/O O.C.	RAN/EMU	21 August 1968
Shipp, LAC N.E.	RAN/EMU	31 May 1969
Vickers, Lt/Cdr P.J.	RAN/EMU	22 February 1968

SELECT BIBLIOGRAPHY

Selected bibliography of sources other than official records — Unit Histories, Combat Reports, Operations Record Books, Log Books, etc. — from the Ministry of Defence, Public Record Office, Commonwealth War Graves Commission, Imperial War Museum, Battle of Britain Museum and RAF Museum in England, and RAAF Historical Section Department of Defence, Australian War Memorial, Australian Archives in Australia:

Baker, C., & Knight, G., *Milne Bay 1942*, Baker-Knight Publications, Loftus, 1991.

Barton, L.L., *The Desert Harassers*, Astor, Mosman, 1991.

Bekker, C., *The Luftwaffe War Diaries*, Corgi, London, 1969.

Brownell, R.J., *From Khaki to Blue*, Military Historical Society of Australia, Canberra, 1978.

Closterman P., *The Big Show*, Cassell, London 1955.

Coulthard-Clark, C.D., *The Third Brother: The Royal Australian Air Force 1921-39*, Allen & Unwin, Sydney, 1991.

Coulthard-Clark, C.D., *The RAAF in Vietnam*, Allen & Unwin, Sydney, 1995.

Cutlack, F.M., *The Australian Flying Corps*, Official History of Australia in the War of 1914-18 Vol.VIII, Angus & Robertson, Sydney, 1923.

Eather, S., *Target Charlie*, Aerospace Publications, Canberra, 1993.

Fairfax, D., *Royal Australian Navy in Vietnam*, Australian Government Publishing Service, Canberra, 1980.

Franks, N., *The Air Battle of Dunkirk*, Kimber, London, 1983.

Gibbons, F., *The Red Knight of Germany*, Cassell, London, 1933.

Gillison, D., *Royal Australian Air Force, 1939-1942*, Australia in the War of 1939-1945 (Air), Australian War Memorial, Canberra, 1962.

Herington, J., *Air War Against Germany and Italy, 1939-1943*, Australia in the War of 1939-1945 (Air), Australian War Memorial, Canberra, 1962.

Johnson, F. (ed.), *RAAF Over Europe*, Eyre & Spottiswoode, London, 1946.

Kilduff, P., *Richthofen — Beyond the Legend of the Red Baron*, Arms and Armour Press, London, 1993.

McCarthy, J., *Australia and the Imperial Defence 1918-1939*, University of Queensland Press, St. Lucia, 1976.

Macmillan, N., *Offensive Patrol,* Jarrolds, London, 1973.

McClelland, James, *Where Australians Fought and Died*, McClelland, Silverdale, 1980.

Mason, F.K., *The Hawker Hurricane*, Aston Publications, Bucks, 1987.

Newton, D., *A Few of 'The Few' — Australians and the Battle of Britain*, Australian War Memorial, Canberra, 1990.

Odgers, G., *Across the Parallel*, William Heinemann, London, 1952.

Odgers, G., *Mission Vietnam*, Australian Government Publishing Service, Canberra, 1974.

Olive, G. & Newton, D., *The Devil at Six O'Clock — Biography of W/Cdr Gordon Olive, MBE, DFC*, unpublished.

Rawlings, J.D.R., *Fighter Squadrons of the RAF and Their Aircraft*, Macdonald and Jane's, London, 1976.

RAAF Directorate of Public Relations, *These Eagles*, Australian War Memorial, Canberra, 1942.

RAAF Directorate of Public Relations, *RAAF Log*, Australian War Memorial, Canberra, 1943.

RAAF Directorate of Public Relations, *RAAF Saga*, Australian War Memorial, Canberra, 1944.

RAAF Directorate of Public Relations, *Victory Roll*, Australian War Memorial, Canberra, 1945.

Robertson, B. (ed), *Von Richthofen and the 'Flying Circus'*, Harleyford, Kings Langley, 1964.

Sakaida, H., *Winged Samurai*, Champlin Fighter Museum Press, Arizona, 1985.

Shores, C. & Williams, C., *Aces High*, Grub St, London, 1994.

Shores, C. & Ring, H., *Fighters Over the Desert*, Spearman, London, 1969.

Terraine, John, *The Right of the Line*, Hodder & Stoughton, London, 1985.

Wilson, D., *The Decisive Factor*, Banner, Canberra, 1991.

Wilson, D., *Lion Over Korea*, Banner, Canberra, 1994.

Wilson, S., *Wirraway, Boomerang and CA-15 in Australian Service*, Aerospace Publications, Canberra, 1991.

INDEX